Worshipping a Crucified Man

Worshipping a Crucified Man

Christians, Graeco-Romans and Scripture in the Second Century

Jeremy Hudson

James Clarke & Co

JAMES CLARKE & CO

P.O. Box 60
Cambridge
CB1 2NT
United Kingdom

www.jamesclarke.co
publishing@jamesclarke.co

Hardback ISBN: 978 0 227 17734 1
Paperback ISBN: 978 0 227 17735 8
PDF ISBN: 978 0 227 17734 4
ePub ISBN: 978 0 227 17735 1

British Library Cataloguing in Publication Data
A record is available from the British Library

First published by James Clarke & Co, 2021r
Copyright © Jeremy Hudson, 2021

Contents

Acknowledgements

This book had its origins in a University of Cambridge PhD thesis with the somewhat more prosaic title: *The Use of the Jewish Scriptures by Early Christian Greek Apologists 140-190 CE: Justin Martyr, Tatian and Theophilus of Antioch*. I would like to record with gratitude all the support I received from staff and fellow students at both the Faculty of Divinity and Wolfson College at Cambridge while I was studying for my PhD.

I am particularly grateful to my supervisor, Professor Judith Lieu, who provided me with patient guidance over the seven years during which I worked part-time on my thesis. Her exemplary combination of encouragement and challenge kept me on the rails and enabled me to carry through my project to a successful conclusion.

I am also grateful to my PhD examiners, Dr James Carleton Paget and Professor Josef Lössl, who provided helpful guidance that has enabled me to improve on the thesis (I hope!) in revising it for publication. Needless to say, the shortcomings in this book remain entirely my own.

I would also like to acknowledge the help and support I received at King's College London where I undertook my Master's degree and launched on the study of early Christianity.

Many people have encouraged and supported me in this enterprise – too numerous to itemise individually – and I appreciate them all; but, like all students of early Christianity, I owe a huge debt to the largely anonymous scribes, who over centuries copied and re-copied precious ancient texts for, without their efforts, we would not today be able to read the words written nearly two thousand years ago. It is to them that this book is dedicated.

Preface

In the mid-second century CE the Christian convert, Justin Martyr, wrote: 'For . . . they declare our madness to be manifest saying that we give the second place after the unchangeable and eternal God and begetter of all to a crucified man'; and again: 'For by what reason should we believe that a crucified man is the first-begotten of the unbegotten God and that he himself will pass judgement on the whole human race?'

He asks, in other words, how Christians could hope to persuade anyone else of the wisdom of following – and, indeed, worshipping – Jesus, a mere human being and one who had been so humiliatingly crucified.

Justin, and other Christian writers of the second century, devoted time and energy to addressing questions of this kind. Understanding the arguments they used to justify, and to promote, belief in the new religion of Christianity and how they used the ancient Jewish scriptures for that purpose is the subject of this book.

By 150 CE it was over a century since the life and death of Jesus in the mid-first century and those who had known him were long dead. The conversion of the Roman Emperor Constantine to Christianity in the early fourth century, which gave the new religion a central role in the Empire, was far in the future. Christianity was still only a small-scale movement; but it was a missionary one and its reach, through proselytising efforts, had extended well beyond its Palestinian Jewish origins, so that adherents were now to be found in numerous communities around the Mediterranean.

This spread of Christianity brought its followers into close contact with the long-established Graeco-Roman culture that dominated all aspects of life in the Roman Empire. Indeed, those who espoused Christianity had in many cases been brought up and educated in Graeco-Roman ways before being converted to the new faith. The authors whose works are considered in the chapters that follow were converts in this mould.

This book is about the arguments these authors put forward in their writings. The texts they wrote were addressed (in form at least) to non-Christian audiences whose beliefs and practices they had formerly shared. They sought to present arguments in favour of Christianity in ways that would appeal to those audiences and in doing so they had to ask themselves whether acceptance of the new faith was compatible with continued adherence to all – or even any – aspects of the Graeco-Roman cultural tradition.

Christianity inherited from its Jewish origins the ancient scriptures of the Jewish people. Christians reinterpreted these texts in the light of their new faith and the Jewish scriptures became the Old Testament of the Christian Bible. The Jewish scriptures were unlike anything in the Graeco-Roman literary tradition; but they became a central feature of Christianity and some Christian writers, converted from Graeco-Roman backgrounds, used them to support the arguments they made in promoting their new faith. How and why this was the case is explored in the following pages.

Abbreviations

1A	Justin Martyr's *First Apology*
AA	Theophilus of Antioch's *Ad Autolycum*
AC	*Anonymous Commentary on Plato's* Theaetetus (*Commentarium in Platonis* Theaetetum)
Aristeas	*Letter of Aristeas*
BCE	Before the Common Era
BETS	*Bulletin of the Evangelical Theological Society*
BJRL	*Bulletin of the John Rylands Library*
BNJ	*Brill's New Jacoby*, ed. by I. Worthington (Leiden: Brill, 2007-) (accessed via online edn [2007-])
BNP	*Brill's New Pauly: Encyclopaedia of the Ancient World*, ed. by H. Cancik and H. Schneider, English edition, ed. by C.F. Salazar (Leiden: Brill, 2002-) (accessed via online edn [2006-])
CE	Common Era
CAH11	*The Cambridge Ancient History: Volume 11: The High Empire, A.D. 70-192*, ed. by A.K. Bowman, P. Garnsey and D. Rathbone, 2nd edn (Cambridge: Cambridge University Press, 2000)
CAH12	*The Cambridge Ancient History: Volume 12: The Crisis of Empire, A.D. 193-337*, ed. by A.K. Bowman, P. Garnsey and A. Cameron, 2nd edn (Cambridge: Cambridge University Press, 2005)
CHC1	*The Cambridge History of Christianity: Volume 1: Origins to Constantine*, ed. by M.M. Mitchell and F.M. Young (Cambridge: Cambridge University Press, 2006)
DT	Justin Martyr's *Dialogue with Trypho*
HE	Eusebius, *The History of the Church from Christ to Constantine*, trans. by G.A. Williamson, rev. and ed. with a new introduction by A. Louth (London: Penguin, 1989) (*Historia Ecclesiastica*)
HP	Heraclitus, *Homeric Problems*
HTR	*Harvard Theological Review*
JBL	*Journal of Biblical Literature*
JECS	*Journal of Early Christian Studies* (1992-)
JEH	*Journal of Ecclesiastical History*

JJS   *Journal of Jewish Studies*
JTS   *Journal of Theological Studies*
LCL   Loeb Classical Library
LSJ   Liddell, H.G., R. Scott and H.S. Jones, *A Greek-English Lexicon*,
          9th edn, rev. and augmented (Oxford: Clarendon Press, 1996)
NCHB1   *The New Cambridge History of the Bible: Volume 1: From the
          Beginnings to 600*, ed. by J. Carleton Paget and J. Schaper
          (Cambridge: Cambridge University Press, 2013)
NETS   *A New English Translation of the Septuagint and the Other Greek
          Translations Traditionally Included under that Title*, by A. Pietersma
          and B.G. Wright (New York: Oxford University Press, 2007) (*NETS*)
Oratio Tatian's *Oratio ad Graecos*
RAC   *Reallexikon für Antike und Christentum: Sachwörterbuch zur
          Auseinandersetzung des Christentums mit der antiken Welt*,
          by T. Klauser, F.J. Dölger, G. Schöllgen, E. Dassmann and
          H. Leitzmann, 27 vols (Stuttgart: Hiersemann, 1950-)
RHE   *Revue d'histoire ecclésiastique*
SBL   Society of Biblical Literature
SecCent *Second Century: A Journal of Early Christian Studies* (1981-1992)
SMSR   *Studi e materiali di storia delle religioni*
SP   *Studia Patristica*
ST   *Studia Theologica*
TLG   Thesaurus Linguae Graecae, digital library ed. by M.C. Pantelia
          (Irvine: University of California, 2001-)
TLZ   *Theologische Literaturzeitung*
VC   *Vigiliae Christianae*
ZAC   *Zeitschrift für Antikes Christentum*
ZNW   *Zeitschrift für die neutestamentliche Wissenschaft und die Kunde der
          älteren Kirche*

Chapter 1

Introduction

Background

By the mid-second century the movement inaugurated by followers of the crucified Jesus of Nazareth had existed for over a century. Emerging from its roots in Jewish Palestine, it had spread widely across the Roman Empire and established itself in a number of locations.[1] From the outset, Christianity sought to make converts and was consequently brought into close contact with the wider non-Jewish population of the Empire.[2] Its adherents were few in number compared with the total population and Christian communities were small-scale when set against those of the Jews.[3]

Christians inherited from their Jewish origins authoritative texts, which are referred to here as the Jewish scriptures[4] and which came to be called the Christian Old Testament. From an early date Christians also produced their own texts. Some of these were later gathered together to form the collection now known as the New Testament,

---

1. M.M. Mitchell et al., 'Part IV: Regional Varieties of Christianity in the First Three Centuries', in CHC1, pp. 295-412; M.J. Edwards, 'Christianity A.D. 70-192', in CAH12, pp. 573-88.
2. CHC1, pp. 314-412; R. MacMullen, *Christianizing the Roman Empire (A.D. 100-400)* (New Haven: Yale University Press, 1984).
3. For the size of the Jewish population in antiquity, see M. Simon, *Verus Israel: A Study of the Relations between Christians and Jews in the Roman Empire AD 135-425*, trans. by H. McKeating (Oxford: Oxford University Press, 1986), pp. 33-34; for numbers of Christians, see R. Stark, *The Rise of Christianity: A Sociologist Reconsiders History* (Princeton: Princeton University Press, 1996), and F. Trombley, 'Overview: The Geographical Spread of Christianity', in CHC1, pp. 302-13.
4. This term describes the Jewish scriptures translated into Greek which were used by early Christians (sometimes referred to as the Septuagint or the LXX).

while other Christian texts were written, copied and preserved.[5] It has therefore fairly been said that 'the earliest Christians . . . created a literary culture'.[6]

A number of texts extant from the mid-second century onwards, commonly referred to as apologetic, mark a new stage in Christian literature. They were, at least ostensibly, addressed to Graeco-Roman[7] audiences; whether these were their real audiences will be considered below. At least some of their authors were converts to Christianity who had received a Graeco-Roman literary education. A striking feature of some of these texts is the extent to which they refer to the Jewish scriptures[8] and it is not immediately obvious why this should be so. In debates with Jews, Christian writers, understandably, discussed the Jewish scriptures; both parties were familiar with the texts concerned and how they should be interpreted was part of the dialogue between them.[9] The position was not the same when the Christian gaze moved from the Jewish to the broader Graeco-Roman world. For, if knowledge of the Jewish scriptures did not extend beyond Jewish communities before the advent of Christianity – an assumption which will be tested below – it is reasonable to ask why a Christian apologist in debate with non-Jewish non-Christians would refer to these texts so extensively.[10]

The Greek Apologists

Apologetic works either promote Christianity to non-Jewish non-Christians or defend it against criticism from them. Such a text cannot stand alone since it must form part of a dialogue between a

---

5. E.g. B.D. Ehrman, ed., *The Apostolic Fathers*, LCL 2 vols (Cambridge, MA: Harvard University Press, 2003).

6. M.M. Mitchell, 'The Emergence of the Written Record', in CHC1, pp. 177-94, 191.

7. The term 'Graeco-Roman' is used throughout to describe the people and culture of the Roman Empire in the second century CE (excluding Jews and Christians) and denoting, somewhat imprecisely, the mainstream culture of the time. It can be criticised on grounds of accuracy – Jews and Christians may also be described as Graeco-Romans – but is preferred to the term 'pagans' which has too many extraneous connotations.

8. Noted in J. Carleton Paget, 'The Interpretation of the Bible in the Second Century', in NCHB1, pp. 549-83, 562, but not pursued further.

9. J.M. Lieu, *Image and Reality: The Jews in the World of the Christians in the Second Century* (London: T. & T. Clark, 1996), pp. 280-81.

10. E. Gibbon, *The Decline and Fall of the Roman Empire*, 6 vols (London: Dent, 1910), 1, p. 498, asserted long ago that such an argument would be ineffective: 'But this mode of persuasion loses much of its weight and influence when it is addressed to those who neither understand nor respect the Mosaic dispensation.'

Christian writer and a person or persons located outside the Christian community, even if there were no other written elements in the dialogue, or if whatever did exist does not survive. The emphasis here is on the arguments put forward in apologetic texts, so it is the contents of the works and the intentions behind them (so far as they can be captured) that are important, rather than the form in which a text is framed and the identity of the addressee(s) named in it.

Scholars have debated how the term 'apologetic' should be used, which works should be included within its scope and which authors should be referred to as apologists. They have reached different conclusions. The earliest apologetic works of which notice survives, those by Quadratus and Aristides, were addressed to the Emperor Hadrian on behalf of Christians.[11] Later works were also addressed to the emperor, notably, Justin Martyr's *Apologies*, and the term 'apologetic' can be restricted to petitions on behalf of Christians addressed to emperors or others in authority. Thus, Parvis defines apologetic texts as works 'that address those with the power to decide policy concerning the execution of Christians, at either an empire-wide or a local level'.[12] She restricts the term to a series of texts beginning with Justin Martyr and ending with Tertullian, excluding, for example, works by Tatian and Theophilus of Antioch which are not addressed to figures in authority. In contrast with this attention to the *form* of a text, however, other scholars emphasise the *intentions* of the authors. Norris, for instance, while recognising the genesis of second-century Christian apologetics in petitions to the Emperor, favours a broader definition. He describes the apologists as 'a series of authors who in the course of the second century composed and circulated addresses and pleas . . . to emperors and others in public authority on behalf of their fellow Christians'[13] but goes on to point out that: 'apology in this narrow sense might, of course, pass over into direct refutation of critics of Christianity or attempts to establish the superiority of the Christian faith'.[14]

Similar sentiments are found in works by Grant and Young, both echoing the emphasis on argument and intention. Thus, Grant describes the apologist as a writer located within a minority group

11. R.M. Grant, *Greek Apologists of the Second Century* (London: SCM Press, 1988), pp. 35-39.

12. S. Parvis, 'Justin Martyr and the Apologetic Tradition', in S. Parvis and P. Foster, eds, *Justin Martyr and His Worlds* (Minneapolis: Fortress Press, 2007), pp. 115-27, 117.

13. R.A. Norris Jr, 'The Apologists', in F.M. Young, L. Ayres and A. Louth, eds, *The Cambridge History of Early Christian Literature* (Cambridge: Cambridge University Press, 2004), pp. 36-44, 36.

14. Ibid., p. 36.

seeking to interpret the culture of that group to wider society[15] and includes within his *Greek Apologists of the Second Century* all Greek Christian writings of the period addressed to non-Christian non-Jewish audiences.[16] Young's survey covers a similarly wide range of texts, her definition being that: '"apology" is . . . the end or purpose of a speech, particularly a speech for the defence in court, and then more loosely a defence or excuse offered in a less precise context or genre'.[17] The approach adopted here reflects the broad descriptions of apologetic offered by these two scholars.

Apologetic Writings and Their Audiences

Who the apologists' audiences were is a difficult issue which has been much discussed, although it has never been clearly resolved. Arguably, however, it is unnecessary to reach a definitive conclusion for the purposes of this book, since the main concerns here are with the contents of the apologetic texts and the arguments they contain. Each text can therefore be examined as a repository of arguments which have been framed for the purposes of dialogue between Christians and non-Christians whatever the precise context in which it was written.

The precise contexts in which the apologetic texts were written are unknown. The form in which these works are couched is that they address named audiences outside Jewish and Christian communities and that they refer to questions posed and objections raised by the non-Christian addressees. Texts appear to assume some prior knowledge of the matters under discussion and to be part of an ongoing debate; issues are introduced without background explanation and the audience is presented as having at least a degree of prior knowledge of Christianity. Some commentators have been inclined to treat apologetic works at face value: Daniélou, for instance, describes them as 'the missionary literature of the second century, the presentation of the Gospel to the pagan world', contrasting them with internally-directed works of 'catechetical literature' aimed at 'expounding the faith to converts'.[18] A

---

15. Grant, *Greek Apologists*, p. 9.
16. Ibid., pp. 5-6.
17. F.M. Young, 'Greek Apologists of the Second Century', in M.J. Edwards, M.R. Goodman, S.R.F. Price and C. Rowland, eds, *Apologetics in the Roman Empire: Pagans, Jews and Christians* (Oxford: Oxford University Press, 1999), pp. 81-104, 91.
18. J. Daniélou, *Gospel Message and Hellenistic Culture*, trans. by J.A. Baker (London: Darton, Longman & Todd, 1973), p. 9.

similar view is espoused by Grant, who argues that: 'apologists wrote for non-Christian groups or individuals to tell outsiders about Christian truth'.[19]

The form of a text in the ancient world could, however, merely be the frame in which an author presents his material[20] and it is possible that, despite appearances, the audiences for apologetic works were actually to be found among Christians. The apologists make frequent use of techniques of literary artifice that were part of the rhetorical discourse of the time and the putative addressees could quite plausibly not be the real audiences.[21] Thus, some scholars have been inclined to treat the texts not so much as part of actual dialogues between Christians and Graeco-Romans, but rather as works that were in practice read wholly (or overwhelmingly) by Christians.[22] Sceptical positions of this kind reflect the terms of a similar debate on writings of the Hellenistic-Jewish period[23] and particularly the contribution of Tcherikover. In a widely-quoted article he argued that, although such literature was externally-directed apologetic in form, it was not, in fact, part of a dialogue between Jews and non-Jews but was written predominantly, if not exclusively, for – and read by – internal Jewish audiences.[24]

Even if, in spite of these arguments, apologetic works were aimed at non-Christians, it does not necessarily follow that they ever reached, or, *a fortiori*, significantly influenced, their intended audiences. As the editors of the 1999 collection, *Apologetics in the Roman Empire* put it: 'matter and style ensured that the apologists would not have been much read outside the Church'.[25] No reference to specific Christian apologetic texts is found in surviving non-Christian literature of the period, although this is an argument from silence, and the low rate of textual survival,

---

19. Grant, *Greek Apologists*, p. 11.
20. A good example is pseudonymous letter collections, see P.A. Rosenmeyer, *Ancient Epistolary Fictions: The Letter in Greek Literature* (Cambridge: Cambridge University Press, 2001), pp. 193-233.
21. M.J. Edwards, M.R. Goodman, S.R.F. Price and C. Rowland, 'Introduction: Apologetics in the Roman World', in Edwards et al., eds, *Apologetics*, pp. 1-13, 8-9. For apologists' use of rhetorical discourse, see R.M. Grant, 'Forms and Occasions of the Greek Apologists', *SMSR*, vol. 52 (1986), pp. 213-26.
22. E.g. M.J. Edwards, 'Apologetics', in S.A. Harvey and D.G. Hunter, eds, *The Oxford Handbook of Early Christian Studies* (Oxford: Oxford University Press, 2008), pp. 549-64, 550-51.
23. The term 'Hellenistic' refers to the period from the fourth century BCE to the second century CE.
24. V. Tcherikover, 'Jewish Apologetic Literature Reconsidered', *Eos*, vol. 48 (1956), pp. 169-93.
25. Edwards et al., 'Introduction', in Edwards et al., eds, *Apologetics*, p. 9.

coupled with the Christian bias to what does survive, prompts caution in drawing firm conclusions. Some non-Christian authors of the second century display an awareness of arguments in favour of Christianity, notably Galen[26] and Celsus,[27] although their writings do not reveal the sources of their knowledge and do not refer to specific Christian works. Some modern scholars, notably, Andresen and, following him, Droge,[28] have argued that the late second-century, anti-Christian writer Celsus wrote in response to Justin's *Apologies* and must therefore have known the latter's work directly. The case is, however, based on perceived similarities in the arguments discussed by Justin and Celsus, rather than on any close textual connections or references, leaving many scholars unconvinced.[29] Indeed, the most direct links between Justin and Celsus proposed by Andresen have been undermined very effectively by detailed critical scrutiny of the surviving texts.[30]

To regard the apologists' audiences as necessarily *either* internal *or* external may, however, be to oversimplify. These works may have been intended for both Christian and non-Christian readerships, rather than exclusively for one or the other; or it may be that texts aimed primarily at external readerships were extensively read internally. Moreover, the

---

26. Galen's writings date from the mid- to late second century CE. He is best-known for his work on medicine, but he also had a strong interest in philosophical issues. A few references to Christianity found in the large quantity of his surviving *oeuvre* betray a curiosity about Christian apologetic arguments, see R. Walzer, *Galen on Jews and Christians* (London: Oxford University Press, 1949). For Galen's *oeuvre*, see R.J. Hankinson, 'The Man and His Work', in R.J. Hankinson, ed., *The Cambridge Companion to Galen* (Cambridge: Cambridge University Press, 2008), pp. 1-33.

27. Celsus was an anti-Christian writer on philosophical issues of whom very little is known. His work, *True Doctrine*, is normally dated to the late second century and survives in significant quantity because the Christian writer Origen composed a comprehensive refutation of it in the mid-third century – *Against Celsus* – which included extensive quotations from Celsus' work. However, while he certainly betrays considerable knowledge of Christian ideas, Celsus makes no references to specific apologetic works, see Origen, *Contra Celsum*, trans. by H. Chadwick (Cambridge: Cambridge University Press, Cambridge 1953).

28. C. Andresen, *Logos und Nomos: Die Polemik des Kelsos wider das Christentum* (Berlin: de Gruyter, 1955), pp. 345-72; A.J. Droge, *Homer or Moses? Early Christian Interpretations of the History of Culture* (Tübingen: J.C.B. Mohr [Paul Siebeck], 1989), pp. 76-77.

29. E.g. E.F. Osborn, *Justin Martyr* (Tübingen: J.C.B. Mohr [Paul Siebeck], 1973), pp. 168-70.

30. G.T. Burke, 'Celsus and Justin: Carl Andresen revisited', *ZNW*, vol. 76 (1985), pp. 107-16.

boundaries between Christian and non-Christian were not necessarily clear,[31] and target audiences could have been located somewhere on the border between the Christian and the non-Christian, among new or potential converts, or among existing Christians considering abandonment of their new faith. It is to readings of this kind that recent scholars, such as Nyström and Pretila, have been drawn.[32]

Scholarly debates over the nature of the original audiences may, however, be less important than they initially appear to be. The subject matter of these apologetic works clearly lies in debates then current between Christians and non-Christians, since their authors would hardly have devoted their energies to discussing issues which were not live at the time. It is, however, quite possible that the apologists fashioned for use within their own communities texts which addressed concerns arising in externally-facing debates; so, even if their texts were written entirely for internal consumption, they were still concerned with issues of controversy between Christians and non-Christians, with how best to promote a Christian case to an external audience and how to respond to objections raised. Thus, even where uncertainty persists concerning the nature of its original audience, examination of the contents of a text and of the arguments it contains can still fruitfully be undertaken.

The term 'audience' can be used in a number of different senses and the discussion by Barclay, in the introduction to his translation of the Jewish writer Josephus' apologetic work *Against Apion*, written at the end of the first century,[33] provides helpful clarification on the issue. He distinguishes three senses of the term 'audience': the declared audience, that is those who are addressed by the text; the implied audience, that is the ideal readers presupposed or 'constructed' by the text; and the intended audience, that is those whom the author hopes will read it. Barclay points out that, while the declared and implied audiences are 'products' of the text itself, determining who the intended audience is may involve drawing on evidence from outside the text – where this is available – and it is the most difficult audience to identify.[34] Applying

---

31. J.M. Lieu, *Christian Identity in the Jewish and Graeco-Roman World* (Oxford: Oxford University Press, 2004), pp. 98-146.

32. D.E. Nyström, *The Apology of Justin Martyr: Literary Strategies and the Defence of Christianity* (Tübingen: Mohr Siebeck, 2018), pp. 19-66; N.W. Pretila, *Reappropriating 'Marvellous Fables': Justin Martyr's Strategic Retrieval of Myth in 1 Apology* (Eugene: Pickwick Publications, 2014), pp. 25-32.

33. Text in Josephus, *Contra Apionem*, ed. by H. St J. Thackeray, LCL 186 (Cambridge, MA: Harvard University Press, 1926); trans. in Flavius Josephus, *Against Apion*, by J.M.G. Barclay (Leiden: Brill, 2007).

34. Barclay, *Against Apion*, pp. xlv-li.

Barclay's categories to Christian apologetic texts, the declared audiences are the named Graeco-Roman addressees, while the implied audiences are to be found among educated Graeco-Romans more generally. The intended audiences are, however, not so straightforwardly defined; they may be found either among non-Christian Graeco-Romans or among members of Christian communities or, perhaps, among both.

Barclay's category of implied audience fits best with the approach to audiences for apologetic texts which is adopted here. What constitutes such an audience can therefore be determined from within the text itself. Audiences will, however, always be referred to here as if they are external to Christianity; this is primarily a matter of convenience, designed to avoid the convoluted phraseology that would be necessary to recognise at every turn the different possibilities for actual audiences which have been discussed here. It is also in line with the way the texts present themselves.

Apologetic Texts

This book does not try to deal with apologetic arguments as a whole but, specifically, with the use they make of the Jewish scriptures. 'Use' can take a number of forms and all of them will be found in different contexts in the works of the Greek apologists. First, there are direct quotations from the scriptural texts – which can be of varying lengths – that are included to support apologetic arguments and are often accompanied by explanations indicating how the texts should be read. Then, there are allusions to specific texts, some more and some less obvious, which again are employed to support the arguments being put forward. Finally, there are allusions which, in the course of an argument, refer to a literary tradition as a source rather than to a specific text. The terms used here to describe use of the scriptures should not be seen as precise definitions, however. In his *Echoes of Scripture in the Gospels* Hays categorises scriptural references by employing the terms 'quotation', 'allusion' and 'echo', although he also adds the wise cautionary note: 'These terms are approximate markers on the spectrum of intertextual linkage, moving from the most to the least explicit forms of reference.'[35]

Of the Greek Christian apologetic texts which are extant from the second century three stand out because they are substantial in themselves and because they make extensive use of the Jewish scriptures: Justin Martyr's *First Apology*, Tatian's *Oratio ad Graecos* and the *Ad Autolycum*

---

35.   R.B. Hays, *Echoes of Scripture in the Gospels* (Waco: Baylor University Press, 2016), p. 10.

of Theophilus of Antioch.[36] Other texts (or what survives of them) are either too brief – such as the works of Apollinaris and Melito[37] – or, if more substantial, rule themselves out because they refer to the Jewish scriptures only very sparingly; thus, Aristides' *Apology*[38] and Athenagoras' *Legatio*,[39] both of which present arguments in favour of Christianity, but neither of them on the basis of Jewish scriptural references,[40] exclude themselves from consideration. Limiting examination to three texts enables issues to be examined in detail and allows comparisons and contrasts to be explored which enrich understanding of the texts, individually and collectively. The following three chapters do contain some discussion of the authors of the texts although, in reality, relatively little is known about them, particularly when compared with authors from later centuries. So, it is the texts themselves, surviving as they do more or less complete, rather than their authors, that are the focus of this book.

Apologetic works are read here as texts about texts and, more specifically, as Christian texts about Jewish scriptures. The apologists present portraits of Christianity which are constructs that may reflect reality, in whole or part, but that are also a representation of reality created by their authors, and it may be hard to see where reflection finishes and creation begins. The Jewish scriptures which these authors discuss, quote from and interpret to their audiences are a central feature of the 'reality' of Christianity which they describe, and, to some extent, create,[41] so an appreciation of the way they portray the scriptures is important for a proper understanding of these works. How they present and make use of the scriptures is not predetermined; it is likely to vary

36. Bibliographical references to the texts are given in the relevant chapter.
37. Apollinaris is mentioned in Eusebius, *The History of the Church from Christ to Constantine*, trans. by G.A. Williamson, rev. and ed. with a new introduction by A. Louth (London: Penguin, 1989) (*HE*), 4.27 and 5.5. Extracts from Melito are quoted in Eusebius, *HE* 4.26. Grant, *Greek Apologists*, pp. 83-99 discusses both authors.
38. *The Apology of Aristides on Behalf of the Christians,* ed. by J.R. Harris with an Appendix by J.A. Robinson (Cambridge: Cambridge University Press, 1891).
39. Athenagoras, *Legatio and De Resurrectione*, ed. by W.R. Schoedel (Oxford: Clarendon Press, 1972).
40. *Apology of Aristides*, ed. by Harris, pp. 82-84, in the Appendix by Robinson, he identifies a mere eight references to 'Scripture', only one of which is to the Jewish scriptures (2 Maccabees 7:28), the remainder being to New Testament texts. Twelve references to the Jewish scriptures are listed in Athenagoras, *Legatio*, p. 154.
41. For the role of texts in creating identities, see Lieu, *Christian Identity*, pp. 27-61.

according to the context in which an author is making his argument. So, similarities and differences in the texts' handling of the scriptures, and how these relate to the literary contexts from which the texts emerged, need to be explored.

The Apologists and the Jewish Scriptures

Given the centrality of the Jewish scriptures for this book, it is necessary to understand something of their nature and of the form in which they might have been available to Christian apologists. It is also important to appreciate the significance of describing them as scriptures.

The Jewish scriptures were the products of ancient Jewish communities, originally composed largely in Hebrew over an extended period of time.[42] Texts came to be grouped as Torah,[43] Prophets and the much looser category called Writings and to be regarded by the Jews as authoritative scriptures. The processes by which this happened – and where the boundaries lay, around and between the different groupings of texts – are recognised by scholars as complex and controversial issues.[44] There were also texts, now commonly referred to as 'apocryphal', because they were ultimately excluded from some later biblical canons,[45] which may also be included under the umbrella heading of Jewish scriptures.

The Hebrew scriptures were translated into Greek, probably by the Jews themselves, during, or after, the third century BCE and probably over several centuries.[46] It is these Greek texts, circulating

---

42. Recent summaries of the issues, with references to some of the extensive literature, are E. Ulrich, 'The Old Testament Text and its Transmission', and J. Schaper, 'The Literary History of the Hebrew Bible', in NCHB1, pp. 83-104 and 105-44, respectively.

43. 'Law' is a common translation for Torah, although some scholars prefer 'Teaching', see B.M. Metzger and M.D. Coogan, eds, *The Oxford Guide to Ideas and Issues of the Bible* (Oxford: Oxford University Press, 2001), p. 493.

44. For a recent summary of the scholarly debates, with copious references to the literature, see J. Barton, 'The Old Testament Canons', in NCHB1, pp. 145-64.

45. J.J. Collins, 'The "Apocryphal" Old Testament', in NCHB1, pp. 165-89.

46. There is a large literature on the origin and development of the Jewish scriptures in Greek. General works containing extensive references to the scholarship are: G. Dorival, M. Harl and O. Munnich, *La Bible grecque des Septante: Du Judaïsme hellénistique au Christianisme ancien* (Paris: Éditions du Cerf, 1988); N. Fernández Marcos, *The Septuagint in Context: Introduction to the Greek Version of the Bible,* trans. by W.G.E. Watson (Leiden: Brill, 2000); K.H. Jobes and M. Silva, *Invitation to the Septuagint* (Grand Rapids: Baker Academic, 2000); and J.M. Dines, *The Septuagint* (Edinburgh: T. & T. Clark, 2004). For the broader cultural role of the Septuagint in ancient Judaism, see T.

among Hellenistic-Jewish communities, which were familiar to early Christians[47] and which are referred to as the Jewish scriptures. They are sometimes called the Septuagint, a term originally applied only to the Greek translation of the Torah,[48] although commonly used in modern literature to refer to Greek translations of the Hebrew scriptures more generally.[49] The term 'Septuagint' is helpful in distinguishing that set of translations from other renderings into Greek undertaken from the second century CE onwards, such as those of 'the Three', which were used by Jews (generally) rather than Christians.[50] The Jewish scriptures in Greek were the core texts of Hellenistic-Jewish culture; they were regarded as authoritative by Jews, as is evident from surviving Hellenistic-Jewish literary works from the second century BCE to the first century CE, such as the *Letter of Aristeas*[51] and the works of Philo[52] and Josephus.[53] The term 'Jewish scriptures' is imprecise, however, and

---

Rajak, *Translation and Survival: The Greek Bible of the Ancient Jewish Diaspora* (Oxford: Oxford University Press, 2009).

47. Considered in literature on the development of the 'Christian Bible', e.g. M. Hengel, *The Septuagint as Christian Scripture: Its Prehistory and the Problem of Its Canon*, trans. by M.E. Biddle (Edinburgh: T. & T. Clark, 2002). For a perspective from a scholar of Judaism, see Rajak, *Translation*, pp. 278-313.

48. The earliest surviving version of the so-called 'legend of the Septuagint', in the *Letter of Aristeas*, identifies seventy-two translators (later versions of the legend amended the number to seventy – hence, Septuagint) and refers only to the translation of the Torah, see *Aristeas to Philocrates: Letter of Aristeas*, ed. and trans. by M. Hadas (Eugene: Wipf & Stock, 1951), and A. Wasserstein and D.J. Wasserstein, *The Legend of the Septuagint from Classical Antiquity to Today* (Cambridge: Cambridge University Press, 2006).

49. As is shown by the titles of some of the works on the Greek Jewish scriptures noted above, see Rajak, *Translation*, pp. 14-16.

50. The relationship between the translations of 'the Three', Aquila, Symmachus and Theodotion, and the Septuagint is discussed in Jobes and Silva, *Invitation*, pp. 37-43, Fernández Marcos, *Septuagint*, pp. 109-54 and Rajak, *Translation*, pp. 290-313.

51. *Aristeas* is discussed below. The text contains lavish praise of the scriptures, e.g. on the part of the Egyptian King, see *Aristeas*, paras. 312-20.

52. Seen generally in the respectful way in which Philo approaches the Greek scriptures in his various commentaries (J.R. Royse, 'The Works of Philo', in A. Kamesar, ed., *The Cambridge Companion to Philo* [Cambridge: Cambridge University Press, 2009] pp. 32-64) and specifically in his account of the legend of the Septuagint; Philo, *De Vita Mosis*, ed. by F.H. Colson, LCL 289, 2 vols (Cambridge, MA: Harvard University Press, 1935), 2, 25-44.

53. Seen in the way Josephus retells the scriptural narrative in his *Jewish Antiquities*, ed. by H. St J. Thackeray, R. Marcus and L.H. Feldman, LCL, 9 vols (Cambridge, MA: Harvard University Press, 1930-1965), and in his comments on the scriptures in *Against Apion*, trans. by Barclay, 1.37-42.

should not be taken to indicate that there was necessarily a defined set of texts grouped into a collection whose make-up was clearly established by the second century CE.[54]

The earliest Christians were, of course, Jews and invoking the scriptures inherited from Judaism was a significant feature of early Christian texts. This is seen in different ways in New Testament texts – in the canonical gospels, the letters of Paul and in Revelation – and, in acknowledgment of this, study of 'the Old Testament in the New Testament' is a recognised area of scholarship.[55] The significance of the Jewish scriptures is also evident in other first- and second-century Christian texts, such as those written by the authors known as the Apostolic Fathers.[56]

The importance of the scriptures for Christians was in large measure associated with the promotion of Jesus Christ as the Jewish Messiah. Their distinctly Christian interpretations of the scriptures differed from, and, indeed, placed them in conflict with, those Jews who retained an allegiance to the traditions of Judaism. In the second century the Jewish scriptures have thus been described as being *inter alia* 'a tool in polemical encounters with Jews'[57] in the hands of Christian writers. A notable example is the *Epistle of Barnabas* which argues forcefully in favour of Christian and against traditional Jewish interpretations of the scriptures.[58] Use of these texts was therefore not something new in the apologists' writings; what was novel was reference to them in texts addressed, ostensibly at least, to audiences outside Christianity or Judaism.

Christian authors of the second century did not necessarily have access to complete texts of the Jewish scriptures and material may have reached them through extracts, summaries, or perhaps orally, or possibly through quotations and references in the writings of others. Written texts were scarce in the ancient world; 'publication' was only achieved by manual copying[59] and the Jewish scriptures represented a large corpus

---

54. L.M. McDonald, 'Canon', in J.W. Rogerson and J.M. Lieu, eds, *The Oxford Handbook of Biblical Studies* (Oxford: Oxford University Press, 2006), pp. 777-809; and M.W. Holmes, 'The Biblical Canon', in Harvey and Hunter, eds, *Oxford Handbook of Early Christian Studies*, pp. 406-26.

55. Examples of the extensive literature are: C.H. Dodd, *According to the Scriptures: The Sub-Structure of New Testament Theology* (London: Nisbet & Co., 1952); and S. Moyise, *Evoking Scripture: Seeing the Old Testament in the New* (London: T. & T. Clark, 2008).

56. Ehrman, *The Apostolic Fathers*.

57. Carleton Paget, 'Interpretation of the Bible', p. 549.

58. J. Carleton Paget, *The Epistle of Barnabas: Outlook and Background* (Tübingen: J.C.B. Mohr [Paul Siebeck], 1994), pp. 69-70.

59. H.Y. Gamble, *Books and Readers in the Early Church: A History of Early*

of texts. Indeed, scholars recognise that handbooks and collections of extracts were forms in which material from literary and philosophical works was transmitted[60] and there is evidence that among Jews ideas and texts from the Jewish scriptures were accessed in the form of extracts or summaries.[61] Such practices influenced emerging Christianity and the theory that *testimonia*, or collections of prophetic proof-texts from scripture, were in circulation in early Christian communities has gained considerable currency. This was initially prompted by the work of Dodd[62] and then developed by other scholars; Albl has provided a review of this scholarly field.[63] The most notable application of the *testimonia* thesis to the second century is Skarsaune's work on the sources used by Justin, which shows how his scriptural quotations were derived from more than one distinct testimonial tradition.[64]

Scripture

The term 'scripture' has been used up to now in the phrase 'Jewish scriptures' without explanatory comment. It is a modern term, and a term of convenience, which is useful in the current context, although its meaning requires clarification.[65] In the context of the debate on the development of the biblical canon Ulrich[66] has provided the following helpful definition: 'A book of scripture is a sacred authoritative work

---

Christian Texts (New Haven: Yale University Press, 1995).

60. H. Chadwick, 'Florilegium', in RAC, 7, pp. 1131-43, and M.C. Albl, *'And Scripture Cannot Be Broken': The Form and Function of the Early Christian* Testimonia *Collections* (Leiden: Brill, 1999), pp. 73-81.

61. Albl, *'And Scripture Cannot Be Broken'*, pp. 81-93. For Qumran evidence, see G.J. Brooke, 'Thematic Commentaries on Prophetic Scriptures', in M. Henze, ed., *Biblical Interpretation at Qumran* (Grand Rapids: Eerdmans, 2005), pp. 134-57.

62. Dodd, *According to the Scriptures*, especially pp. 28-110.

63. Albl, *'And Scripture Cannot Be Broken'*, pp. 7-69 for a literature review and pp. 97-158 for Christian *testimonia* collections. A note of caution is, however, struck in Carleton Paget, 'Interpretation of the Bible', p. 556: 'In the absence of unambiguous evidence for the existence of testimony books, certitude about their existence is impossible.'

64. O. Skarsaune, *The Proof from Prophecy: A Study in Justin Martyr's Proof-Text Tradition: Text-Type, Provenance, Theological Profile* (Leiden: Brill, 1987), pp. 139-242.

65. This is not always provided in the literature. The chapter entitled 'The Uses of Scripture in Hellenistic Judaism' in Rajak, *Translation*, pp. 210-38, uses the term 'scripture' without discussing what it means.

66. E. Ulrich, 'The Notion and Definition of Canon', in L.M. McDonald and J.A. Sanders, eds, *The Canon Debate* (Peabody: Hendrickson, 2002), pp. 21-35.

believed to have God as its ultimate author, which the community, as a group and individually, recognizes and accepts as determinative for its belief and practice for all time and in all geographical areas.'[67]

This is quite a precise definition, which views scripture as necessarily determinative for belief and practice, not simply as inspired (and inspirational) text. Use of the word 'authoritative', however, begs the question as to what that term means; again, Ulrich provides a definition: 'An authoritative work is a writing which a group, secular or religious, recognizes and accepts as determinative for its conduct, and as of a higher order than can be overridden by the power or will of the group or any member.'[68]

Once more the idea of a text being determinative for conduct is present, and it is striking that both definitions stress what a group or community 'recognizes and accepts'. Thus, there is not something inherent in a text which qualifies it as scripture; what is critical is the attitude taken towards it and how it is viewed and treated by those who possess or use it.

These definitions fit well the texts sacred to the Jews and the term 'Jewish scriptures' is therefore appropriately applied to them. It is worth noting, however, that the Graeco-Roman literary tradition did not have an analogous set of sacred texts fitting the definition of scripture employed here.[69] The Homeric epics have sometimes been seen as a parallel for the Jewish scriptures, but the comparison is a misleading one. Finkelberg and Stroumsa draw a helpful distinction between literary and religious canons, placing the works of Homer in the first category and the Jewish scriptures in the second.[70] In a further work Finkelberg[71] has developed the concept of the 'foundational text' which she defines as having three

---

67. Ibid., p. 29.
68. Ibid.
69. There were, of course, religious texts outside the Jewish tradition, but neither the Egyptian priestly records referred to by Diodorus Siculus, *Library of History*, ed. by C.H. Oldfather, LCL, 12 vols (Cambridge, MA: Harvard University Press, 1933-67), 1, 69.7, nor the Roman *Books of the Pontifices* referred to in ancient sources (J.A. North, 'The Books of the *Pontifices*', in C. Moatti, ed., *La mémoire perdue: recherches sur l'administration romaine* [Rome: École Française de Rome, 1998], pp. 45-63) are analogous to the Jewish sacred texts.
70. M. Finkelberg and G.G. Stroumsa, 'Introduction: Before the Western Canon', in M. Finkelberg and G.G. Stroumsa, eds, *Homer, the Bible and Beyond: Literary and Religious Canons in the Ancient World* (Leiden: Brill, 2003), pp. 1-8.
71. M. Finkelberg, 'Canonising and Decanonising Homer: Reception of the Homeric Poems in Antiquity and Modernity', in M.R. Niehoff, ed., *Homer and the Bible in the Eyes of Ancient Interpreters* (Brill, Leiden 2012), pp. 15-28.

criteria: that it occupies the central place in education; that it is the focus of exegetical activity aimed at defending it from any form of criticism; and that it should be the vehicle by which the identity of the community to which it belongs is articulated.[72] She claims that both Homer and the Bible meet these criteria and that both should therefore be seen as foundational texts. The standard for scripture set out above is, however, much more exacting than the one Finkelberg sets for her 'foundational text'; it includes the notions that a text is 'believed to have God as its ultimate author' and that it is recognised and accepted 'as determinative for its belief and practice for all time'. These features are characteristic of the Jewish scriptures but not the Homeric epics; so, while both texts may be described as foundational, the latter cannot be described as scripture.

The Jewish Scriptures and the Graeco-Roman World

It has been the implication so far that non-Christian non-Jews were not familiar with the Jewish scriptures already and that the apologists brought these texts to their attention for the first time. This assumption needs to be tested, however, and there are a number of ways of doing this. First, the question can be asked whether Judaism was a proselytising religion; if it was, then the scriptures, which were central to Judaism, would doubtless have featured in any dialogues with non-Jews that aimed to attract converts. Second, Hellenistic-Jewish literature can be explored to see whether it shows Jewish writers actively promoting their scriptures to non-Jewish audiences. Third, Graeco-Roman writings can be examined to establish whether their authors reveal knowledge or awareness of the Jewish scriptures. Analysis of these three strands of evidence will show that the extent to which the apologists' Graeco-Roman audiences were familiar with the Jewish scriptures before the advent of Christianity was at best very limited.

Alexander the Great's conquests in the fourth century BCE provided the impetus to accelerate the movement of Jews outside Palestine and encourage the growth of diaspora Jewish communities in Greek cities of the Eastern Mediterranean.[73] This brought Jews into close proximity with non-Jews and, although the extent to which they integrated or remained separate has been debated,[74] opportunities clearly existed for

---

72. Ibid., p. 16.
73. J.M.G. Barclay, *Jews in the Mediterranean Diaspora: From Alexander to Trajan (323 BCE-117 CE)* (Edinburgh: T. & T. Clark, 1996).
74. Analysed by Barclay in ibid., pp. 92-102, in terms of assimilation, acculturation and accommodation.

proselytising activity. Some scholars, from Harnack onwards, have argued that such activity was significant and, indeed, successful.[75] Studies by McKnight[76] and Goodman[77] have, however, concluded (independently) that Jewish missionary activity was not of great significance in the ancient world. For both scholars, the argument is essentially the same: that the evidence is simply insufficient to support the case. They acknowledge that Jews may have been receptive to proselytes and that there are examples of non-Jews becoming sympathisers towards, or even converts to, Judaism; but they both regard such evidence as limited and insufficient to support the contention that missionary activity was widespread; and their conclusions have been endorsed in another, more recent, work by Riesner.[78] Other scholars, notably, Bird[79] and, especially, Carleton Paget,[80] have supplied something of a corrective in suggesting that missionary activity was perhaps a more significant phenomenon than McKnight and Goodman allowed for. Importantly, however, this has not led them to contend that any such missionary activity provided a route by which the Jewish scriptures became well known outside Jewish circles to any significant extent, and that is the critical point at issue here.[81]

---

75. A. Harnack, *The Expansion of Christianity in the First Three Centuries*, trans. by J. Moffat, 2 vols (London: Williams & Norgate, 1904-05), 1, pp. 1-18; E. Schürer, *The History of the Jewish People in the Age of Jesus Christ* (*175 BC-AD 135*), Vol. 3.i, ed. by G. Vermes, F. Millar and M. Goodman, new English rev. version (Edinburgh: T. & T. Clark, 1986), pp. 150-76; more recently, L.H. Feldman, *Jew and Gentile in the Ancient World: Attitudes and Interactions from Alexander to Justinian* (Princeton: Princeton University Press, 1993), pp. 288-382.

76. S. McKnight, *A Light among the Gentiles: Jewish Missionary Activity in the Second Temple Period* (Minneapolis: Fortress Press, 1991).

77. M. Goodman, *Mission and Conversion: Proselytising in the Religious History of the Roman Empire* (Oxford: Clarendon Press, 1994).

78. R. Riesner, 'A Pre-Christian Jewish Mission?', in J. Ådna and H. Kvalbein, *The Mission of the Early Church to Jews and Gentiles* (Tübingen: Mohr Siebeck, 2000), pp. 211-50.

79. M.L. Bird, *Crossing Land and Sea: Jewish Missionary Activity in the Second Temple Period* (Peabody: Hendrickson, 2010).

80. J. Carleton Paget, *Jews, Christians and Jewish Christians in Antiquity* (Tübingen: Mohr Siebeck, 2010), pp. 149-83.

81. That Judaism could embrace a 'universalist' outlook has been well argued by T.L. Donaldson, *Judaism and the Gentiles: Jewish Patterns of Universalism* (*to 135 CE*) (Waco: Baylor University Press, 2007), in which universalism is identified with four factors: a spectrum of sympathisers, converts, ethical monotheism and participants in eschatological redemption. Donaldson is, however, clear that universalism does not necessarily entail proselytism.

Surviving Hellenistic-Jewish literature provides some evidence of Jewish history and culture being promoted to external audiences. This did not entail bringing the scriptures to their attention to any marked extent, however, and where the externally apologetic impetus is clearest – with Josephus – there is no apparent desire to promote the actual texts of the scriptures to non-Jews.

The most substantial item of Hellenistic-Jewish literature, the Septuagint translation, made it possible for Greek-speaking non-Jews to read the Jewish scriptures, at least if they were able to gain access to it. The text itself provides scant clues as to why translation from Hebrew into Greek was undertaken. There is one tantalising reference in the Prologue to Sirach, at a point where the author is discussing translation and says: 'it is necessary that . . . those who love learning be capable of service to outsiders, both when they speak and when they write.'[82] This could be taken to indicate that translation into Greek was, at least in part, undertaken for the benefit of those outside Jewish communities, although the reference is ambiguous and far from conclusive. *The Letter of Aristeas* which is the earliest surviving text to contain a version of the so-called 'legend of the Septuagint' was probably written in the second century BCE.,[83] It describes how the translation project was initiated by Ptolemy of Egypt in the third century BCE so that a copy of the Greek version could be deposited in the famous Library at Alexandria, where it would be available for non-Jews to read.[84] It thus provides evidence of a tradition – clearly extant in the ancient world – that the Septuagint was regarded from its inception as performing an apologetic function. There are obviously fictional elements to *Aristeas*[85] and some elements of its narrative do not appear very credible.[86] The whole account is not without historical value, however, for it appears to preserve a tradition of early interest in the translation of the Jewish scriptures into Greek on the part of the Ptolemaic rulers of Egypt. Some scholars have treated the essence of the story as quite plausible, not least because they have found

82. *NETS*, Sirach, Prologue, 5.
83. Dating can only be tentative; scholars place the text somewhere in the second century BCE. For discussion of the debate, see Schürer, *History of the Jewish People*, 3.i, pp. 677-84.
84. *Aristeas*, paras. 38 and 317.
85. The author presents himself as a Greek royal emissary, although modern scholars are unanimous in the view that he was an Alexandrian Jew. The arguments are summarised in *Aristeas*, Introduction, pp. 3-9.
86. E.g. the lengthy account of the philosophical question-and-answer sessions involving Ptolemy and the Jewish scholars and the detailed description of the gifts Ptolemy sent to Jerusalem, see *Aristeas*, paras. 182-300 and 51-82.

it difficult to conceive that such a large-scale literary enterprise could have been carried through by Alexandrian Jews without royal support.[87] With or without such assistance, however, the Septuagint translation has tended to be regarded by modern scholarship as an initiative of the Jewish community of Alexandria itself, carried out not to support proselytising activity, but for the benefit of Greek-speaking Jews themselves.[88]

In addition to the Septuagint, fragments of Hellenistic-Jewish literature survive in the works of later Christian authors. These fragments are thought to date from between the third and first century BCE and to emanate from Alexandria,[89] although their fragmentary nature means that the original works cannot be judged as whole entities. As they are, however, these texts do not constitute strong evidence that their authors were promoting the scriptures to non-Jews. Their contents do include material clearly derived from the Jewish scriptures[90] – sometimes with additions to, and sometimes with quite marked divergences from, the scriptural accounts – but the surviving fragments at least do not quote from the scriptures or even refer to them as sources.

These works are couched in Hellenistic-Greek literary forms[91] but diaspora Jewish communities were extensively Hellenised, writing in Greek and with a culture strongly influenced by Greek traditions,[92] so it

---

87. S. Honigman, *The Septuagint and Homeric Scholarship in Alexandria: A Study in the Narrative of the* Letter of Aristeas (London: Routledge, 2003), pp. 136-39; Rajak, *Translation*, pp. 64-91.

88. Barclay, *Jews in the Mediterranean*, pp. 424-26; Rajak, *Translation*, pp. 210-38.

89. *Fragments from Hellenistic Jewish Authors*, ed. by C.R. Holladay, 4 vols (Chico and Atlanta: Scholars Press, 1983-96), *Volume 1: Historians* (1983) and *Volume 2: Poets* (1989). Individual texts are discussed in: Schürer, *History of the Jewish People*, 3.i, pp. 513-66; P.M. Fraser, *Ptolemaic Alexandria*, 3 vols (Oxford: Clarendon Press, 1972), 1, pp. 687-716; J.J. Collins, *Between Athens and Jerusalem: Jewish Identity in the Hellenistic Diaspora*, 2nd edn (Grand Rapids: Eerdmans, 2000), pp. 29-63; E.S. Gruen, *Heritage and Hellenism: The Reinvention of Jewish Tradition* (Berkeley: University of California Press, 1998), pp. 110-88.

90. For example, Demetrius the Chronographer deals predominantly with events in Genesis and Exodus, Eupolemus largely with Solomon and the building of the Temple and Artapanus mainly with material from Exodus, see Holladay, *Fragments 1*, pp. 51-243.

91. Chiefly historical forms, e.g. Eupolemus and Pseudo-Aristeas, see Holladay, *Fragments 1*, pp. 93-156 and 261-75, but also poetic drama, e.g. 'The Exodus' of Ezekiel the Tragedian, see *The* Exagoge *of Ezekiel*, ed. by H. Jacobson (Cambridge: Cambridge University Press, 1983), and Hellenistic-Oriental romance, e.g. Artapanus, see Holladay, *Fragments 1*, pp. 189-243, and M. Braun, *History and Romance in Graeco-Oriental Literature* (Oxford: Blackwell, 1938), pp. 26-31.

92. Barclay, *Jews in the Mediterranean*, pp. 88-124.

cannot be assumed that they were written with an intended audience in view which was among non-Jews as opposed to Hellenised Jews.[93] They are probably best seen as akin to the 'Rewritten Bible' texts which were a prominent feature of the literature of Second Temple Judaism and which were written for internal Jewish consumption.[94]

The work of the first-century-CE Alexandrian Jew Philo[95] survives in impressive quantity, much of it comprising commentaries on the Pentateuch of various kinds written in Greek.[96] There is no external evidence to indicate who Philo's audience was, nor does he himself say for whom he was writing, so judgements on these issues must be made from evidence in the texts themselves.[97]

Philo's surviving texts which relate to the scriptures are conventionally divided into three groups: the Allegorical Commentaries, the Questions and Answers and the Exposition of the Law. The Allegorical Commentaries appear to assume prior knowledge of the Pentateuch; they do not provide introductions to the texts but are written to deepen readers' understanding of their meaning. Scholars have therefore understandably concluded that these texts were written for already

93. The argument in the influential article by Tcherikover, 'Jewish Apologetic Literature Reconsidered', has already been noted. G.E. Sterling, *Historiography and Self-Definition: Josephos, Luke-Acts and Apologetic Historiography* (Leiden: Brill, 1992) argues that Jewish historical literature is aimed at self-definition rather than external presentation.

94. G. Vermes, *Scripture and Tradition in Judaism: Haggadic Studies*, 2nd rev. edn (Leiden: Brill, 1973), pp. 67-126; P.S. Alexander, 'Retelling the Old Testament', in D.A. Carson and H.G.M. Williamson, eds, *It Is Written: Scripture Citing Scripture: Essays in Honour of Barnabas Lindars, SSF* (Cambridge: Cambridge University Press, 1988), pp. 99-121; D.A. Machiela, 'Once More, with Feeling: Rewritten Scripture in Ancient Judaism – A Review of Recent Developments', *JJS*, vol. 61 (2010), pp. 308-20.

95. For family and personal background, see D.R. Schwartz, 'Philo, His Family, and His Times', in A. Kamesar, ed., *The Cambridge Companion to Philo* (Cambridge: Cambridge University Press, 2009), pp. 9-31.

96. Royse, 'The Works of Philo', pp. 32-64.

97. There is a large literature on Philo. The following are useful for the issues discussed here: E.R. Goodenough, 'Philo's Exposition of the Law and his *De Vita Mosis*', *HTR*, vol. 26 (1933), pp. 109-25; P. Borgen, *Philo of Alexandria: An Exegete for His Time* (Leiden: Brill, 1997); E. Birnbaum, *The Place of Judaism in Philo's Thought: Israel, Jews and Proselytes* (Atlanta: Scholars Press, 1996); D.M. Hay, ed., *Both Literal and Allegorical: Studies in Philo of Alexandria's Questions and Answers on Genesis and Exodus* (Atlanta: Scholars Press, 1991); D.T. Runia, *Exegesis and Philosophy: Studies on Philo of Alexandria* (Aldershot: Variorum, 1990); M. Niehoff, *Philo on Jewish Identity and Culture* (Tübingen: Mohr Siebeck, 2001).

believing Jews. The Questions and Answers – those on Genesis and Exodus survive – are simpler works, which explain the sacred texts in a question-and-answer form and at a much more basic level.[98] They appear best fitted to being an educative tool for use in a catechetical context within Jewish communities and this is how scholars have come to regard them.[99]

The Exposition of the Law is the set of Philo's texts which could most plausibly be directed at an audience external to Judaism and could therefore be a vehicle for bringing the scriptures to the attention of a Graeco-Roman audience. Some Philo scholars have been drawn to the idea of such an audience, for instance, Goodenough[100] in the early twentieth century and Runia[101] in the late twentieth century. More recently, Niehoff has also argued that the Exposition texts were aimed at a Graeco-Roman audience, although she has done this in the context of a biographical reading of Philo's *oeuvre* which remains extremely controversial among scholars.[102] In one of the Exposition texts, the *Life of Moses*, Philo expresses the wish that the Jewish scriptures should become better known among non-Jews[103] and should indeed be accepted by them; he even suggests that the rationale for the Septuagint translation was to bring the scriptures to the attention of Greeks.[104] Comments of this kind are, however, very

98. Philo, *Questions on Genesis*, trans. by R. Marcus, LCL 380, and *Questions on Exodus*, trans. by R. Marcus, LCL 401 (Cambridge, MA: Harvard University Press, 1953).

99. M. Niehoff, *Jewish Exegesis and Homeric Scholarship in Alexandria* (Cambridge: Cambridge University Press, 2011), pp. 152-68.

100. Goodenough, 'Philo's Exposition of the Law'.

101. Runia, *Exegesis and Philosophy*, argues for an audience of both Jews and non-Jews.

102. M. Niehoff, *Philo of Alexandria: An Intellectual Biography* (New Haven: Yale University Press, 2018). She presents an 'intellectual biography' of Philo suggesting that his visit to Rome in 38-41 CE led to a shift in the audience at which his works were directed from internal Jewish to external Graeco-Roman, with the texts of the Exposition of the Law (which she argues were composed later in Philo's life) as externally-directed. The thesis is speculative, not least since Philo's texts do not provide any clear evidence for dating or even sequencing.

103. 'But, if a fresh start should be made to brighter prospects, how great a change for the better might we expect to see! I believe that each nation would abandon its peculiar ways, and, throwing overboard their ancestral customs, turn to honouring our laws alone': Philo, *De Vita Mosis*, 2, 44.

104. 'Then it was that some people, thinking it a shame that the laws should be found in one half only of the human race, the barbarians, and denied altogether to the Greeks, took steps to have them translated': Philo, *De Vita Mosis*, 2, 27.

rare in Philo's extant works and they are probably best read as the wishes and hopes of a fervent Jew, rather than as evidence of a serious apologetic intention.

In the *Life of Moses*, as indeed in other Exposition of the Law texts, Philo's practice is not to quote from the Jewish scriptures, as such, but rather to paraphrase or summarise them. Thus, even if Philo's audience was external to the Jewish community in Alexandria, little or no support is provided for the argument that he wishes to encourage non-Jews to become directly acquainted with the sacred texts. So, like the fragmentary text survivals discussed earlier, Philo's writings do not furnish evidence that the Jewish scriptures were becoming known outside Jewish communities.

The final Hellenistic-Jewish writer to consider is Josephus, who wrote as an exile in Rome towards the end of the first century CE[105] and who addresses a non-Jewish audience. In his *Jewish Antiquities*[106] Josephus re-presents scriptural material as a historical narrative in the Graeco-Roman manner, and the story of the Jewish people is told as a series of lives of great men whose deeds exhibit cardinal virtues.[107] He appears to want to acquaint his audience with the contents of the Jewish scriptures but not to expose them to the actual texts. He acknowledges his debt to the scriptures as the prime source for his history of the Jewish people.[108] However, the actual wording of his account is not close to that of the scriptures. He paraphrases and elaborates rather than translating.[109] In *Against Apion*, his apologetic work on behalf of Judaism, Josephus writes to demonstrate the antiquity of the Jewish people to a Graeco-Roman audience[110] but he deliberately draws on evidence from non-Jewish historical sources rather than from the Jewish scriptures.[111]

---

105. For Josephus generally, see T. Rajak, *Josephus, the Historian and His Society* (London: Duckworth, 1983).
106. Complete text in Josephus, *Jewish Antiquities*, LCL. Translations and commentaries in: Flavius Josephus, *Judean Antiquities: Books 1-4*, trans. by L.H. Feldman (Leiden: Brill, 2004), *Judean Antiquities: Books 5-7* and *Judean Antiquities: Books 8-10*, trans. by C.T. Begg and P. Spilsbury (Leiden: Brill, 2005). See also L.H. Feldman, *Josephus's Interpretation of the Bible* (Berkeley: University of California Press, 1998), and L.H. Feldman, *Studies in Josephus' Rewritten Bible* (Leiden: Brill, 1998).
107. Feldman, *Josephus's Interpretation*, pp. 74-131. This literary form has been termed 'apologetic historiography': Sterling, *Historiography and Self-Definition*, pp. 226-310.
108. Josephus, *Jewish Antiquities*, 1.17.
109. Feldman, *Josephus's Interpretation*, pp. 14-73.
110. Barclay, *Against Apion*, pp. xlv-liii.
111. Ibid., 1.73-218 discusses Egyptian, Phoenician, Chaldean and Greek evidence

Josephus wants to tell his audience about the scriptures and praises them lavishly[112] but he does not quote from them and refers to them only in general terms. He says that non-Jewish writers do not read the Jewish scriptures[113] and he is neither encouraging nor expecting his audience to read them directly.

As well as writings from Hellenistic Judaism, the surviving corpus of non-Jewish Graeco-Roman literature can be examined for evidence as to whether the Septuagint was known outside Jewish circles before the advent of Christianity. Some of these works reveal a positive interest in the history and culture of the Jews. References to the Jewish scriptures are, however, isolated and fragmentary, and insufficient to demonstrate strong familiarity on the part of the Graeco-Roman authors. Indeed, it seems likely that exposure to the Jewish scriptures outside Jewish communities was only ever very partial. The volume of the scriptural texts is, of course, very large; the early chapters of Genesis feature significantly in the examples quoted below, so this material may have been better known than the rest. It is also possible that collections of extracts or summaries or paraphrases circulated rather than full texts and that, while the Jewish scriptures may have been the ultimate source for some Graeco-Roman writers, their contents were mediated through shorter or more simplified texts rather than being derived from the scriptures themselves.[114]

Surviving references to the Jews in Graeco-Roman literature have been conveniently collected by Stern.[115] Notable examples are: Strabo's *Geography*, which devotes extensive space to the history, religion and political arrangements of the Jewish people;[116] Alexander Polyhistor's *On the Jews*, which is known to have been a well-researched account of the Jewish people;[117] Book IV of Plutarch's *Table Talk*, which discusses Jewish

---

for the history of the Jews, rather than Jewish, arguing that these will be credible to a Graeco-Roman readership whereas Jewish sources would not be (1.69-72).

112. Ibid., 1.37-42.

113. Ibid., 1.217.

114. Rajak, *Translation*, p. 269, says as much of Pseudo-Longinus (discussed further below): 'Longinus will have read, if not the Greek Bible, at least a form of rewritten Bible which, for my argument, is worth almost as much.'

115. *Greek and Latin Authors on Jews and Judaism*, ed. by M. Stern, 3 vols (Jerusalem: Israel Academy of Sciences and Humanities, 1974-84).

116. Ibid., 1, pp. 261-315. Strabo is dated by Stern from the 60s of the first century BCE to the 20s of the first century CE.

117. It only survives in fragments: ibid., pp. 157-64. Alexander Polyhistor dates from the first century BCE.

religion;[118] and Book V of Tacitus' *Histories*, which displays considerable curiosity about the history of the Jews, recounting no fewer than six different versions of their origins as a people.[119] Graeco-Roman interest in the Jews coalesced around a number of themes: their antiquity and their foundation story in the Exodus from Egypt, the figure of Moses their founder and great leader,[120] certain customs peculiar to the Jews (abstention from pork, circumcision and Sabbath observance) and their severely aniconic monotheism.

The material on which Graeco-Roman writers drew must in large part have come ultimately from Jewish traditions but whether to any extent from the Jewish scriptures themselves is unclear. Reticence in Graeco-Roman texts about the sources being drawn on makes judgement difficult; the Jewish scriptures are not quoted or even cited as a source but references to them have been detected in some works. Cook, who has made a special study of the subject, argues that Nicolaus of Damascus 'undoubtedly had access to a LXX even if he did not know it well'[121] and, somewhat more cautiously, that Apollonius Mollon[122] and Pompeius Trogus[123] had access to scriptural traditions, if not actually to the Septuagint. Graeco-Roman writers sometimes mention the Jewish sacred books, showing at least that they were aware of their existence: Diodorus Siculus writes of the Jewish holy books 'containing the xenophobic laws' when relating the story of the profanation of the Temple by Antiochus IV,[124] Alexander Polyhistor refers to Jewish sacred books[125] and the poet Juvenal to Moses' 'secret tome'.[126] There are also a few allusions to the text of the Jewish scriptures in surviving Graeco-Roman works, in Ocellus Lucanus, Pseudo-Ecphantus and Pseudo-Longinus. The work of Ocellus Lucanus dates from the second century BCE and contains an

---

118. Ibid., pp. 545-76. Plutarch dates from the 40s of the first century CE to the 20s of the second century.
119. Stern, *Greek and Latin Authors*, 2, pp. 1-93.
120. The subject of a study in its own right: J.G. Gager, *Moses in Greco-Roman Paganism* (Nashville: Abingdon Press, 1972).
121. J.G. Cook, *The Interpretation of the Old Testament in Greco-Roman Paganism* (Tübingen: Mohr Siebeck, 2004), p. 20.
122. Ibid., pp. 11-13; Stern, *Greek and Latin Authors*, 1, pp. 148-56. Apollonius Mollon dates from the first century BCE.
123. Cook, *Interpretation*, pp. 23-25; Stern, *Greek and Latin Authors*, 1, pp. 332-43. Pompeius Trogus dates from the end of the first century BCE to the beginning of the first century CE.
124. Stern, *Greek and Latin Authors*, 1, p. 183; Cook, *Interpretation*, pp. 16-18.
125. Ibid., pp. 13-15; Stern, *Greek and Latin Authors*, 1, p. 158.
126. Juvenal, *Satires*, ed. by S.M. Braund, LCL 91 (Cambridge, MA: Harvard University Press, 2004), 14.102.

apparent reference to Genesis 1:28;[127] the quotation is not exact but the verbal similarity signals the connection to be a very plausible one (to Stern a 'probable allusion').[128] Two texts in Pseudo-Ecphantus, noted by Stern, also appear to exhibit semantic similarities – again not exact – with Genesis 2:7 and 1:26, respectively.[129] In *On the Sublime* by Pseudo-Longinus,[130] a reference to Genesis 1:3, 9 and 10, which is described as being from a work by 'the lawgiver of the Jews',[131] that is, Moses, is much clearer. The introduction of this reference, with minimal explanation, suggests that the Genesis passage was familiar, not just to the author, but also to his readers; it is noteworthy not only that the reference is made, but that Moses is described as 'no mean genius',[132] with his ideas being described in positive terms.

In a somewhat different category is the work already referred to of the anti-Christian polemicist, Celsus. His *True Doctrine* is important because it is the only anti-Christian work of any substance to survive from the second century. Extracts from it included in Origen's *Against Celsus* – written to refute it – show that Celsus was well-informed about Christianity and had some knowledge of the contents of the Jewish scriptures, notably of parts of Genesis and Exodus.[133] There is, however, only one actual scriptural quotation in the extensive surviving extracts from *True Doctrine* and it therefore cannot be said with any certainty that Celsus had direct knowledge of the Jewish scriptures. Cook's conclusion that his knowledge of the Jewish scriptures was 'very spotty'[134] is well-judged. Like the Graeco-Roman authors already discussed, Celsus appears to have had some, albeit limited, familiarity with the contents of the Jewish scriptures; but this could easily have been acquired from intermediate sources and traditions, rather than from the texts themselves.

---

127. Stern, *Greek and Latin Authors*, 1, pp. 131-33.
128. Ibid., p. 131. Cook, *Interpretation*, pp. 8-9, argues that it could be an allusion to the Septuagint but notes Dorival's view that it might be verbal coincidence.
129. Stern, *Greek and Latin Authors*, 3, pp. 33-37. Dating of Pseudo-Ecphantus is uncertain, Stern suggesting 'First to second centuries C.E.?' Cook, *Interpretation*, pp. 34-35, again acknowledges the possibility of verbal coincidences.
130. Stern, *Greek and Latin Authors*, 1, pp. 361-65; 'Longinus', *On the Sublime*, ed. by D.A. Russell (Oxford: Clarendon Press, 1964), pp. 11-12 (text) and 92-94 (commentary); Cook, *Interpretation*, pp. 32-34. The work is dated by Stern to the first century CE, albeit tentatively. The quotation from Genesis is not exact – it combines elements from three verses – but the reference is unmistakable.
131. 'Longinus', *On the Sublime*, p. 93.
132. Ibid.
133. Cook, *Interpretation*, pp. 55-149.
134. Ibid., p. 57.

Scholars have varied in their overall assessments of the evidence from Graeco-Roman literature for their authors' familiarity with the Jewish scriptures before the advent of Christianity. Reference has already been made to the work of Tcherikover, who argued for a minimalist position: 'The fact, however, is that the translation of the Holy Scriptures into Greek made no impression whatever in the Greek world, since in the whole of Greek literature there is no indication that the Greeks read the Bible before the Christian period.'[135]

Cook takes a much less negative view and, while acknowledging that the evidence is very limited, concludes with due caution that some pagan authors 'are aware of the LXX (or the Jewish books of laws) although extant quotations are sparse' and that others 'seem to be aware of the existence of the LXX'.[136] The most recent review of the evidence, by Rajak, is even more positive.[137] Of the Graeco-Roman texts discussed here, she refers only to those by Ocellus Lucanus and Pseudo-Longinus; she concludes that cultural contact between Jews and non-Jews was in fact considerably more extensive than has been generally supposed:

> It would be absurd to claim the books of the Bible, in whatever language, were literature in which pagans without a special interest would be able to immerse themselves. . . . There were literate pagans, above all philosophers, who, quite simply, did have an interest sufficient to take them some distance into the Jewish writings. . . . They were able to do so because the books of the Bible were part of their world and were not an unknown entity.'[138]

The difference between Cook and Rajak is perhaps one of emphasis rather than substance. Both acknowledge the limited and fragmentary nature of the evidence. Nevertheless, they both conclude that *some* Graeco-Roman authors had *some* familiarity with the Jewish scriptures, Cook being the more cautious in his assessment, Rajak the more expansionist.

---

135. Tcherikover, 'Jewish Apologetic Literature Reconsidered', p. 177.
136. Cook, *Interpretation*, p. 52.
137. Rajak, *Translation*, pp. 267-70. Feldman, *Jew and Gentile*, pp. 311-14, takes an even more optimistic view, arguing that the Septuagint positively *was* known to the Graeco-Roman world, but his suggestion that all the Greek and Roman authors who wrote about the Jews must have had direct access to the Septuagint strains credibility.
138. Rajak, *Translation*, p. 270.

The Scholarly Context

This review of the ancient literature suggests that the Jewish scriptures were probably very little known outside Jewish and Christian circles before the apologists wrote their texts. Before going on to explain how the apologists' works will be approached in this book, however, previous scholarship will be considered. Works on individual texts are discussed in the relevant chapter, so it is those which relate to more general themes that are reviewed here. Second-century apologetic writings have been the subject of much critical attention but surprisingly little of it has been devoted to the concerns addressed in this book. This may be because analyses of apologetic arguments are here brought together with discussion of approaches to biblical interpretation; previous scholarship has tended to address only one or other of these issues.

Scholarship on arguments in apologetic texts has, unsurprisingly, been concerned with the analysis of ideas, and frequently with placing them in a wider context. Themes that recur in the literature include efforts to identify material which can help either to chart the development of Christian theology[139] or to relate the contents of Christian writings to prevailing Greek philosophical ideas.[140] Other scholarly work which draws heavily on apologetic texts has been thematical in nature, exploring, for example, Christian doctrines of Creation[141] or relations between Christians and Jews.[142] These works examine ideas in apologetic texts but they do not, to any significant extent, consider the way the scriptures are employed in apologetic arguments.[143]

Scholarly literature has also discussed second-century scriptural interpretation and done so extensively, with general surveys of the field

---

139. E.g. J.N.D. Kelly, *Early Christian Doctrines*, 4th edn (London: Adam & Charles Black, 1968); E.F. Osborn, *The Emergence of Christian Theology* (Cambridge: Cambridge University Press, 1993).

140. E.g. H. Chadwick, *Early Christian Thought and the Classical Tradition: Studies in Justin, Clement and Origen* (Oxford: Clarendon Press, 1966).

141. G. May, *Creatio ex Nihilo: The Doctrine of 'Creation out of Nothing' in Early Christian Thought*, trans. by A.S. Worrall (London: T. & T. Clark, 1994).

142. Lieu, *Image and Reality*, pp. 155-97.

143. As is evident from general works on ancient Christian apologetics: M. Fiedrowicz, *Apologie im frühen Christentum: Die Kontroverse um den christlichen Wahrheitsanspruch in den ersten Jahrhunderten* (Paderborn: Ferdinand Schöningh, 2000); B. Pouderon and J. Doré, eds, *Les apologistes chrétiens et la culture grecque* (Paris: Beauchesne, 1998); M. Pellegrino, *Studi su l'antica apologetica* (Rome: Edizioni di Storia e Letteratura, 1947).

by Grant and Tracy,[144] Simonetti[145] and Carleton Paget.[146] More specific studies have looked at individual authors or schools and what emerges strikingly is the variety in approaches that have been identified, with different strands of second-century Christianity approaching the Jewish scriptures very differently.[147] There is only space here to touch on the work of three second-century writers, Valentinus, Marcion and Irenaeus, to illustrate this. In the Valentinian *Gospel of Truth*,[148] the narrative of Genesis is merged with Gnostic myth in a way that 'erases the line between text and commentary, as interpretation becomes new composition';[149] Marcion's approach to the Jewish scriptures has been characterised as treating them as 'a primary evidential authority, although not a moral or spiritual one';[150] while in the work of Irenaeus emphasis is placed on interpreting the scriptures in the light of the gospels proclaimed by the Apostles.[151] These are clearly very different. The objective in this book is not, however, to present a further approach to scripture to set alongside them, but rather to show how the writers considered here approach the scriptures and to relate what they say to their apologetic context.

Where scholars have discussed the apologists' use of the scriptures, they have tended to discuss specific textual issues, such as identifying the form of the scriptural texts to which the authors are referring, understanding how the individual texts cited are being interpreted, the nature of the sources for particular textual readings and how *testimonia* traditions are drawn on.[152] What has tended to be ignored is the use

---

144. R.M. Grant and D. Tracy, *A Short History of the Interpretation of the Bible*, 2nd edn, rev. and enlarged (London: SCM Press, 1984), pp. 39-51.

145. M. Simonetti, *Biblical Interpretation in the Early Church: An Historical Introduction to Patristic Exegesis*, trans. by J.A. Hughes (Edinburgh: T. & T. Clark, 1994), pp. 1-33.

146. Carleton Paget, 'Interpretation of the Bible'.

147. Modern scholarship emphasises the diversity to be found in the different Christian 'schools' in the second century: W.A. Löhr, 'Das antike Christentum in zweiten Jahrhundert – neue Perspektiven seiner Erforshung', *TLZ*, vol. 127 (2002), pp. 247-62.

148. 'The Gospel of Truth', ed. by E. Thomassen and M. Meyer, in M. Meyer, ed., *The Nag Hammadi Scriptures* (New York: HarperOne, 2007), pp. 31-47: discussed in D. Dawson, *Allegorical Readers and Cultural Revision in Ancient Alexandria* (Berkeley: University of California Press, 1992), pp. 145-70.

149. Dawson, *Allegorical Readers*, p. 128.

150. J.M. Lieu, *Marcion and the Making of a Heretic* (Cambridge: Cambridge University Press, 2015), p. 357.

151. J. Behr, *Irenaeus of Lyons: Identifying Christianity* (Oxford: Oxford University Press, 2013), pp. 124-40.

152. These issues are discussed further in the chapters on individual authors.

made of the scriptures in apologetic arguments.[153] There are two brief exceptions to this, the first being an article by Horbury[154] which includes a section on the apologists' use of scripture.[155] The discussion is necessarily very short but Horbury does address the role of the scriptures in the arguments of apologetic texts directed towards the Graeco-Roman world and highlights some of the themes which will feature in this book: the perceived antiquity of the scriptures, their function as prophecy and the significance of the moral precepts they contain. The second work to note is a short article by Boccabello on the use Justin and Theophilus make of the Book of Zechariah,[156] in which he links references to texts from Zechariah with the apologetic intentions of authors interacting with Graeco-Roman audiences (or at least purporting to do so). He suggests, somewhat cautiously, that Christian writers could find the Jewish scriptures useful in providing support for their arguments in debates with non-Christians:

> it is probably best to draw rather limited conclusions – the apologists saw Zechariah as useful in addressing issues which were clearly raised by the Christian interaction with paganism. This is true regardless of the extent to which these texts themselves represent just such an interaction. We can see perceived usefulness whether they are talking to pagans or merely talking to each other about pagans.[157]

Looking more broadly at scholarship in the field, there are two significant and influential works, by Droge and Young, which in some measure bear on the subject matter of this book, even if the apologetic use of scripture is not precisely their concern. One merit of both of them is the emphasis they place on the Graeco-Roman context in which Christian apologists wrote and the way their works engage intensively with Graeco-Roman culture. They both present Christianity as being at once in dialogue but also in competition with the mainstream culture.

---

153. E.g. Grant and Tracy, *Short History*, pp. 39-51, discuss second-century biblical interpretation without reference to the apologists' use of scripture.
154. W. Horbury, 'Old Testament Interpretation in the Writings of the Church Fathers', in M.J. Mulder, ed., *Mikra: Text, Translation, Reading and Interpretation of the Hebrew Bible in Ancient Judaism and Early Christianity* (Assen: Van Gorcum, 1988), pp. 727-87.
155. Ibid., pp. 740-44.
156. J.S. Boccabello, 'Why Would a Pagan Read Zechariah? Apologetics and Exegesis in the Second-Century Greek Apologists', in C. Tuckett, ed., *The Book of Zechariah and Its Influence* (Aldershot: Ashgate, 2003), pp. 135-44.
157. Ibid., p. 143.

Droge's theme[158] is the development by second-century Christian apologists of a distinctive interpretation of the history of culture which emphasises the antiquity of the traditions inherited from the Jews. This is an important theme in second-century apologetic writings but, while Droge necessarily draws on the apologists' use of the scriptures as an important source for their arguments, he does not overtly discuss how they read and understand the scriptures as texts, which is the key concern in this book. Droge's contribution is, nevertheless, one of the essential building blocks for this work.

The overarching theme of Young's work,[159] which ranges across the whole patristic field from the first to the fifth century, is how Christian literary culture came to supersede that of the Graeco-Roman tradition, absorbing in the process many features of the culture it replaced. At the core of the new Christian culture were the scriptures, both Old and New Testament, the seminal texts around which Christian learning coalesced. Much of Young's work is concerned with the later patristic centuries but one section discusses the second century.[160] Her key theme is the 'battle of the literatures'[161] or the way Christian writers promoted their scriptures as an alternative to challenge the dominance of the long-established Graeco-Roman literary tradition. This is, again, an important theme in second-century apologetic writings and highly relevant to the consideration here of the way the scriptures are used; Young's contribution therefore provides a second essential building block for this work.

Christian Apologists and the Graeco-Roman Literary Context

Previous scholarship, and particularly the work of Droge and Young, provides the background and context for this book which explores the part played by the Jewish scriptures in the literary strategies of three chosen texts. The approach taken here entails treating seriously and centrally the apologetic form and nature of these texts and reading them as they present themselves. More specifically, the focus is on two issues: the place of the Jewish scriptures in apologetic arguments and the portrait of the Jewish scriptures which emerges from those arguments. Each text presents itself as a dialogue between a Christian writer and

---

158. Droge, *Homer or Moses?*
159. F.M. Young, *Biblical Exegesis and the Formation of Christian Culture* (Cambridge: Cambridge University Press, 1997).
160. Ibid., pp. 49-57.
161. Ibid., p.57.

a non-Christian Graeco-Roman audience, so the relationship between texts and their audiences is critically important. Ideally, the texts would be examined in the context of the intellectual milieu from which they emerged, with each text viewed as one component in an exchange of ideas and arguments with other parties, rather in the way that a text from a later century would be examined in its 'argumentative context' when significantly more evidence is available.[162] The specific contexts in which each of these apologetic texts was written and the nature of the audiences to which they were first addressed remain unknown, however, or at least matters of speculation. It is not now possible to access any of the other elements in the dialogues of which they may originally have formed a part, since any that did exist do not survive. The contents of the texts may or may not reflect discussions that actually took place and, while each text gives some account of arguments and criticisms levelled against the author and to which he is responding, this material is only available in the form in which he himself presents it, and so cannot be treated as a source that is independent of the writer of the text.[163]

There are clearly dangers in reading texts without a knowledge of their actual contexts. Writing about seventeenth-century English political texts David Wootton puts the point well:

> To read them in isolation, without attention to the views of their contemporaries, is to lose sight of the arguments they were trying to overcome and the causes they were trying to assist. It is comparable to listening to the prosecution or the defence in a criminal trial without hearing the other side's case: without some sense of the strengths and weaknesses of the opponent it is impossible to grasp why apparently promising lines of argument are never pursued, while at other times what seem to be trivial distinctions and secondary issues are subjected to lengthy examination.[164]

---

162. Q. Skinner, *Visions of Politics: Volume 1: Regarding Method* (Cambridge: Cambridge University Press, 2002), pp. 103-27, cited phrase on p. 116. The potential value for early Christian studies of the work of the so-called 'Cambridge School', and specifically that of Skinner, is highlighted in C. Markschies, *Christian Theology and Its Institutions in the Early Roman Empire: Prolegomena to a History of Early Christian Theology*, trans. by W. Coppins (Waco: Baylor University Press, 2015), pp. xiii-xiv.

163. This contrasts sharply with Origen's *Against Celsus* in which the arguments of Celsus are presented verbatim.

164. D. Wootton, *Divine Right and Democracy: An Anthology of Political Writing in Stuart England* (Harmondsworth: Penguin, 1986), p. 10.

Wootton here draws attention to some real difficulties which arise in the reading of apologetic texts. There are, however, ways of addressing them. For it is possible, despite the limitations, to examine second-century Christian apologetic works in a contemporary context and to see them against the background of the Graeco-Roman literary environment of the time but one that is conceived more generally. The apologists' textual strategies can be examined for the way they would have engaged with the concerns and interests of an audience educated in the Graeco-Roman literary culture of the second century, about which a considerable amount is known. Audiences are presented in these texts as having a measure of education, with references to literary works and to mythological and philosophical ideas from the Graeco-Roman tradition introduced without comment or explanation. Justin, Tatian and Theophilus were themselves all converts to Christianity who had received a Graeco-Roman education before their conversion. Thus, the authors and their implied audiences share a common Graeco-Roman cultural background and this provides the generalised argumentative context in which their engagement with each other can be examined.

The nature of Graeco-Roman literary culture is therefore all-important. Education in the Graeco-Roman world was highly structured and centred on the study of a corpus of classic texts,[165] with works written in Greek centuries before still being very much read and studied in the second century CE. From an early stage of its existence the Greek tradition categorised texts;[166] a basic distinction was drawn between poetry and prose,[167] with texts then being classified into a number of distinct forms including, most prominently, epic, comedy, tragedy, oratory, philosophy and history.[168] There was also a well-established tradition of literary criticism, involving the self-conscious examination

---

165. For discussion of the nature of ancient Graeco-Roman education: H.I. Marrou, *A History of Education in Antiquity*, trans. by G. Lamb (London: Sheed & Ward, 1956); M.L. Clarke, *Higher Education in the Ancient World* (London: Routledge & Kegan Paul, 1971); T.J. Morgan, *Literate Education in the Hellenistic and Roman Worlds* (Cambridge: Cambridge University Press, 1998); H.G. Snyder, *Teachers and Texts in the Ancient World: Philosophers, Jews and Christians* (London: Routledge, 2000).

166. E.g. the comparison drawn between tragedy and epic in Aristotle's *Poetics*, see *Ancient Literary Criticism: The Principle Texts in New Translations*, ed. by D.A. Russell and M. Winterbottom (Oxford: Clarendon Press, 1972), pp. 123-25.

167. See Aristotle's separate treatments of poetic and prose styles, the former in his *Poetics* and the latter in his *Rhetoric*, in ibid., pp. 85-132 and 134-70.

168. D.A. Russell, *Criticism in Antiquity*, 2nd edn (London: Duckworth, 1995), pp. 148-58.

of literature and the application of critical techniques to the study of classic texts. This tradition included both theoretical works, concerned with the classification of texts and with what made for good literature or a good literary style – notably, in the field of rhetoric[169] – and also works of practical criticism, including commentaries and other works which interpreted classic texts.[170]

A pronounced bias in favour of the traditional and a high regard for what was ancient and long-established over what was novel and without precedent strongly influenced attitudes towards both ideas and works of literature.[171] In Young's apt phrase: 'Nothing could be both new and true.'[172] Moreover, a number of cultural developments occurred in the late Hellenistic period that were concerned in some way with looking back to the past. The first was a revival, and an intensification, of interest in the ancient founding texts of the Greek philosophical schools[173] and in their authors, most notably Plato and Aristotle,[174] together with an interest in the very earliest thinkers, those proponents of Ancient Wisdom who were believed to have pre-dated the emergence of the various philosophical schools.[175] The second was a burgeoning interest

169. See, generally, G.A. Kennedy, *The Art of Rhetoric in the Roman World 300 BC-AD 300* (Princeton: Princeton University Press, 1972), and, more specifically, R.N. Gaines, 'Roman Rhetorical Handbooks', in W. Dominik and J. Hall, eds, *A Companion to Roman Rhetoric* (Oxford: Blackwell Publishing, 2007), pp. 163-80.

170. Russell, *Criticism in Antiquity*, and Russell and Winterbottom, eds, *Ancient Literary Criticism*.

171. A.H. Armstrong, 'Pagan and Christian Traditionalism in the First Three Centuries A.D.', in E.A. Livingstone, ed., *Studia Patristica* (*SP*), vol. 15, no. 1 (Berlin: Akademie-Verlag, 1984), pp. 414-31; G.R. Boys-Stones, *Post-Hellenistic Philosophy: A Study of Its Development from the Stoics to Origen* (Oxford: Oxford University Press, 2001).

172. Young, *Biblical Exegesis*, p. 52.

173. M.A. Frede, 'Epilogue', in K. Algra, J. Barnes, J. Mansfeld and M. Schofield, eds, *The Cambridge History of Hellenistic Philosophy* (Cambridge: Cambridge University Press, 1999), pp. 771-97, 784-85 has been influential. See also G. Betegh, 'The Transmission of Ancient Wisdom: Texts, Doxographies, Libraries', in L.P. Gerson, ed., *The Cambridge History of Philosophy in Late Antiquity* (Cambridge: Cambridge University Press, 2010), pp. 25-38; M. Hatzimichali, 'The Texts of Plato and Aristotle in the First Century BC', in M. Schofield, ed., *Aristotle, Plato and Pythagoreanism in the First Century BC: New Directions for Philosophy* (Cambridge: Cambridge University Press, 2013), pp. 1-27.

174. D. Sedley, 'Philosophical Allegiance in the Greco-Roman world', in J. Barnes and M. Griffin, eds, *Philosophia Togata: Essays on Philosophy and Roman Society* (Oxford: Clarendon Press, 1989), pp. 97-119, refers to 'a virtually religious commitment to the authority of a founder figure' (p. 97).

175. Boys-Stones, *Post-Hellenistic Philosophy*.

in primeval history, in the origins and early history of humankind, with sometimes lengthy works written which charted the history of human affairs from very earliest times.[176] The third was the literary and cultural phenomenon known as the Second Sophistic, which fostered a conscious referencing back to the literature of ancient Greece and spawned texts imitating the language and style of highly-esteemed classical Athenian literature.[177]

Into this literary environment stepped the apologists introducing discussion of texts which, although translated into Greek, had their origins in an alien, barbarian culture outside the Graeco-Roman literary tradition. The strategies which the apologists adopted for presenting these texts in their engagement with audiences from a Graeco-Roman cultural background are at the core of this book. As well as analysis of the arguments deployed, other issues to be addressed include the nature and provenance of the scriptures, the source of their authority and the techniques used to interpret them. This book therefore enters the territory of literary criticism where it engages with questions such as the way in which admired literary works were discussed in the Graeco-Roman tradition and the critical approaches which were used to comment on and explain them.

To achieve their objectives the apologists created their own literary works. This book explores the forms and styles which they chose to employ to frame their material in various different ways and how these relate to the Graeco-Roman context in which their works were presented. It also considers how they used rhetorical and other strategies from the Graeco-Roman literary tradition to assist with making their arguments.

The apologists' writings feature two obvious protagonists, Christian and non-Christian, but there is also a third, namely the Jews, since it is their scriptures which are being promoted. The apologists present these texts as Christian. However, they know, and their audiences know, that the texts derive from the Jews who originally produced them, to

---

176. R. Mortley, *The Idea of Universal History from Hellenistic Philosophy to Early Christian Historiography* (Lampeter: Edwin Mellen Press, 1996).

177. G. Anderson, *The Second Sophistic: A Cultural Phenomenon in the Roman Empire* (London: Routledge, 1993); S. Goldhill, ed., *Being Greek under Rome: Cultural Identity, the Second Sophistic and the Development of Empire* (Cambridge: Cambridge University Press, 2001); T. Whitmarsh, *The Second Sophistic* (Oxford: Oxford University Press, 2005). The relevance of the Second Sophistic for understanding early Christian literature is increasingly recognised, e.g. A.P. Johnson, 'Early Christianity and the Classical Tradition', in D.S. Richter and W.A. Johnson, eds, *The Oxford Handbook of the Second Sophistic* (Oxford: Oxford University Press, 2017), pp. 625-38.

whom they are still sacred and who are still very much present in the Graeco-Roman world. The strategies the apologists adopt to position Christianity relative to Judaism in their dialogues with Graeco-Roman audiences therefore also form an important ingredient in the discussion.

The next three chapters examine in turn apologetic works by Justin Martyr, Tatian and Theophilus of Antioch. Discussion will show the part that the Jewish scriptures play in the writings of each and will identify similarities and differences. The final chapter will then draw out some concluding themes.

Chapter 2

The 'Proof from Prophecy' in Justin Martyr's *First Apology*

The first of the three texts to be considered in this book is Justin Martyr's *First Apology*.[1] It is a long and involved work which presents itself as a petition to the emperor on behalf of persecuted Christians, although it also includes a considerable amount of material aimed at persuading readers of the truth of Christianity. To support his case for Christianity, Justin includes extensive references to the Jewish scriptures.[2] These are concentrated in Chapters 30-53, the section known as the 'Proof from Prophecy', and this is necessarily the chief focus of attention here.[3]

Before commencing a detailed examination of the Proof from Prophecy, some background will be provided on Justin and on his *First Apology*. Previous scholarship and the differing approaches that scholars have taken to the text will then be considered and the approach adopted in this book will be explained.

Background

Little is known about Justin Martyr's life, although there is general agreement among scholars on the basic facts.[4] He originally came from

---

1. Justin, Philosopher and Martyr: *Apologies*, ed. by D. Minns and P. Parvis (Oxford: Oxford University Press, 2009) (*1A*). References to the text are to chapter and verse numbers in this edition. Translations are also from this edition, adapted where appropriate. Other modern editions consulted: Justin Martyr, *Apologiae pro Christianis*, ed. by M. Marcovich (Berlin: de Gruyter, 1994); Justin, *Apologie pour les Chrétiens*, ed. by C. Munier (Paris: Éditions du Cerf, 2006).
2. For lists of the scriptural references: Minns and Parvis, *Apologies*, pp. 339-40; Marcovich, *Apologiae*, pp. 171-72; Munier, *Apologie*, pp. 371-73.
3. Although Chapters 30-53 contain the main body of the Proof from Prophecy, there are also references to prophecy in later chapters and these sometimes feature in the discussion here.
4. For biographical issues: Minns and Parvis, *Apologies*, pp. 32-33; L.W. Barnard,

Flavia Neapolis (modern-day Nablus) in Syria Palestina and was probably born around 100 CE. A gentile by birth and education, he at some stage converted to Christianity, claiming in his *Dialogue with Trypho* that it was exposure to the Jewish scriptures which triggered his conversion.[5] He visited Rome, settled there in later life and was martyred in the 160s. The *First Apology* is dated to the early 150s when Justin was established in Rome;[6] the text survives in only one source of independent value, the fourteenth-century Byzantine manuscript, *Parisinus graecus 450*.[7] There is no external evidence extant which would locate the *First Apology* in a context of contemporary debates and, although the writing of such a huge work is likely to have been prompted by some particular circumstance, what this might have been cannot now be recovered.[8]

The *First Apology* presents itself at the outset as an address and petition (*προσφώνησις καὶ ἔντευξις*),[9] directed at the Emperor Antoninus Pius and his two adopted sons Marcus Aurelius and Lucius Verus, and put forward on behalf of Christians to plead for relief from persecution.[10] Some argue that

---

Justin Martyr: His Life and Thought (Cambridge: Cambridge University Press, 1967), pp. 1-13; Munier, *Apologie*, pp. 9-19; P. Lampe, *From Paul to Valentinus: Christians at Rome in the First Two Centuries*, trans. by M. Steinhauser (London: Continuum, 2003), pp. 257-60.

5.   Justin Martyr, *Dialogus cum Tryphone*, ed. by M. Marcovich (Berlin: de Gruyter, 1997), pp. 7 and 8 (*DT*). For an English translation: Justin Martyr, *Dialogue with Trypho*, trans. by T.B. Falls, rev. by T.P. Halton and ed. by M. Slusser (Washington, DC: Catholic University of America Press, 2003). References to *DT* are to the Marcovich edition.

6.   Justin Martyr, *The First and Second Apologies*, trans. by L.W. Barnard (Mahwah: Paulist Press, 1997), p. 11; Minns and Parvis, *Apologies*, p. 44; Marcovich, *Apologiae*, p. 11.

7.   Minns and Parvis, *Apologies*, p. 3. The fourteenth-century manuscript includes the text of another work by Justin known as the *Second Apology*. The relationship between the two works has been a matter of intense debate in the literature, exposing complex issues that are beyond the scope of this book. Since the *Second Apology* contains no references to the Jewish scriptures, however, its contents do not feature in the discussion here.

8.   Grant, *Greek Apologists*, pp. 53-54, argues that the *First Apology*'s composition was occasioned by the martyrdom of Polycarp in 155 or 156, but he fails to adduce strong evidence for this.

9.   *1A* 1.1. Justin also uses βιβλίδιον (petition) to refer to the text itself at 69.1 in the section which Minns and Parvis transfer from the *Second Apology*. (Their arguments for doing so are set out in Minns and Parvis, *Apologies*, pp. 27-30.) Scholars often use the Latin term '*libellus*' to describe the text.

10. The addressees (Minns and Parvis, *Apologies*, pp. 34-41) are named at *1A* 1.1 and subsequently referred to in the second-person plural at a number of points, e.g. 2.2-2.4, 23.1, 32.6 and 68.3.

it should be accepted as such, with those named the actual addressees and the text a genuine petition.[11] Imperial rule had a strong personal element, despite the Empire's huge size; petitions to the emperor from individuals and small communities were not uncommon[12] and a number survive.[13] Other scholars doubt that the *First Apology* was a genuine petition, however, and it arguably stretches credulity to regard this long and involved work as falling into the same category as relatively short and straightforward requests for the alleviation of abuses.[14] It has also been well argued that the tone of the work is insufficiently respectful for a genuine address to an emperor.[15]

The contents of the *First Apology* are also problematic since much of the work is not concerned with the alleviation of abuses. Some critics emphasise the work's rambling and digressive character and claim that it has little in the way of coherent structure.[16] Such judgements are unduly harsh, however, for it is possible to identify a general flow to the argument and to divide the work into sections in a reasonably coherent way, as a number of commentators have done.[17] A relatively straightforward view of the structure of the work involves the identification of two major themes: arguments for the relief of Christians from persecution and arguments for the promotion of Christianity, the first of them strongest

---

11. E.g. P. Keresztes, 'The Literary Genre of Justin's First Apology', *VC*, vol. 19 (1965), pp. 99-110; F. Millar, *The Emperor in the Roman World* (*31 BC-AD 337*) (London: Duckworth, 1977), p. 563; O. Skarsaune, 'Justin and the Apologists', in D J Bingham, ed., *The Routledge Companion to Early Christian Thought* (Abingdon: Routledge, 2010), pp. 121-36, especially pp. 122-24; P. Parvis, 'Justin Martyr', in P. Foster, ed., *Early Christian Thinkers: The Lives and Legacies of Twelve Key Figures* (London: SPCK, 2010), pp. 1-14.

12. W. Eck, 'Provincial Administration and Finance', in CAH11, pp. 266-92, 268-72; Millar, *The Emperor in the Roman World*, pp. 240-52.

13. T. Hauken, *Petition and Response: An Epigraphic Study of Petitions to Roman Emperors, 181-249* (Bergen: Norwegian Institute at Athens, 1998), pp. 1-256 prints relevant texts.

14. See ibid., pp. 74-139 and 284-85, for a third-century CE petition from Skaptopara in Asia Minor, regarded by its editor, at 477 words, as long, although it is completely dwarfed by the length of the *First Apology*.

15. P.L. Buck, 'Justin Martyr's *Apologies*: Their Number, Destination, and Form', *JTS*, vol. 54 (2003), pp. 45-59, draws attention to five instances at 2.3-4, 5.1, 12.6-7, 45.6 and 68 (although this argument has been challenged, see S. Moll, 'Justin and the Pontic Wolf', in Parvis and Foster, eds, *Justin Martyr and His Worlds*, pp. 145-51).

16. E.g. the influential work of J. Geffcken, *Zwei griechische Apologeten* (Leipzig: Teubner, 1907), p. 101. Marcovich, *Apologiae*, Part VII, comments that 'Justin's . . . train of thought is disorganized, repetitious and occasionally rambling'.

17. Barnard, *Apologies*, pp. 6-9; Marcovich, *Apologiae*, pp. 11-25; Minns and Parvis, *Apologies*, pp. 49-54.

in the early parts of the work (although recurring later on),[18] while the
second is particularly evident in the Proof from Prophecy (although also
found elsewhere in the text).[19]

The *First Apology* begins with arguments for the relief of Christians
from harsh and unfair treatment by the Roman authorities and this theme
continues up to the point where Justin says that he has made his case and
could now conclude: 'We could stop here and add no more, reckoning that
what we ask is just and true.'[20] The work continues, however, but the argument
shifts, in the words of Minns and Parvis, 'from petition to persuasion'[21] and
from here on it is concerned primarily with the promotion of Christianity.[22]
Some critics suggest that the Proof from Prophecy, which makes up the
bulk of this section of the work, comprises pre-existing material which was
incorporated into the *First Apology*; this is quite plausible but impossible to
prove.[23] The issue of relief from persecution is not entirely lost, however,
since Justin returns to this theme later on,[24] and it features strongly at
the end of the work when the text of a rescript of the Emperor Hadrian
concerning the treatment of Christians is included.[25]

Various suggestions have been made regarding the intended audience
and purpose of the *First Apology*, although definitive conclusions on these
issues remain elusive. If it was not a genuine petition to the emperor, such
a form could still have been employed by Justin because, for whatever
reason, he found it convenient to use, with the work still being directed
at an audience external to Christianity.[26] Alternatively, the *First Apology*
could have been aimed at an internal Christian audience, with the Proof
from Prophecy, in particular, being valuable in a catechetical context.[27] The
First Apology was certainly read and preserved by Christians and there is no
convincing evidence that it was known outside Christian communities.[28]

18. *1A* 68.
19. E.g. *1A* 61-67. Analyses of the text's contents recognise that much of it concerns
     a more general promotion of Christianity and not the subject matter of the
     petition: Minns and Parvis, *Apologies*, pp. 49-54; Marcovich, *Apologiae*, pp. 11-
     25; Munier, *Apologie*, pp. 33-38.
20. *1A* 12.11.
21. Minns and Parvis, *Apologies*, p. 50.
22. Parts II to V of the analysis in Marcovich, *Apologiae*, pp. 14-25.
23. Minns and Parvis, *Apologies*, pp. 47-48.
24. E.g. *1A* 20.3 and 24.1.
25. *1A* 68.3-68.10. The rescript may or may not be authentic: Minns and Parvis,
     Apologies, p. 44.
26. Barnard, trans., *Apologies*, pp. 8-9; Marcovich, *Dialogus*, VII.
27. Minns and Parvis, *Apologies*, p. 46.
28. As noted in Chapter 1, Droge, *Homer or Moses?*, follows Andresen, *Logos und
     Nomos*, in arguing that the late second-century, anti-Christian writer Celsus

What might be called a midway view – that it was aimed at those on the margins of Christianity – is taken by two recent scholars who have examined the work from different standpoints. Nyström argues that the audience is to be found among Christians, with an emphasis on those newly converted or on the verge of conversion,[29] while for Pretila the *First Apology* was aimed at those within the Christian community who were considering a return to paganism.[30]

As was noted in Chapter 1 when discussing apologetic works generally, it may be unwarranted to draw a sharp distinction between internal and external audiences, however, since those within the Christian community would be familiar with non-Christian Graeco-Roman culture – many of them converts like Justin – while those outside might already have some knowledge of, and interest in, Christianity.[31] Indeed, the text assumes at times that its readers are already familiar with aspects of Christianity since ideas and events are referred to but not explained. The *First Apology* is concerned in part with comparison and contrast between Christianity, on the one hand, and Graeco-Roman philosophical and mythological traditions, on the other, so its contents could be of interest to both internal and external audiences; indeed, it may be that both were in Justin's sights.

The Scholarly Context

There has been considerable previous scholarship on Justin,[32] although only a limited amount relates to the theme of this book. Three concerns have predominated: first, scholars have examined theological issues in Justin's work, seeking to locate them in the development of early Christian ideas;[33] second, Justin's work has been fertile ground for the

was responding to Justin and therefore must have known his work well. The case is, however, based on similarities of argument rather than any close textual connection and remains unconvincing; the judgement in Osborn, *Justin Martyr*, p. 169 that 'his [Celsus'] direct acquaintance with Justin is an attractive but unnecessary hypothesis' is a sound appraisal.

29. Nyström, *Apology of Justin Martyr*, pp. 19-66.
30. Pretila, *Re-appropriating 'Marvellous Fables'*, p. 32.
31. As noted in Chapter 1, Lieu, *Christian Identity*, pp. 98-146, cautions against too rigid a view of confessional identities and boundaries in this period.
32. For a different analysis of recent Justin scholarship, see M. Slusser, 'Justin Scholarship: Trends and Trajectories', in Parvis and Foster, eds, *Justin Martyr and His Worlds*, pp. 13-21.
33. Examples are general works, e.g. Osborn, *Justin Martyr*, and Barnard, *Justin Martyr*, and studies of specific themes, e.g. R. Holte, 'Logos Spermatikos: Christianity and Ancient Philosophy according to St. Justin's Apologies', *ST*, vol. 12 (1958), pp. 109-68; D.C. Trakatellis, *The Pre-existence of Christ in Justin*

study of Christian-Jewish relations;[34] and, third, scholars have long been interested in the relationship between Justin's ideas and Greek philosophy.[35]

Some studies have, however, been specifically concerned with Justin and the scriptures. Smit Sibinga and Prigent have, separately, made detailed examinations of the scriptural sources on which Justin drew.[36] Shotwell has described Justin's methods of scriptural exegesis, stressing influences from Palestinian Judaism.[37] Aune has examined Justin's use of the Old Testament, noting how his readings sometimes follow those found in New Testament texts, sometimes follow non-canonical sources and are sometimes original to him.[38] A dominating presence in the field is the magisterial work of Skarsaune, who undertook an extensive analysis of Justin's use of the Jewish scriptures, although his concern was with the *testimonia* sources on which Justin drew rather than with the way he deployed scriptural material in his arguments.[39]

One feature of the scholarship has been a tendency to analyse the contents of the *First Apology* together with those of *Dialogue with Trypho*, the latter being a work concerned with dialogue between Christians and Jews, real or imagined. Combining material from the two texts produces a composite account of Justin's approach to the Jewish scriptures.[40] The *Apology* and the *Dialogue* are, however, separate texts and it must be allowed that an author

　　　Martyr (Missoula: Scholars Press, 1976); T. Stylianopoulos, *Justin Martyr and the Mosaic Law* (Missoula: Scholars Press, 1975).

34.　E.g. Lieu, *Image and Reality*; D. Rokéah, *Justin Martyr and the Jews* (Leiden: Brill, 2002).

35.　E.g. C. Andresen, 'Justin und der mittlere Platonismus', *ZNW*, vol. 44 (1952/53), pp. 157-95; N. Hyldahl, *Philosophie und Christentum: Eine Interpretation der Einleitung zum Dialog Justins* (Kopenhagen: Prostant apud Munksgaard, 1966); Chadwick, *Early Christian Thought*; M.J. Edwards, 'On the Platonic Schooling of Justin Martyr', *JTS ns*, vol. 42 (1991), pp. 17-34; C. Nahm, 'The Debate on the "Platonism" of Justin Martyr', *SecCent*, vol. 9 (1992), pp. 129-51.

36.　J. Smit Sibinga, *The Old Testament Text of Justin Martyr: I: The Pentateuch* (Leiden: Brill, 1963); P. Prigent, *Justin et l'Ancient Testament: L'argumentation scripturaire du Traité de Justin contre toutes les hérésies comme source principale du Dialogue avec Tryphon et de la Première Apologie* (Paris: Libraire Lecoffre, 1964).

37.　W.A. Shotwell, *The Biblical Exegesis of Justin Martyr* (London: SPCK, 1965). He is refuting an older view, championed in E.R. Goodenough, *The Theology of Justin Martyr* (Jena: Frommann, 1923), pp. 113-17, that Justin's approach to scripture was influenced by the Jewish writer, Philo of Alexandria.

38.　D.E. Aune, 'Justin Martyr's Use of the Old Testament', *BETS*, vol. 9 (1966), pp. 179-97.

39.　Skarsaune, *Proof from Prophecy*.

40.　E.g. Aune, 'Justin Martyr's Use'; Shotwell, *Biblical Exegesis*; Skarsaune, *Proof from Prophecy*.

may take a different view of a subject at different times, depending on the context in which he is addressing it, the audience for which he is writing and the issues with which he is concerned. Thus, the approach to the Jewish scriptures in the *Dialogue* may well differ from that in the *Apology* and, when the two texts are examined together as if they were one, what emerges may not represent accurately the arguments in either.[41] An example of how this can be avoided is a paper by Skarsaune analysing Justin's ethnic discourse in the *Apology* and the *Dialogue* in a way that is not misleading. He considers first the account in the *Dialogue* and then the treatment of the same issue in the *First Apology*;[42] comparing and contrasting the two, and not seeking to merge them, results in neither text being misrepresented.[43] Distortion of Justin's arguments is also avoided here, since the concern is with Justin's engagement with Graeco-Roman and not Jewish audiences, and the *Apology* alone is examined to the exclusion of the *Dialogue*.

The main argument in Justin's discussion of the Jewish scriptures, the 'Proof from Prophecy', has attracted surprisingly little attention in the secondary literature. Skarsaune's large-scale work, in spite of a title suggesting an interest in Justin's arguments, is, as already noted, actually concerned with the source material which underpins Justin's Proof, rather than the Proof itself. Chadwick's article on Justin's defence of Christianity,[44] which again might be expected to focus on the Proof from Prophecy, is largely concerned with the way Justin handles criticisms of Christians and with his theological ideas. It devotes little space to the Proof and really only addresses one feature of the argument, namely Justin's use of evidence that prophecies have been fulfilled.[45] Chadwick rightly recognises the importance of this for the credibility of the Proof from Prophecy but argues that Justin struggles to make his case because 'he has not yet got a book called

---

41. Indeed, references to the *Dialogue with Trypho* have tended to dominate discussion in the literature, with the *First Apology* receiving less attention, e.g. Shotwell, *Biblical Exegesis*; Aune, 'Justin Martyr's Use'.

42. O. Skarsaune, 'Ethnic Discourse in Early Christianity', in J. Carleton Paget and J. Lieu, eds, *Christianity in the Second Century* (Cambridge: Cambridge University Press, 2017), pp. 250-64, 257-60.

43. A similarly careful approach to analysing the thought of an author who wrote multiple works addressing the same issues is found in Jacobsen's work on Origen's soteriology and christology. Rather than looking at Origen's *oeuvre* as an entity and producing a composite picture of his views, he first examines each work individually and only after having done this does he seek (and find) commonality of ideas: A-C Jacobsen, *Christ – the Teacher of Salvation: A Study on Origen's Soteriology and Christology* (Münster: Aschendorff, 2015).

44. H. Chadwick, 'Justin Martyr's Defence of Christianity', *BJRL*, vol. 47 (1965), pp. 275-97.

45. Ibid., pp. 281-83.

"The New Testament" which he can thrust into the hands of benevolent inquirers.[46] Whether or not 'New Testament texts' were available to Justin, this argument is misleading, since the authority of texts for the apologists depended on their antiquity and recent Christian texts could therefore not provide compelling evidence. The approach which Justin actually adopts to demonstrate the fulfilment of prophecies will be explained below.

Nyström's recent contribution[47] is welcome for a number of reasons. He looks exclusively at the *First Apology* (leaving aside the *Dialogue with Trypho*) and his interest is in analysing the strategies deployed to defend and promote Christianity, singling out the 'logos doctrine' the 'theft theory' and the 'Proof from Prophecy'. He discusses Justin's use of arguments and recognises the importance of the Proof for Justin's case in ways that previous scholars have not.[48] It will emerge in due course, however, that a different view of the Proof from Prophecy is taken here from that of Nyström. His interest in examining arguments in the *First Apology* is shared by other recent scholars; the theme of Haddad's book is Justin's arguments for 'religious liberty and judicial justice',[49] while Pretila examines the role of pagan mythology in Justin's case for Christianity.[50]

The Approach Taken Here

Thus, Justin's *First Apology* can be – and indeed has been – read in different ways. The approach taken here follows the work of recent scholars like Nyström and Haddad in its concern with Justin's arguments but charts a new direction in considering the role of the Jewish scriptures in those arguments.

Analysis of arguments in a text is normally done most effectively by reference to the audience to whom those arguments are addressed. It has, however, already been noted that it is not possible to reach definitive conclusions on who the audience for the *First Apology* was. It is therefore helpful to return to Barclay's analysis of apologetic audiences described in Chapter 1 and to map his categories onto Justin's *Apology*. Thus, the declared audience is the imperial addressees named at the outset, the implied audience is to be found among educated Graeco-Romans more generally – since much of the material in the text is concerned with the promotion of Christianity

46. Ibid., p. 283.
47. Nyström, *Apology of Justin Martyr*.
48. Ibid., pp. 105-31.
49. R.M. Haddad, *The Case for Christianity: St Justin Martyr's Arguments for Religious Liberty and Judicial Justice* (Lanham: Taylor Trade, 2010).
50. Pretila, *Re-appropriating 'Marvellous Fables'*.

and not simply with securing for Christians relief from harsh and unfair treatment – while the intended audience could be either Graeco-Romans external to Christianity or members of Christian communities or those on the borderland between the two (or perhaps a combination of these).

It was argued in Chapter 1 that it was unnecessary to determine the precise nature of an intended audience, however, since an apologetic text can be treated as a repository of arguments in favour of Christianity and analysed with reference to its implied audience, irrespective of who the intended audience may have been. That is the approach taken here. It was also suggested in Chapter 1 that to avoid unnecessarily convoluted phraseology, and in accordance with the way an apologetic text presents itself, the audience for the work should be described as if it is external to Christianity. Again, that is the approach followed here.

Justin's arguments originate in a desire to explain the status of Jesus Christ and this issue is examined first. Then, the texts from the Jewish scriptures which Justin uses to make his case are considered. This entails discussion of the authority of these texts, which is found to be rooted in the legend of the Septuagint. Finally, the prophetic material in the texts – concerned with events in the life of Jesus and the early spread of Christianity through the preaching of the Apostles – is examined.

Jesus Christ and the Proof from Prophecy

The starting point for the Proof from Prophecy is Justin's wish to demonstrate the status of Jesus Christ, from whom Christians take their name.[51] The importance attached to the person of Jesus is shown by the range and nature of the terms used to refer to him. On a number of occasions he is described as Teacher[52] and elsewhere as Saviour.[53] There are a series of references to Jesus as Son of God: he is the 'Son and apostle of the Father of all and Lord God',[54] 'Son of God and apostle',[55] 'Son of God',[56] 'Son of the true God',[57] 'first born of God',[58] 'first begotten of the unbegotten God'[59] and 'begotten in a special manner the Son of God,

---

51. *1A* 12.9.
52. *1A* 4.7, 12.9, 19.6, 21.1 and 32.2.
53. *1A* 33.7, 61.3, 66.2 and 67.8.
54. *1A* 12.9.
55. *1A* 63.10.
56. *1A* 22.1.
57. *1A* 13.3.
58. *1A* 46.2.
59. *1A* 53.2.

being his Logos and first-born and power'.[60] Jesus Christ is also referred to
as the incarnate Logos: 'the Logos of God is his Son',[61] 'the Logos himself
who acquired physical form and became a human being and was called
Jesus Christ',[62] 'the Logos which is the first begotten of God',[63] 'the Logos
in whom the whole human race shared'[64] and 'after the Father of all and
Lord God, the first Power and Son is the Logos, who was made flesh and
became a human being'.[65] Jesus is described as the one who will return and
at his second coming judge the human race: 'he will raise the bodies of all
human beings who have lived, he will bestow incorruptibility on those of
the worthy and he will send those of the unjust in everlasting pain to the
eternal fire with the evil demons'.[66] He is also venerated: 'We worship both
this God and the Son who came from him and taught us these things'[67] and
'the one who became the teacher for us of these things, and who was born
for this, Jesus Christ . . . we rationally worship'.[68]

Listing points in this fashion shows the extraordinary extent of
the claims Justin is making on behalf of someone who lived and died
a human being. The position is, however, more surprising than this,
for Jesus was born in lowly and obscure circumstances and died a humiliating death by crucifixion at the hands of the Roman authorities. A
humble birth would not in itself have presented problems for a Graeco-
Roman audience; Plutarch records how both Theseus and Romulus
were born in circumstances of low social status and went on to become
instrumental figures in the establishment of the two greatest cities,
Athens and Rome.[69] Indeed, the miraculous birth of Jesus as a result of
divine intervention marked him out as someone special. Justin draws
attention to the virgin birth on a number of occasions and accords it a
particular prominence;[70] it is stated as a fact not a conjecture and there is
no suggestion that it requires explanation.[71] Miraculous circumstances

---

60. *1A* 23.2.
61. *1A* 63.4.
62. *1A* 5.4.
63. *1A* 21.1.
64. *1A* 46.2.
65. *1A* 32.10.
66. *1A* 52.3.
67. *1A* 6.2.
68. *1A* 13.3.
69. Plutarch, *Lives: I: Lives of Theseus and Romulus. Lycurgus and Numa. Solon and Publicola*, ed. by B. Perrin, LCL 46 (Cambridge, MA: Harvard University Press,), *Life of Theseus* 2, 1-2.
70. *1A* 21.1, 22.2, 22.5, 32.14, 33.1-9, 46.5, 54.8 and 63.16.
71. Justin is keen to clarify that the virgin conceived, not through intercourse, but

surrounded the births of many famous figures in Graeco-Roman tradition and to have one divine and one human parent was a mark of a significant individual.[72]

Similarly, the resurrection and ascension of Jesus were miraculous occurrences, but are not presented by Justin as problematic. They are referred to in a low-key way as events which had been prophesied and have now occurred, with no further explanation provided.[73] The difficult issue is the manner of the death of Jesus. Justin acknowledges that he had died a humiliating death by crucifixion: 'For it is there they declare our madness to be manifest saying that we give the second place after the unchangeable and eternal God and begetter of all to a crucified man.'[74] He later makes the same point in the form of a question: 'For by what reason should we believe that a crucified man is the first-begotten of the unbegotten God and that he himself will pass judgment on the whole human race?'[75] Justin's response to this conundrum is his Proof from Prophecy. Before developing this argument, however, he refers to two other possible explanations for the status of Jesus: first, the value of his teachings and, second, his achievements as a miracle-worker, although neither of them proves able to provide an adequate account.

---

because the power of God overshadowed her (*1A* 33.4 and 6), unlike Greek mythology in which it was said that Zeus 'came to women for the sake of sexual pleasure' (*1A* 33.3). Birth by virginal conception has not conventionally been seen as featuring in the Graeco-Roman tradition and the Christian tradition is normally regarded as unique in this respect: T. Boslooper, *The Virgin Birth* (London: SCM Press, 1962), pp. 185-86; a recent work suggests, however, that priestess cults of virginal conception did exist in the Greek tradition, although normally unacknowledged: M. Rigoglioso, *The Cult of Divine Birth in Ancient Greece* (New York: Palgrave Macmillan, 2009).

72. Boslooper, *The Virgin Birth*, pp. 167-86: for example, Suetonius, *Lives of the Caesars, Volume 1: Julius. Augustus. Tiberius. Gaius. Caligula*, ed. by J.C. Rolfe, LCL 31 (Cambridge, MA: Harvard University Press, 1914), *Augustus* 94.4, reports the legend that Augustus had a divine father, Apollo.

73. *1A* 38.5 for the Resurrection (prophecy from Psalm 3:6) and 51.6-7 for the Ascension (prophecy from Psalm 24:7-8). That a person of great significance went up to heaven at the end of earthly life was a familiar idea to Graeco-Roman audiences from accounts of the lives of famous historical figures (Plutarch, *Lives: I, Comparison of Theseus and Romulus* 4.1, and Cassius Dio, *Roman History*, ed. by H. Cary and H.B. Foster, LCL, 9 vols [Cambridge, MA: Harvard University Press, 1914-27], 7, 56, 42.3 [in relation to Augustus]) and also from the belief that emperors became gods: I. Gradel, *Emperor Worship and Roman Religion* (Oxford: Clarendon Press, 2002), pp. 261-371.

74. *1A* 13.4.

75. *1A* 53.2.

First, Justin recounts some of the teachings of Jesus: 'we thought it worthwhile . . . to make mention of some few of the teachings of Christ himself'.[76] He describes Jesus' teachings on temperance,[77] loving all, sharing with the needy and doing nothing for the sake of glory,[78] being long-suffering,[79] not swearing, always telling the truth and worshipping God alone[80] and paying taxes to, and serving, the emperor.[81] He also describes how Jesus' teachings have transformed the lives of his adherents:

> Formerly we delighted in fornication, now we embrace temperance alone; then we practiced magical arts, now we have dedicated ourselves to the good and unbegotten God; then we loved above all the means of acquiring money and property, now we put even what we have to common use, and share with all those in need.[82]

Although the teachings of Jesus may be admirable, however, and may have had a strong and positive impact on his followers, Justin does not suggest that they are sufficient to demonstrate his special status.

Justin refers, second, to the miracle-working of Jesus, how he healed the sick and raised the dead to life.[83] This is also insufficient to justify his status, however, for Jesus could have performed miracles through magic and still only *seem* to be the Son of God.[84] Justin cites cases of other miracle workers: Simon, a Samaritan from Gitthon 'performed magical deeds in your royal city of Rome';[85] and Menander, a disciple of Simon from Kapparetaia in Samaria, 'when he was in Antioch deceived many through magical arts'.[86] Justin notes how Simon acquired considerable status in Rome: 'he was considered a god, and was honoured with a statue as are the other gods honoured among you'.[87] Thus, Jesus' actions

---

76. *1A* 14.4. The sayings of Jesus quoted in the *First Apology* parallel closely the Synoptic Gospels but are not presented as derived from scriptural texts: A.J. Bellinzoni, *The Sayings of Jesus in the Writings of Justin Martyr* (Leiden: Brill, 1967).
77. *1A* 15.1-15.8.
78. *1A* 15.9-15.17.
79. *1A* 16.1-16.4.
80. *1A* 16.5-16.7.
81. *1A* 17.1-17.3.
82. *1A* 14.2.
83. *1A* 30.1 and 48.1-2.
84. *1A* 30.1.
85. *1A* 26.2.
86. *1A* 26.4.
87. *1A* 56.2.

as a miracle-worker do not mark him out as unique. If, however, teaching and miracle-working are inadequate to demonstrate the special status of Jesus, what does establish it for Justin is the Proof from Prophecy.

The Texts Providing the Proof from Prophecy

The crux of the Proof from Prophecy is that events surrounding the life and death of Jesus and the early growth of Christianity are found to have been foretold in ancient prophetic texts. The argument is spelt out at exceptional length in Chapters 30-53 of the *First Apology*, a text which in all only runs to 68 chapters.[88] It is clearly unfamiliar to his audience, since it is described and explained in detail. Justin says he is bringing the prophecies to his readers for their inspection, as if doing so for the first time.[89] This contrasts with the way that he refers to the myths of Greece and Rome; they are first mentioned without any explanation[90] and, when they reappear, the information provided is scarcely more detailed.[91] Justin says that mythological stories do not need to be rehearsed because they are already familiar to his readers: 'And what sort of stories are told about the doings of those who are called the sons of Zeus it is not necessary to say to those who know.'[92] He never speaks like this about the prophecies, always spelling them out in full and explaining their meanings.

Justin's references to the Jewish scriptures are conveniently listed by Minns and Parvis,[93] with the most numerous being to Isaiah, the Pentateuch and the Psalms.[94]

Justin does not describe the texts as 'scriptures'[95] in the *Apology*, although he does use this term in his *Dialogue with Trypho*, where various cognates of γράφω (write) are employed to refer to the Jewish scriptures:[96]

---

88. Marcovich, *Apologiae*. The text is 70 chapters long in Minns and Parvis, *Apologies*, because the editors transfer material from the *Second Apology* to the *First Apology*.
89. *1A* 44.13.
90. *1A* 21.
91. *1A* 53.
92. *1A* 21.4.
93. Minns and Parvis, *Apologies*, pp. 339-40.
94. Thirty-nine from Isaiah, twenty-five from the Pentateuch and thirteen from the Psalms.
95. The one possible exception is when Justin uses the phrase 'in the writings of Moses' (*1A* 60.2) which occurs when he is discussing Plato's borrowings from Moses (outside the section on the Proof from Prophecy).
96. O. Skarsaune, 'Justin and His Bible', in Parvis and Foster, eds, *Justin Martyr and His Worlds*, pp. 53-76, 55.

αἱ γραφαὶ,[97] τὰς γραφάς,[98] τῶν γραφῶν,[99] ἡ γραφὴ[100] and γέγραπται.[101]
In the *Dialogue*, however, the context is debate between Christians and
Jews, in which the two parties share a common understanding of what
such terms mean. In the *First Apology*, where the context is dialogue
between Christians and non-Jews, this is not the case, since the Jewish
scriptures were not part of a common discourse.

Thus, instead of scriptures, Justin refers to prophecies or 'the Books
of the Prophecies' (τὰς βίβλους τῶν προφητῶν).[102] Such terms reflect the
use he makes of the texts in his arguments, where they are employed to
show that the life and death of Jesus and the growth of Christianity have
previously been foretold. No definition or list of prophetic texts is provided;
'prophets' are referred to in the plural, indicating that the prophecies have
multiple authors, some of whom are named, although virtually nothing is
said about them as individuals. As well as Isaiah, who features on several
occasions,[103] other prophets named are[104] Jeremiah,[105] Ezekiel,[106] Daniel,[107]
Joel,[108] Micah,[109] Zephaniah[110] and Zechariah.[111] There are texts from the
Psalms and the Pentateuch, also described as prophetic and with their
authors named: David, author of the Psalms, is 'king and prophet'[112] and

97.   *DT* 32.1, 39.6 and 86.1.
98.   *DT* 82.4 and 127.5.
99.   *DT* 32.2, 34.1, 39.7 and 61.1.
100. *DT* 56.17.
101. *DT* 58.3.
102. *1A* 31.2.
103. *1A* 33.1, 35.3, 37.1, 44.2 etc. See Marcovich, *Apologiae*, p. 175.
104. Minns and Parvis, *Apologies*, pp. 339-40. Sometimes Justin identifies a saying
      as prophetic without naming the author, e.g. 'listen to the prophecies spoken
      concerning this. They are these' (*1A* 50.1-50.2).
105. The two identifiable quotations from Jeremiah at *1A* 47.5 and 53.11 are actually
      attributed to Isaiah; the one quotation from Lamentations at *1A* 55.5 is only
      ascribed to 'the prophet'.
106. Ezekiel is named at *1A* 52.5.
107. The single quotation from Daniel at *1A* 51.8-51.9 is attributed to Jeremiah.
108. The one quotation from Joel at *1A* 52.11 is part of what Minns and Parvis,
      Apologies, p. 213, n. 2, describe as a 'complex assemblage of quotation and
      allusion' which is attributed by Justin to Zechariah; it also includes words from
      Isaiah.
109. Micah is named at *1A* 34.1.
110. Zephaniah is named in the Septuagintal Greek form, Sophonias, at *1A* 35.10,
      although only the first part of the text quoted is found in Zephaniah (at *1A*
      3.14), with the full text quoted appearing in Zechariah (*1A* 9.9): Minns and
      Parvis, *Apologies*, p. 179, n. 2.
111. *1A* 35.10.
112. *1A* 35.6.

Moses, author of the Pentateuch, is described as 'the first of the prophets'[113] and referred to a number of times as the author of prophetic texts.[114] This places him in a new light as far as the non-Jewish Graeco-Roman world was concerned; Moses was a well-known figure, identified as a lawgiver, the leader of the Exodus or as a magician, but not hitherto as a prophet.[115]

How Justin views the scope of the Books of the Prophecies remains uncertain. He may have in mind the whole corpus of Jewish scriptures as it existed at the time and uses the term he does to emphasise its prophetic nature. It is, however, also possible that he regarded the Books of the Prophecies as a more limited range of texts, comprising, certainly, the books from which he quotes, and perhaps others – for instance, books from the Jewish scriptures which modern scholars class as prophets, such as Hosea and Amos – but not the whole Jewish scriptures. Justin's use of citations in the *Apology* differs from the *Dialogue*; in the former there are no quotations from Joshua, Samuel or Kings, for instance, as there are in the latter.[116] This may be because Justin takes different views in the *Apology* and the *Dialogue* of the scope of the authoritative texts, mirroring the difference noted above in the terms he uses to refer to them; it may, however, simply be that the predominantly historical narrative of, say, Joshua, Samuel and Kings is not useful for the prophetically-based arguments of the *First Apology*.

It should not be assumed that, when quoting from, say, Isaiah or Ezekiel, Justin necessarily had access to complete versions of those texts. In Chapter 1 above the importance of quotation collections at the time was noted and, although Justin cites actual texts rather than paraphrases, it is possible that quotation collections of some sort were his sources. Skarsaune's painstaking analysis of Justin's sources strongly suggests that in the *First Apology* he was drawing on existing clusters of quotations from the Jewish scriptures and not on full scriptural texts and, indeed, that such collections may have been all that was available to him.[117]

The Authority of the Sacred Texts

The Books of the Prophecies are presented by Justin as having an authority which derives from their antiquity and their authorship and

---

113. *1A* 32.1.
114. E.g. *1A* 44.8 and 54.5.
115. Gager, *Moses in Greco-Roman Paganism*.
116. Marcovich, *Dialogus*, pp. 321-22 lists the references.
117. Skarsaune, *Proof from Prophecy*, pp. 133-242. Skarsaune, 'Justin and His Bible', pp. 55-56, maintains that, when he wrote *Dialogue with Trypho*, Justin, by contrast, had access to manuscripts of complete biblical books.

he uses the legend of the Septuagint (referred to in Chapter 1)[118] to demonstrate this. There are a number of versions of the legend,[119] Justin's being the earliest known account by a Christian author.[120] He describes[121] how the prophecies were delivered a long time ago by people who were 'prophets of God' (θεοῦ προφῆται).[122] They wrote the prophecies down themselves and books containing them were preserved by the kings of the Jews. Later, Ptolemy, King of Egypt, when setting up his Library in Alexandria, wished to collect writings of all peoples; he heard about the prophetic books and sought to acquire them. They were sent to him by Herod,[123] King of the Jews, but, finding the texts to be in Hebrew, Ptolemy requested that translators be provided. This was done; the texts were rendered into Greek and preserved in Egypt until Justin's own time. Justin says that they were also preserved in Jewish communities.[124]

There are significant differences between Justin's treatment of the legend and those of his predecessors. He refers to the texts as the Books of the Prophecies, in contrast to descriptions of them as the laws of the Jews in *Aristeas*[125] and as laws made by Moses in Philo's *Life of Moses*.[126] He describes the prophets as having arisen among the Jews (ἐν Ἰουδαίοις) but says nothing further about the Jewish people or the Jewish religion. This contrasts with *Aristeas* where the High Priest[127] and the Jerusalem

---

118. This is the phrase commonly used to describe the tradition although it does not appear in the *First Apology*.

119. Wasserstein and Wasserstein, *Legend of the Septuagint*.

120. Ibid., pp. 98-100.

121. *1A* 31.

122. *1A* 31.1.

123. Minns and Parvis, *Apologies*, pp. 165-67, n. 4 and n. 5, follow W. Schmid, 'Ein rätselhafter Anachronismus bei Justinus Martyr', in W. Schmid, *Ausgewählte philologishe Schriften: Herausgegeben von Hartmut Erbse und Jochem Küppers* (Berlin: de Gruyter, 1984), pp. 333-37, in treating the reference to Herod as a scribal error in the manuscript, while not endorsing the detail of Schmid's explanation. Other authorities do not follow Schmid: Munier, *Apologie*, p. 210, n. 2; Barnard, *Apologies*, pp. 146-147; and Marcovich, *Apologiae*, p. 76n. It is not implausible that Justin's original text contained an anachronistic error and the majority view is followed here in preference to that of Minns and Parvis.

124. *1A* 31.3-31.5.

125. *Aristeas*, para. 10: this refers to the Pentateuch alone.

126. Philo, *De Vita Mosis*, 2, 31 and 34. Philo says that Moses' law or laws consist of two parts, the first historical and the second concerned with commands and prohibitions: Philo, *De Vita Mosis*, 2, 46.

127. The deputation from Alexandria is described as being 'to Eleazar, the High Priest of the Jews' (*Aristeas*, para. 1), who later makes a long speech on the Jewish law (*Aristeas*, paras. 130-66).

Temple[128] feature prominently. Justin makes only passing reference to the translators, who were clearly Jews, although they are not identified as such.[129] In *Aristeas*, by contrast, they are significant figures whose wisdom is emphasised,[130] while in Philo's *Life of Moses* their work is described in miraculous terms, with translators working independently producing identical translations.[131] Justin plays down the Jewish connections in the legend; the prophecies are presented as the work of ancient wise men who just happened to have emerged from among the Jews.[132]

The legend establishes the antiquity of the prophetic books and this is a source of their authority.[133] The accuracy of the surviving texts is also emphasised. Justin provides a complete manuscript history, describing how the texts were written down by their authors, preserved over centuries and lodged in a Greek royal library, so that what can be read now are the very words the prophets spoke long ago.[134] For Justin, the Books of the Prophecies are a multi-authored collection. Each prophet orally delivered and then wrote down his prophecies which were subsequently brought together in a collection. Individual authorship of prophecies was not lost, however, for, with some exceptions,[135] the quotations are attributed to named authors, so the tradition is not an anonymous one. Each quotation is the work of an individual author but the message of the prophecies is a single collective wisdom. Thus, even when a prophecy is actually a composite of a number of different elements traceable to different scriptural books, the 'quotation' is attributed by Justin to one named prophet.[136] Individual prophets are referred to as authors of texts to identify them, not, however, in order to isolate individual messages or to distinguish the ideas of one from those of another and there are no references to the original historical circumstances in which prophecies were delivered.

---

128. *Aristeas*, paras. 84-99, describes the Temple and its ceremonies.
129. *1A* 31.4 only says that Herod 'asked that people be sent who might translate them [the books of the prophecies] into the Greek language'.
130. Particularly for the contributions they make to the debate at the banquet of the Egyptian king: *Aristeas*, paras. 187-261.
131. Philo, *De Vita Mosis*, 2, 37-40.
132. *1A* 31.1. Justin's portrayal of the Jews in the *First Apology* will be discussed further below.
133. For antiquity as a source of authority, see Armstrong, 'Pagan and Christian Traditionalism'.
134. *1A* 31.5.
135. See, e.g. *1A* 38, for a series of quotations from Isaiah and the Psalms not attributed to named prophets.
136. E.g. *1A* 52.10-12 attributed to Zechariah.

Indeed, the prophecies spoken by the 'prophets of God'[137] were, ultimately, not their own words but utterances inspired by the Prophetic Spirit which speaks with a single voice. The phrase 'Prophetic Spirit' ($\pi\rho\sigma\phi\eta\tau\iota\kappa\grave{o}\nu\ \pi\nu\varepsilon\tilde{v}\mu\alpha$)[138] is used many times in the *First Apology*;[139] it plays a key role in Justin's account of the legend of the Septuagint and in his discussion of the prophecies. The term is hardly known previously – it occurs twice in Philo and once in the *Shepherd of Hermas*[140] – so Stanton's suggestion that 'Justin may well have coined the phrase himself' is quite plausible.[141] Justin does not define Prophetic Spirit or discuss what the term means. Its role is to act as the mechanism through which what will occur in the future is revealed to the prophets.[142]

The Prophetic Spirit is portrayed as close to God and twice described as being venerated. On the first occasion, Justin says: 'We venerate and worship both this God and also the Son who came from him and taught us these things, and the host of the other good angels who follow him and are made like him, and also the Prophetic Spirit';[143] and, on the second, introducing an element of hierarchy: 'Jesus Christ . . . we rationally worship . . . For we have learnt that he is the son of the true God, and we hold him in second place and the Prophetic Spirit in the third rank.'[144] Divinely inspired words are revealed to the prophets by the Prophetic Spirit which describe what God ordains should happen: that He will send His Son at the first coming as saviour and at the second as judge.

This account of the authority of the Books of the Prophecies differs from Nyström's.[145] He argues that, since Justin was writing for a non-Jewish audience, the Jewish scriptures could not be cited as authority and Justin's argument for Christianity is therefore based on reason and not scriptural authority: 'Christian tradition/teaching, as identical to logos/reason, is

---

137. *1A* 31.1.
138. G.N. Stanton, 'The Spirit in the Writings of Justin Martyr', in G.N. Stanton, B.W. Longnecker and S.C. Barton, eds, *The Holy Spirit and Christian Origins: Essays in Honor of James D.G. Dunn* (Grand Rapids: Eerdmans, 2004), pp. 321-34.
139. Thirty-seven times in all, twenty-five in the *First Apology*, e.g. 31.1, 32.2, 33.2 and 5, 35.3, 38.1 and 39.1, and twelve in the *Dialogue*: Stanton, 'Spirit in the Writings of Justin', p. 326.
140. Ibid., p. 327.
141. Ibid. The loss to posterity of so much first- and second-century literature should, however, engender a degree of caution about accepting such a judgement too readily.
142. Although it conveys other forms of wisdom as well: see below.
143. *1A* 6.2.
144. *1A* 13.3.
145. Nyström, *Apology of Justin Martyr*, pp. 105-31.

the fundamental authority and the function of the Hebrew prophets is to confirm this fact.'[146] For this to be the case, however, much greater emphasis would need to be given by Justin to arguments from 'logos/reason' (which are referred to in the *First Apology* but not greatly developed) and much less to the Proof from Prophecy. Nyström pays little regard to two factors which are important to Justin's argument: the trouble taken to establish the authority of the ancient prophecies through the legend of the Septuagint and the role of the Prophetic Spirit in linking prophecies to a divine origin.

The Contents of the Prophecies

Having established the sources of the prophecies' authority, Justin then relates them to Jesus. He provides a summary of the contents of the prophecies:

> In the Books of the Prophets, then, we found Jesus our Christ, proclaimed ahead of time as drawing near, being born of a virgin, and growing to manhood, and healing every disease and every illness, and raising the dead, and being resented and unacknowledged, and being crucified, and dying and rising again, and ascending into the heavens, and both being, and being called, the Son of God, and we found certain people sent by him to every race of people to proclaim these things, and that it was rather people from among the gentiles who believed in him.[147]

The main theme of this passage is the principal events in the story of Jesus (his birth, life, death, resurrection and ascension),[148] although two later developments, occurring after the death of Jesus, are mentioned as foretold: proclamation of the gospel by his followers and acceptance of the gospel by the gentiles. Justin's summary is, however, not exhaustive, since prophesied events are referred to later on which are not included here: the second coming of Jesus to judge the world;[149] the rejection of Jesus by the Jews;[150] and the defeat of the Jews by the Romans.[151] More will be said about these later.

---

146. Ibid., p. 112.
147. *1A* 31.7.
148. One of the statements in the passage refers to a prophecy which does not describe an event in the life of Jesus but touches on his unique status: 'both being, and being called, the Son of God'.
149. *1A* 52.3.
150. *1A* 49. There is, however, implicit criticism of the Jews in the statement in *1A* 31.7 that 'it was rather people from among the gentiles who believed in him'.
151. *1A* 47.

The nature of the events listed suggests that prophecies only foretell events of great importance and not random future occurrences. If an event is found to have occurred as foretold, it must be highly significant since God through the Prophetic Spirit has prophesied it. Moreover, the events prophesied are often extraordinary in themselves, such as birth from a virgin, miraculous healing of the sick or resurrection and ascension into heaven, or, if not actually extraordinary, then momentous in some other way. The crucifixion and death of Jesus are in one sense mundane events in the life of a condemned criminal but because they happen to the Son of God they are accorded a special significance.

Justin does not describe a single occurrence only, rather a series of events which have been prophesied and are now being fulfilled. Showing that one event was prophesied and has now occurred would be significant. However, demonstrating this for a whole sequence is much more telling, since the weight of evidence accumulates with multiple cases of prophetic fulfilment. This is all the more so when the sequence of individual occurrences constitutes a coherent narrative of events.

Skarsaune has tracked how in subsequent chapters of the *First Apology* specific prophetic texts support each statement in the summary account and there is no need to repeat that here.[152] To demonstrate that the prophecies are fulfilled, however, events must be identified to match each prophecy. Justin's prophecies can be grouped into three categories: first, those predicting events that pre-date the current generation (but are still comparatively recent);[153] second, those whose fulfilment is apparent to the current generation; and, third, those which have not yet been fulfilled.

The birth of Jesus is described as having taken place 150 years earlier,[154] placing the events of his life and death in the first category, well before the memory of anyone now living. For these events an appeal cannot, by Justin's

---

152. Skarsaune, *Proof from Prophecy*, pp. 139-64.

153. The fulfilment of ancient prophecies in the life of a great man in comparatively recent times – the imperial age of Augustus – would have been familiar to a Graeco-Roman audience from the very popular work of Virgil (Virgil, *Eclogues, Georgics and Aeneid*, ed. by H.R. Fairclough and rev. by G.P. Goold, LCL, 2 vols [Cambridge, MA: Harvard University Press, 1999]), notably in the prophecies in Books 1, 6 and 8 of *The Aeneid* and in the 4th *Eclogue* (discussed in G. Williams, *Technique and Ideas in the* Aeneid [New Haven and London: Yale University Press, 1983], pp. 138-56; and J.J. O'Hara, *Death and the Optimistic Prophecy in Virgil's* Aeneid [Princeton: Princeton University Press, 1990], pp. 128-75). For Virgil's widespread popularity: R.J. Tarrant, 'Aspects of Virgil's Reception in Antiquity', in C. Martindale, ed., *The Cambridge Companion to Virgil* (Cambridge: Cambridge University Press, 1997), pp. 56-72.

154. *1A* 46.1.

time, be made to eye-witness testimony. Christian Gospels are not cited as sources for information about the life of Jesus; Justin relies instead on other sources and he identifies two. First, the description of Jesus' birth in Bethlehem as fulfilment of a prophecy from Micah is accompanied by the comment that this is something 'you can learn from the census-lists made under Quirinius who was your first procurator in Judaea'.[155] A documentary source is clearly being referred to here. Second, Justin twice cites[156] the 'Acts Recorded under Pontius Pilate' as a source for the life of Jesus, commenting on the first occasion: 'And that these things happened you can learn from the "Acts Recorded under Pontius Pilate" [ἐκ τῶν ἐπὶ Ποντίου Πιλάτου γενομένων ἄκτων]'.[157] The precise meaning of this phrase remains elusive. Some commentators suppose that 'Acts Recorded under Pontius Pilate' denotes a documentary source[158] (even if no such source survives), with Munier going so far as to suggest that it refers to official documents from the prefecture of Pontius Pilate preserved in the imperial archives.[159]

It seems most likely that Justin would not refer to a source in the way he does if his audience were aware that it did not exist, since this would undermine his credibility. He clearly wants his readers to accept his statement as good evidence that events had occurred as he describes them. So, he could be referring to a letter from Pilate to the emperor describing his actions. Correspondence certainly took place between emperors and provincial governors in the early imperial period as dictated by the needs of official business; it was, however, *ad hoc* in nature, so far as can be ascertained, with no evidence that there was regular reporting by provincial governors to the centre of the Empire in Rome.[160] No correspondence involving Pontius Pilate survives but two events are recorded by ancient historians which could have prompted Pilate to write to the emperor. The first, described by the first-century, Alexandrian-Jewish writer Philo,[161] occurred when Pilate erected golden shields in Herod's palace in Jerusalem, causing consternation among the local Jewish population and prompting them to complain to Emperor Tiberius. The latter wrote to Pilate rebuking him for his actions, so it is possible that Pilate then wrote back to defend himself.[162] The second incident,

---

155. *1A* 34.2.
156. *1A* 35.9 and 48.3.
157. *1A* 35.9.
158. Barnard, trans., *Apologies*, p. 151, n. 242; Minns and Parvis, *Apologies*, p. 177, n. 9.
159. Munier, *Apologie*, p. 223, n. 5.
160. Millar, *Emperor in the Roman World*, pp. 313-41.
161. Philo, *De Legatione ad Gaium*, ed. by F.H. Colson, LCL 379 (Cambridge, MA: Harvard University Press, 1962), 38.299-305.
162. Particularly as Philo records that Pilate was fearful that a Jewish petition to the

recorded by the first-century Jewish historian Josephus residing in Rome,[163] occurred when Vitellius *legatus* of Syria sent Pilate to Rome to be investigated by the Emperor Tiberius after complaints by the Samaritans of heavy-handed treatment. Again, it is conceivable that Pilate would have written to the Emperor to defend himself. These were specific instances. Nevertheless, it would involve a further stretch to claim that in either case a self-justifying account by Pilate would have had anything to say about Jesus. Conceivably, Pilate could have done so as part of a general defence of his record as governor. However, to speculate that this was actually the case presses the evidence further than it will reasonably go.[164]

The second category of prophecies is those whose fulfilment has occurred in the lifetimes of people now living. Justin says: 'for we see even with our own eyes that things have happened and are happening as they were foretold';[165] and later: 'the phrase "He shall be the expectation of the nations" signified that people from all nations will expect him to come again. It is possible for you to see this with your own eyes and to be persuaded by the reality.'[166]

At various points, references are made to current or recent events, of which contemporaries would have been aware from their own experience or knowledge. There are two in particular: the defeat of the Jews by the Romans and the acceptance of Jesus by the gentiles. On the first, Justin refers to the 'recent Jewish war [the Bar Kokhba Revolt]'[167] and how in the same conflict the Romans 'came to rule over the Jews and gained mastery of all their land'.[168] He also refers to the Romans' plundering of the land of the Jews[169] and to the 'desolation of the land of the Jews' by the Romans.[170] On the second, the gentiles are described as awaiting (present tense: προσδοκῶσι) the return of Jesus,[171] with Justin explaining how the preaching of the Apostles prompted their conversion:

Emperor 'would also expose the rest of his conduct as governor by stating in full the briberies, the insults, the robberies, the outrages and wanton injuries, the executions without trial constantly repeated, the ceaseless and supremely grievous cruelty': ibid., 38.302.

163. Josephus, *Jewish Antiquities* 9.18.85-89.
164. These events are discussed in H.K. Bond, *Pontius Pilate in History and Interpretation* (Cambridge: Cambridge University Press, 1998), pp. 24-93.
165. *1A* 30.1.
166. *1A* 32.4.
167. *1A* 31.6.
168. *1A* 32.3.
169. *1A* 47.1-47.6.
170. *1A* 53.3.
171. *1A* 32.4.

For men twelve in number went out from Jerusalem into the world and they were unskilled in speaking. Through the power of God they made known to the whole human race how they were sent by Christ to teach the word of God to all; and we who formerly were slaying one another not only do not fight against enemies but confessing Christ die gladly.[172]

The fulfilment of this second category of prophecies is validated by eye-witness testimony. Justin appeals to the existing knowledge of his readers, and it must be presumed that he expects this to be sufficient grounds for them to accept his case, since he says nothing more in justification. In mid-second-century Rome the defeat of the Jews by the Romans some fifteen to twenty years earlier would have been a well-known fact of recent history and the growth of Christianity as the result of missionary activity would have been evident to his readers.[173] Scholarship has shown the importance and status of eye-witness testimony for historical writing in the ancient world,[174] so it is not surprising to find Justin making an appeal of this kind.

The third category of prophecies comprises those that have not been fulfilled. Justin wants to show that they are not false prophecies, so instead of rejecting them he maintains that they remain to be fulfilled in the future at the second coming when Christ returns in triumph: 'For the prophets proclaimed beforehand his two comings: one, which has indeed already happened, that of a dishonoured and suffering human being, and the second when it is proclaimed that he will come with glory from the heavens with his angelic army.'[175]

The fact that some prophecies are as yet unfulfilled is, therefore, not a weakness in the Proof. Here then is Justin's answer to the question with which this book began: how can Christians believe in a crucified man?

---

172. *1A* 39.3.

173. For the Bar Kokhba revolt of 132-135 CE: W. Horbury, *Jewish War under Trajan and Hadrian* (Cambridge: Cambridge University Press, 2014).

174. R. Bauckham, *Jesus and the Eyewitnesses: The Gospels as Eyewitness Testimony* (Grand Rapids: Eerdmans, 2006), pp. 5-11. S. Byrskog, *Story as History – History as Story: The Gospel Tradition in the Context of Ancient Oral History* (Tübingen: Mohr Siebeck, 2000), pp. 48-65, reviews material from ancient historians concerning the importance of eye-witness testimony not just for historians who were eye-witnesses themselves, such as Thucydides and Josephus, but also for others such as Polybius and Tacitus. Polybius comments that the historian's interrogation of eye-witnesses to events 'is exceedingly valuable and is the most important part of history': Polybius, *The Histories*, ed. by W.R. Paton and rev. by F.W. Walbank and C. Habicht, LCL, 6 vols (Cambridge, MA: Harvard University Press, 2010-2012), 4.12.27.6.

175. *1A* 52.3.

Descriptions of Jesus in the prophecies as a humiliated figure refer only to his first coming, for at his second coming he will appear in glory as a triumphant figure. It is, however, only reading the prophecies that reveals this.

Justin's account of the prophecies has built up a narrative of events, some of which have taken place in recent history and some of which will occur in the future. It is a selective account but the selection is not random or accidental. The Prophetic Spirit's narrative consists of a sequence of divinely-ordained events, comprising not just the life and death of Jesus and the growth of Christianity among the gentiles, but also the rejection of Jesus by the Jews, the Jews' defeat by the Romans, their exclusion from the land of Judaea and their future condemnation at the last judgement.[176] One event which is not part of this sequence of prophesied events, however, is the persecution of Christians by the Romans. Thus, while Justin recognises that such ill-treatment has occurred, it was not something that was previously prophesied and should not, therefore, be regarded as part of God's plan for the world. Persecution of Christians by the Romans can be brought to an end – as Justin wishes that it should be – without contravening the divine plan.

Justin uses the insights provided by the prophecies to set up pairs of opposites. First, there is the contrast between those who follow Jesus and those who follow Graeco-Roman mythological gods. Second, the Jews, who reject Jesus Christ and persecute Christians, are contrasted with the gentiles, who accept the gospel preached by the Apostles. Third, the Jews are contrasted with the Romans, with whom they have been in violent conflict and by whom they have been defeated. Finally, the Christians, who at the last judgement will be saved, are contrasted with the Jews, who will be condemned.

Justin's argument has turned full circle. He began the *First Apology* by protesting against the unfair treatment of Christians by the Roman authorities and then moved to a more general defence of Christianity. His Proof from Prophecy showed that some recent occurrences have been divinely ordained. However, his catalogue of events does not include the persecution of Christians by the Roman authorities. The plea for good relations between Christians and the Roman authorities with which Justin began is therefore shown to be consistent with, and, moreover, supported by, his Proof from Prophecy.

---

176. Justin also refers to the Jews' persecution of Christians during the Bar Kokhba war: *1A* 31.6. For a summary of Justin's overall portrayal of the Jews in the *First Apology*: S.G. Wilson, *Related Strangers: Jews and Christians 70-170 C.E.* (Minneapolis: Fortress Press, 1995), p. 31.

Indeed, not only need there not be enmity between the Christians and the Romans, but a shared opposition to the Jews appears to unite them. The Romans have defeated the Jews in war and laying waste to their land is a form of persecution. Justin never refers to these events in terms that are critical of the Romans; but he does criticise the Jews for their rejection of Jesus and their persecution of Christians and he interprets the prophecies as foretelling the condemnation of the Jews at the second coming. Thus, through the insights provided by the ancient prophecies, Christianity's position in the world is characterised by reference to two other parties, the Jews and the Romans, and its relationship with them.

The Proof from Prophecy and Graeco-Roman Culture

Since Justin's Proof from Prophecy presents itself as addressed to a Graeco-Roman audience, it is unsurprising that clear connections should be evident in the text between the arguments he presents and a number of aspects of Graeco-Roman culture. These links reveal both parallels and contrasts. The features in question are the Graeco-Roman traditions of prophecy and Ancient Wisdom, the well-established traditions of Greek philosophy – including the attachment to rationality in argument – and myth-based Graeco-Roman religion. These will now be examined in turn.

The Graeco-Roman Prophetic Tradition

Justin's account of the prophecies and their fulfilments is addressed to an audience previously unfamiliar with them. The prophecies emanate from among the Jews, even though their Jewish origin is played down. To those who were culturally Greek, the Jews were one of the barbarian (or non-Greek) peoples, so the prophecies are barbarian in origin. Justin does not characterise the prophecies in these terms, however; 'barbarian' appears rarely in the *First Apology* and never in connection with the Proof from Prophecy.[177]

Justin's presentation tends rather to emphasise connections with the separate Graeco-Roman prophetic tradition with which his audience would have been familiar. This tradition was of long standing[178] and

---

177. There are four occurrences of βάρβαρος/οί βάρβαροι (barbarian/s) at 5.4, 7.3, 46.3 and 60.11: Marcovich, *Apologiae*, p. 183.

178. Works dealing with this issue: J.A. North, 'Diviners and Divination at Rome', in M. Beard and J.A. North, *Pagan Priests: Religion and Power in the Ancient World* (London: Duckworth, 1990), pp. 51-71; H.-J. Klauck, *The Religious Context of Early Christianity: A Guide to Graeco-Roman Religions*, trans. by B. McNeil

fostered widespread acceptance of the notion that the future could be foretold. Certain special individuals or groups were thought to have prophetic powers, which came to them from a divine source; indeed, they were often thought to be speaking the words of a god and sometimes to be uttering prophecies in a manic state of divine possession. Particular places – temples or sanctuaries – were often the location of oracles where prophecies were dispensed, Delphi being the most celebrated. Prophecies could be delivered orally and later written down. Some were thought to have originated long ago, to have been preserved in writing and sometimes grouped together in collections. They could be composed in poetry or in more special poetic forms, such as acrostic, and they were frequently enigmatic or paradoxical. Thus, a prophecy commonly needed interpretation if its present-day relevance was to be understood and this required skill and insight. Interpretations could be correct or incorrect and the true meaning of a prophecy could be a matter of dispute. Prophecies could foretell events which were positive or beneficial in nature or they could be prophecies of doom; in the latter case, they could be interpreted as warnings, with actions required to propitiate the gods, such as offering sacrifices or building a new temple. It was a common practice, when important decisions needed to be taken, to consult oracles for guidance, for instance, by putting questions to, and soliciting answers from, an oracle.

Looking at the prophecies presented by Justin against this background, a number of similarities are evident. Justin's prophecies were of ancient provenance; they were uttered by prophets who were more than ordinary human beings and who received their insights from a divine source, in his case the Prophetic Spirit. Like Graeco-Roman prophecies, Justin's could be enigmatic or paradoxical in form, sometimes bordering on the incomprehensible, and they required skilled interpretation to be deciphered and for their relevance to the present day to be understood.[179]

Some features of the Graeco-Roman tradition were, however, not found in Justin's account. His prophets were not associated with specific shrines or temples and are not described as coming from particular locations. There was no suggestion that prophecies were uttered in states

---

(London: T. & T. Clark, 2000), pp. 177-209; D. Potter, *Prophets and Emperors, Human and Divine Authority from Augustus to Theodosius* (Cambridge, MA: Harvard University Press, 1994); F. Santangelo, *Divination, Prediction and the End of the Roman Republic* (Cambridge: Cambridge University Press, 2013); D.E. Aune, *Prophecy in Early Christianity and the Ancient Mediterranean World* (Grand Rapids: Eerdmans, 1983), pp. 23-79.

179. Issues of interpretation are considered further below.

of mania, when a prophet was the object of divine possession.[180] The prophecies were not couched in verse or acrostic forms[181] but expressed in plain language. Moreover, they are not presented as being delivered in response to enquiries;[182] indeed, nothing is said about what prompted the prophets to utter them except that they were inspired by the Prophetic Spirit.

There are, however, particular parallels to be drawn between Justin's ancient prophecies and the tradition of Sibylline prophecy which was strong in Rome where Justin was writing.[183] Prophecies uttered by the Sibyl of Cumae in very ancient times were brought together in book collections. They were acquired by the Romans in legendary circumstances,[184] preserved by them and frequently consulted.[185] Just as royal figures – the kings of the Jews and the Greek kings of Egypt – were instrumental in the preservation of prophetic texts in Justin's version

---

180. Justin twice (*1A* 33.9 and 35.3) refers to prophets as possessed by God (using θεοφορέομαι) but a state of mania is not suggested in either instance.

181. As is the case with the only extant Sibylline prophecy: A. Giannini, ed., *Paradoxographorum Graecorum Reliquiae* (Milan: Institutio Editorale Italiano, 1966), pp. 200-7; trans. in W. Hansen, trans., *Phlegon of Tralles' Book of Marvels* (Exeter: University of Exeter Press, 1996), pp. 40-43.

182. Again, most famously in the oracle at Delphi.

183. The Sibylline tradition attracted considerable attention from ancient historians: H. Diels, *Sibyllinische Blätter* (Berlin: Georg Reimer, 1890); *Book III of the Sibylline Oracles and Its Social Setting: With an Introduction, Translation and Commentary*, ed. by R. Buitenwerf (Leiden: Brill, 2003); *The Sibylline Oracles: With Introduction, Translation and Commentary on the First and Second Books*, ed. by J.L. Lightfoot (Oxford: Oxford University Press, 2007); H.W. Parke, *Sibyls and Sibylline Prophecy in Classical Antiquity*, ed. by B.C. McGing (London: Routledge, 1988); J. Scheid, 'Les Livres Sibyllins at les archives des quindécemvirs', in C. Moatti, ed., *La mémoire perdue: recherches sur l'administration romaine* (Rome: École Française de Rome, 1998), pp. 11-26; W. den Boer, *Private Morality in Greece and Rome: Some Historical Aspects* (Leiden: Brill, 1979), pp. 93-128; Santangelo, *Divination*, pp. 128-48.

184. For the story of the acquisition of the Sibylline Books by the early Roman king Tarquinius, see Dionysius of Halicarnassus, *Roman Antiquities*, ed. by E. Cary, LCL, 7 vols (Cambridge, MA: Harvard University Press, 1937-50), 4.62. Dionysius stresses the subsequent importance of the Books for the Roman people: 'there is no possession of the Romans, sacred or profane, which they guard so carefully as they do the Sibylline oracles' (4.62.5).

185. B. MacBain, *Prodigy and Expiation: A Study in Religion and Politics in Republican Rome* (Brussels: Latomus, 1982). The first-century Roman poet Lucan describes how the Cumaean Sibyl put her inspiration at the service of Rome in particular: Lucan, *Pharsalia*, ed. by J.D. Duff, LCL 220 (Cambridge, MA: Harvard University Press, 1928), 5.183-86.

of the Septuagint legend, so the Roman emperors had an important role in relation to the Sibylline Books. They were responsible for their preservation, for the arrangements for consulting and interpreting them and for weeding out false from true prophecies.[186] So, it is not surprising to find that at one point Justin mentions the Books of the Sibyl in the same breath as his Books of the Prophecies.[187]

Analogies between Justin's prophecies and the Sibylline tradition should not be pressed too far, however, since there are also significant differences, notably in the purpose of prophetic activity. Sibylline prophecies were consulted when events suggested that the *pax deorum* (peace of the gods) had been broken, to identify remedial steps necessary to propitiate the gods. For Justin the purpose of prophecies was to demonstrate the status of Jesus and to attract new converts to Christianity;[188] so while he employed prophetic language and used concepts which would have had some familiarity for his readers, he was nevertheless drawing on a separate prophetic tradition and using his prophecies to achieve a radically different purpose.

Moreover, Justin's approach was novel in that it brought prophecy into the sphere of the literary. In Graeco-Roman culture prophecy was a subject which was discussed by literary writers who might treat the contents of prophetic utterances with respect; but prophetic insights were seen as the product of a different form of discourse, one external to literary culture. That culture placed a high premium on rational arguments, whereas prophetic insights were regarded as being of a different order,

---

186. In 28 BCE Augustus had the Sibylline Books transferred from the Temple of Jupiter to the new Temple of Apollo that he had had built on the Palatine close to his own residence. Later, in 12 BCE, he acted to put an end to the private ownership of oracles, ordering that all extant prophecies be surrendered and examined; the genuine (Sibylline) oracles (which were found to be a minority) were admitted to the official collection and the remainder were destroyed: Parke, *Sibyls and Sybilline Prophecy*, pp. 141-42. See also Suetonius, *Augustus*, LCL 31; Tacitus, *Annals*, ed. by J. Jackson, LCL (Cambridge, MA: Harvard University Press, 1937), 6.12. In 19 CE the Emperor Tiberius had all prophetic books examined to sort genuine from bogus prophecies, retaining the former and rejecting the latter: Cassius Dio, *Roman History*, LCL 7.57.18.3-4.

187. *1A* 44.12. Aune, *Prophecy in Early Christianity*, p. 37, comments that most Sibylline oracles were oracles of doom, mirroring those of Justin's prophecies which relate to the Eschaton and the fate of the Jews; however, the bulk of the prophecies quoted by Justin contain positive messages relating to the life of Jesus and the growth of Christianity.

188. There are extant cases of multiple Sibylline prophecies relating to the same set of circumstances, but not of a series of prophecies providing a narrative of events such as Justin portrays: MacBain, *Prodigy and Expiation*, pp. 82-106.

deriving from non-rational sources. The work of two Greek authors, Plato and Plutarch, will illuminate this: Plato as the originator of one of the major strands of Greek philosophy and still hugely influential in the second century CE and Plutarch as a writer of much more recent date with a strong interest in both philosophy and prophecy.

Plato saw value in prophecy. He accepted that alongside reason, the source of knowledge, other forms of insight might be provided by prophecy and divination which were divinely inspired.[189] Prophecy is not a subject to which he ever gives extended treatment but his works contain a number of references to it. In the *Phaedrus*, when discussing the prophetic inspiration of the Sibyl, he refers to 'the noblest of arts, which foretells the future'.[190] In *Ion* he likens poets to prophets and emphasises the divine origin of their inspiration:

> God takes away the mind of these men [the poets] and uses them as his ministers, just as he does soothsayers and godly seers, in order that we who hear them may know that it is not they who utter these words of great price, when they are out of their wits, but that it is God himself who speaks and addresses us through them.[191]

In *Meno* Plato compares prophets and statesmen and comments that, when in the throes of divine inspiration, neither of them understands what they are saying: 'statesmen . . . have nothing more to do with wisdom than soothsayers and diviners; for these people utter many a true thing when inspired, but have no knowledge of anything they say'.[192] Finally, in the *Timaeus* Plato describes the liver as the organ of divination in the human body and a part of the divinely-created order 'that it might in some degree lay hold on truth'[193] and says that, while divination can yield insights, these are distinct from the conclusions reached by reflections of the rational mind.[194]

189. E.R. Dodds, *The Greeks and the Irrational* (Berkeley: University of California Press, 1951), pp. 207-35.
190. Plato, *Phaedrus*, ed. by H.N. Fowler, LCL 36 (Cambridge, MA: Harvard University Press, Cambridge Mass 1914), 244B.
191. Plato, *Ion*, ed. by H.N. Fowler and W.R.M. Lamb, LCL 164 (Cambridge, MA: Harvard University Press, 1925), 534C-D.
192. Plato, *Meno*, ed. by W.R.M. Lamb, LCL 165 (Cambridge, MA: Harvard University Press, 1924), 99C.
193. Plato, *Timaeus*, ed. by R.G. Bury, LCL 234 (Cambridge, MA: Harvard University Press, 1929), 71E.
194. Ibid., 71E-72B.

Closer to Justin's own time, Plutarch,[195] who had a strong interest in philosophy,[196] also engaged extensively with religious issues.[197] He was a priest in the temple at Delphi and wrote several works relating to oracles,[198] which he discussed in rational terms,[199] as well as a treatise on the Egyptian myth of Osiris and Isis, in which he approached myth from a philosophical standpoint.[200] Plutarch had a sympathy with prophecy,[201] which sat alongside his enthusiasm for philosophy and rational argument. His view, in van Nuffelen's words, was that 'philosophy and religious tradition lead to knowledge of the same truth.'[202] In extant texts Plutarch never discusses the relationship between the non-rational insights that could be gained from prophecy and the knowledge which comes from the rational methods of philosophy, so his views on this issue are unknown.[203] Importantly indeed, insights from prophecy are not brought into his rational arguments; he treats the two as distinct, with prophetic insight at Delphi and rational inquiry in philosophical discussions.

Thus, Plato and Plutarch, both writers sympathetic to prophecy, do not use prophetic statements as part of their rational arguments and their writings are emblematic of Greek culture in this respect. Written prophecies were known and consulted but the literary and the prophetic were separate cultural stands. By contrast, prophecy *was* part of the literary culture of Hellenistic Judaism and prophetic material occupied a significant portion of the contents of its core text, the Septuagint. Justin was drawing on this

---

195. On Plutarch generally, see R. Lamberton, *Plutarch* (New Haven: Yale University Press, 2001). His dates are c. 45 BCE-120 CE.

196. E.g. Plutarch, *Platonicae Quaestiones* and *De Animae Procreatione in Timaeo* in *Moralia, Volume 13, Part 1* and *De Stoicorum Repugnantiis* and *De Communibus Notitiis adversus Stoicos* in *Moralia, Volume 13, Part 2*, ed. by H. Cherniss, LCL 427 and 470, respectively (Cambridge, MA: Harvard University Press, 1976).

197. For Plutarch's religion: J. Oakesmith, *The Religion of Plutarch: A Pagan Creed of Apostolic Times* (London: Longmans, Green & Co., 1902); F.E. Brenk, *In Mist Appareled: Religious Themes in Plutarch's Moralia and Lives* (Leiden: Brill, 1980).

198. Plutarch, *De E Apud Delphos, De Pythiae Oraculis* and *De Defectu Oraculorum*, ed. by F.C. Babbitt, LCL 306 (Cambridge, MA: Harvard University Press, 1936).

199. Lamberton, *Plutarch*, pp. 155-72.

200. Plutarch, *De Iside et Osiride*, ed. by J.G. Griffiths (Cardiff: University of Wales Press, 1970).

201. Brenk, *In Mist Appareled*, pp. 184-255.

202. P. van Nuffelen, *Rethinking the Gods: Philosophical Readings of Religion in the Post-Hellenistic Period* (Cambridge: Cambridge University Press, 2011), pp. 48-71 (quotation on p. 50). See also H.D. Betz, *Plutarch's Theological Writings and Early Christian Literature* (Leiden: Brill, 1975), pp. 36-37.

203. Lamberton, *Plutarch*, pp. 52-59.

culture when he accessed the Books of the Prophecies but, in bringing prophecies from the Jewish tradition into his apologetic arguments, he was doing something which was unfamiliar to Greek literary culture.

Justin's novelty in this respect is reflected in the vocabulary he employs to describe prophecy, which differs from that of the classical literary tradition. In the latter there was no single term for prophecy and the prophetic, with three terms being employed: '*μάντις*', '*προφήτης*' and '*χρησμός*' (with their cognates),[204] of which *προφήτης* was the least common.[205] *Προφήτης* is, however, Justin's term for his prophets, to the exclusion of the others,[206] and he also uses cognates of *προφήτης*, which were either uncommon in classical Greek, such as the verb *προφητεύω*,[207] or were unknown before the second century, such as the noun *προφητεία*.[208] Thus, Justin uses a distinctive vocabulary to describe prophecy that reflects his particular perspective, following the semantic usage which entered Greek from Hellenistic Judaism. The Hebrew term '*nabi*' was rendered into Greek as *προφήτης* by the Septuagint translators[209] and it was this term, regularly used by Hellenistic-Jewish writers such as Philo and Josephus, which appears in the *First Apology*.[210]

The Proof from Prophecy and Ancient Wisdom

Justin's argument in the Proof from Prophecy connects with another strand of Graeco-Roman culture, in addition to the prophetic, that of Ancient Wisdom. Boys-Stones has traced the development during the later Hellenistic period of the idea of a golden age of philosophical wisdom in very ancient times, first among Stoics and later among Platonists.[211] These ideas are associated particularly with the philosophers Posidonius in the first century BCE and Cornutus in the first century CE.[212] According

---

204. Aune, *Prophecy in Early Christianity*, pp. 23-48; and LSJ entries for *μάντις*, *προφήτης* and *χρησμός*.

205. TLG searches for *μάντις*, *προφήτης* and *χρησμός*.

206. *Μάντις* and *χρησμός* do not appear in *First Apology*: Marcovich, *Apologiae*, pp. 197 and 211.

207. LSJ entries for *προφητεύω* and *προφητεία*; TLG searches for cognates of *προφήτης*; and Marcovich, *Apologiae*, p. 205.

208. G. Kittel and G. Friedrich, eds, *Theological Dictionary of the New Testament*, ed. and trans. by G.W. Bromiley, 10 vols (Grand Rapids: Eerdmans, 1964-76), 6, pp. 781-861, 784; and Marcovich, *Apologiae*, p. 205.

209. E. Fascher, ΠΡΟΦΗΤΗΣ: *Eine sprach- und religionsgeschichtliche Unter-suchung* (Giessen: Alfred Töpelmann, 1927), pp. 102-8; and TLG search for *προφήτης*.

210. TLG searches for *μάντις*, *προφήτης* and *χρησμός* in Philo and Josephus.

211. Boys-Stones, *Post-Hellenistic Philosophy*.

212. Ibid., pp. 44-59.

to this tradition, the earliest era of humankind was dominated by sages whose thinking displayed a unity of ideas that disappeared later when the different, and competing, philosophical schools developed.

Justin's account of his prophets resonates with this Ancient Wisdom tradition.[213] He emphasises their great antiquity: 'And this was prophesied before he [Jesus] appeared, sometimes five thousand years before, sometimes three thousand, sometimes two thousand, and again a thousand and elsewhere eight hundred';[214] and stresses how their writings, dating from a distant age, exhibit the unanimity of ideas found in the Ancient Wisdom tradition. The prophecies may have been delivered by different individuals but they convey a common message. Justin contrasts this with the Greek philosophical schools, several times highlighting that different philosophers do not agree and, indeed, that they contradict one another. He says, for example, that: 'those among the Greeks who taught whatever pleased them are called in every case by the single title "philosopher" even though they contradicted one another in their opinions'.[215]

Justin considers that his prophets are not only ancient, but pre-date the development of Greek philosophy: 'Moses is older even than all the writers in Greek.'[216] This chronological priority is shown by the fact that Greek philosophers actually learnt some of their ideas from Justin's ancient prophets: 'And everything which both the philosophers and the poets said concerning the immortality of the soul or punishments after death or contemplation of heavenly things or similar doctrines they were enabled to understand and they explained because they took their starting-points from the prophets.'[217] Justin provides a specific example of such borrowing when he cites the reference in the *Timaeus* to God having made the world by changing formless matter and claims that Plato took this idea from Genesis. Quoting from Genesis 1 Justin says: 'In this way both Plato and those who say the same things and we ourselves learnt that the whole world came into being by the Word of God out of previously existing things spoken of by Moses. And you can also be persuaded of this.'[218] It was not original to Justin that Moses pre-

---

213. Ibid., pp. 184-88, briefly discusses Justin but makes no reference to his use of ancient prophecies.

214. *1A* 31.8.

215. *1A* 7.3; see also 4.8 and 26.6.

216. *1A* 44.8.

217. *1A* 44.9.

218. *1A* 59.5. The translation here follows Minns and Parvis' emendation of the manuscript text (Minns and Parvis, *Apologies*, p. 233, n. 4), *pace* Marcovich and Munier, and follows Marcovich's use of a capital Λ in Λόγῳ, *pace* Minns and Parvis and Munier.

dated Greek culture and that later Greek philosophers borrowed from the writings of Moses; that idea – sometimes called the 'theft theory' – had become well-established in Hellenistic-Jewish historiography before taking root among Christian writers.[219]

The Proof from Prophecy and Greek Philosophy
Justin's comments on Greek philosophy referred to above appear critical and at times even disparaging. The overall picture in the *First Apology* is, however, a mixed one, for Justin on occasion is more positive. At the outset, the addressees of the *Apology* are described, flatteringly, as philosophers[220] and references of this kind are repeated later.[221] Justin sometimes couples philosophy with piety[222] and then treats it sympathetically, saying, for example, 'you [the addressees] hear on all sides that you are called pious and philosophers and guardians of justice and lovers of learning.'[223] When philosophy is referred to on its own, however, Justin's comments can be more critical in tone, emphasising the divisions that exist among philosophers.[224]

Overall, however, philosophy features comparatively little in the *First Apology*.[225] Two chapters are devoted to discussion of Plato's ideas, although they are mainly concerned with showing that the tradition of thought derived from Moses is superior.[226] There are explicit references to similarities between Christian doctrines and ideas from the Greek philosophical schools of Platonism and Stoicism: 'For when we say that all things were fashioned and came into being through God we will seem to

---

219. Droge, *Homer or Moses?*, pp. 12-48; W. Löhr, 'The Theft of the Greeks: Christian Self-Definition in the Age of the Schools', *RHE*, vol. 95 (2000), pp. 403-26; Nyström, *Apology of Justin Martyr*, pp. 82-86.

220. *1A* 2.2.

221. E.g. *1A* 12.5.

222. E.g. *1A* 3.2, 12.5 and 70.4. See A.-M. Malingrey, *'Philosophia' Études d'un groupe de mots dans la littérature grecque, des présocratiques au IVe siècle après J.-C.* (Paris: C. Klincksieck, 1961), pp. 124-26; and H.H. Holfeder, 'Εὐσέβεια καὶ φιλοσοφία: Literarische Einheit und politischer Kontext von Justins Apologie (Teil I)', *ZNW*, vol. 68 (1977), pp. 48-66.

223. E.g. *1A* 2.2.

224. E.g. *1A* 4.8, 7.3 and 26.6.

225. R. Joly, *Christianisme et philosophie: études sur Justin et les apologistes grecs du deuxième siècle* (Brussels: University of Brussels, 1973), pp. 9-83, argues for the importance in Justin's work of the confrontation between Christianity and philosophy, but he does this mainly on the basis of *DT* 1-7: 'The text of Justin which illustrates most directly the conflict between philosophy and Christianity is without doubt the Prologue of the *Dialogue with Trypho*' (p. 9).

226. *1A* 59-60.

speak the doctrine of Plato, and in saying that there will be a conflagration, we will seem to speak that of the Stoics.'[227] This point is not developed, however, and Justin limits himself to noting commonalities in ideas.[228] The one occasion on which he does address a philosophical issue is in Chapter 43 when he discusses whether his argument based on prophecy implies 'that we say that the things which happen happen through the necessity of fate.'[229] This is a philosophical objection which can reasonably be made to the argument in the Proof from Prophecy, as Justin is aware, and his response is to set out a case for free will and against determinism:

> But that by free choice they [human beings] both act rightly and stumble we demonstrate as follows. We see the same human being in pursuit of opposite things. But if he were fated to be either wicked or virtuous, he would never be capable of opposite things and would not have changed many times. But neither would some human beings be virtuous and some wicked, since we would then be maintaining that fate is the cause of the wicked and acts in opposition to itself; or else the opinion mentioned earlier would seem to be true, that neither virtue nor vice exists, but that good and evil are only matters of opinion.[230]

This argument is presented in a form which would be at home in a philosophical treatise.[231] Justin seeks to show that taking a position different from his own leads either to illogicality ('we would then be asserting that fate is the cause of the wicked and does things contrary to itself') or falsity ('that neither virtue nor vice exists, but that good and evil are matters of opinion only'). It is noteworthy that Justin makes no

227. *1A* 20.4.
228. M. Bonazzi and C. Helmig, eds, *Platonic Stoicism-Stoic Platonism: The Dialogue between Platonism and Stoicism in Antiquity* (Leuven: Leuven University Press, 2007): in the 'Introduction', pp. vii-xv, the editors characterise Greek philosophical discourse of the time as a debate between Platonism and Stoicism, with influences in both directions. Justin appears to be deliberately avoiding a preference for one school over the other.
229. *1A* 43.1.
230. *1A* 43.4-43.6.
231. Fate was an established issue of debate in Graeco-Roman philosophical discourse, not least because of its importance for Stoic thought: BNP article on 'Fate' by D. Frede; M.A. Frede, *A Free Will: Origins of the Notion in Ancient Thought*, ed. by A.A. Long (Berkeley: University of California Press, 2011). For a treatise on the subject written a few decades after Justin's *First Apology*, see Alexander of Aphrodisias, *On Fate: Text, Translation and Commentary*, ed. by R.W. Sharples (London: Duckworth, 1983) discussed further below.

references here to evidence or argument from the Jewish scriptures; he engages with a philosophical question, using arguments appropriate to a philosophical debate, and the passage stands out as the only place in the *First Apology* where he does this.

Thus, in the *Apology* Greek philosophy plays only an incidental rather than a central role. Justin has been seen by some commentators as very sympathetic to Greek philosophy and as a writer who positively seeks to identify common ground between Christianity and Greek philosophy.[232] The evidence from the *First Apology* does not support this, however. Indeed, one striking feature of the work is that, especially in the Proof from Prophecy section, references to philosophy are so few; Justin's proof does not seek to present Christianity as the alternative to Greek philosophy or to show resemblances between them.

This contrasts with Chapters 1-9 of the *Dialogue with Trypho* where Justin exposes deficiencies in various schools of Greek philosophy, particularly Platonism,[233] and then presents the ideas of the ancient prophets, revealed to him by a mysterious old man, as the alternative to be embraced instead.[234] The ideas of these prophets are the origin of Christian thinking and Christianity is referred to as a philosophy. Thus, Justin describes the words of Christ as 'the only sure and useful philosophy'[235] and says that as a consequence he himself is now a philosopher.[236] In the *First Apology*, however, Justin does not describe the prophetic texts as philosophy or refer to the prophets as philosophers; instead, he uses the terms prophecy and prophets throughout. Nor does he call himself a philosopher anywhere in the *Apology*; so, while the Greek philosophical schools are Justin's main target in the *Dialogue*, Chapters 1-9, this is not the case with the Proof from Prophecy in the *Apology*.

Rationality and Proof in the First Apology
It is noteworthy that Justin never refers to prophecy, which is at the core of his argument, as magical, miraculous or irrational. Indeed, he is at pains to present his case as rational.[237] It may be that Justin is here

---

232. E.g. Chadwick, *Early Christian Thought*, pp. 9-22. This has, of course, been disputed: e.g. Hyldahl, *Philosophie und Christentum*, although that is a study of the *Dialogue with Trypho* and not the *First Apology*.

233. The discussion between Justin and the old man in *DT* 3-7 is presented in the form of a philosophical dialogue.

234. *DT* 7.

235. *DT* 8.1.

236. *DT* 8.2.

237. A point emphasised in relation to the apologists generally by Joly, *Christianisme et philosophie*, who devotes a whole chapter to 'Le Christianisme rationnel des

responding to contemporary criticisms of Christians for ignoring proofs and arguments, criticisms found, for instance, in the work of Galen and Lucian.[238] Before even reaching the chapters on the Proof from Prophecy, he gives prominence in the *First Apology* to the concept of rationality by referring to it a number of times; thus, when pleading for relief from persecution, Justin appeals to reason and rejects irrationality:

> For it was not to flatter you with this document nor to gain your favour by our speech that we approached you, but rather to demand that you give judgement in accordance with careful and exacting reason [λόγον], not being gripped by prejudice or the wish to please the superstitious nor driven by irrational impulse or long-entrenched rumours.[239]

Later he refers to the 'rational powers' (λογικῶν δυνάμεων)[240] which God has bestowed on humankind and to human beings as 'rational' (λογικοί)[241] creations.

Similar sentiments are found in the Proof from Prophecy. Justin asks: 'For by what reason [λόγῳ] would we believe in a crucified man that he is the first-begotten of the unbegotten God'[242] – a question which in effect he has already answered much earlier when he said that 'we will prove [ἀποδείξομεν] that the one who became the teacher for us of these things, and who was born for this, Jesus Christ... we rationally worship [μετὰ λόγου τιμῶμεν]'.[243] The demonstration Justin refers to here is the kernel of the Proof from Prophecy and he seeks to portray it as a rational argument. He begins with the words 'we shall now make proof, not trusting those who make assertions' (τὴν ἀπόδειξιν ἤδη ποιησόμεθα, οὐ τοῖς λέγουσι πιστεύοντες),[244] and goes on to say that he will provide 'the greatest and truest proof' (μεγίστη καὶ ἀληθεστάτη ἀπόδειξις).[245] Thus, Justin goes beyond describing his argument as rational, using forms of λόγος and its cognates and refers to his argument prominently as a proof, ἀπόδειξις.[246] He does not, however,

---

apologistes', pp. 85-154.

238. J. Barnes, 'Galen, Christians, Logic', in J. Barnes, *Logical Matters: Essays in Ancient Philosophy II*, ed. by M. Bonelli (Oxford: Clarendon Press, 2012), pp. 1-21, 4-5.

239. *1A* 2.3.

240. *1A* 10.4.

241. *1A* 28.3.

242. *1A* 53.2.

243. *1A* 13.3.

244. *1A* 30.1.

245. Ibid.

246. It appears ten times in the *First Apology*: 14.4, 20.3, 23.3, 30.1 (twice), 46.6

present his argument as a *philosophical* proof, to combat the claims of the Greek philosophical schools and replace them with a Christian alternative. Instead, Justin uses ἀπόδειξις in an everyday, non-philosophical, sense, intending to challenge the claims of the mythologically-based religion of Greece and Rome rather than their philosophical traditions.

Ἀπόδειξις is the term in Greek philosophy for a logical proof, used by Aristotle in the *Posterior Analytics*[247] and also in Stoic logic, which emerged to rival (or complement) the Aristotelian tradition.[248] In later Hellenistic centuries both these philosophical traditions were still live, with Peripatetic writers debating issues of Aristotelian logic,[249] while the Stoic position on what constituted a proof was actively discussed,[250] and the work of the third-century-CE Sceptic Sextus Empiricus is testimony to sceptically-generated attacks on the possibility that proofs could exist at all.[251] Justin's younger contemporary, Galen, also based in Rome and known chiefly for his works on medicine, displayed a strong interest in logic;[252] he wrote a fifteen-book treatise on the subject, of which only small fragments survive,[253] and a short introductory text which survives complete.[254]

(twice), 54.1, 58.2 and 63.10, in all cases either with reference to Justin's own argument or to the lack of proof in those of his opponents.

247. Aristotle, *Posterior Analytics*, ed. by H. Tredennick, LCL 391 (Cambridge, MA: Harvard University Press, 1960): examples of use of ἀπόδειξις at 1.71b.17 and 1.72a.8; see also Aristotle, *Posterior Analytics*, trans. by J. Barnes, 2nd edn (Oxford: Clarendon Press, 1993).

248. For texts on Stoic logic: *The Hellenistic Philosophers: Volume 1: Translations of the Principal Sources with Philosophical Commentary*, ed. by A.A. Long and D. Sedley (Cambridge: Cambridge University Press, 1987), pp. 208-20; *The Hellenistic Philosophers: Volume 2: Greek and Latin Texts with Notes and Bibliography*, ed. by A.A. Long and D. Sedley (Cambridge: Cambridge University Press, 1989), pp. 209-21.

249. J. Barnes, 'Peripatetic Logic: 100 BC-AD 200', in R.W. Sharples and R. Sorabji, eds, *Greek and Roman Philosophy 100 BC-200 AD*, 2 vols (London: Institute of Classical Studies, University of London, 2007), 2, pp. 531-46.

250. J. Brunschwig, 'Proof Defined', and J. Barnes, 'Proof Destroyed', in M. Schofield, M. Burnyeat and J. Barnes, eds, *Doubt and Dogmatism: Studies in Hellenistic Epistemology* (Oxford: Clarendon Press, 1980), pp. 125-60 and pp. 161-81, respectively.

251. Sextus Empiricus, *Outlines of Pyrrhonism*, ed. by R.G. Bury, LCL 273 (Cambridge, MA: Harvard University Press, 1933); Sextus Empiricus, *Outlines of Scepticism*, trans. by J. Annas and J. Barnes (Cambridge: Cambridge University Press, 1994), 2.134-203.

252. T. Tieleman, 'Methodology', in R.J. Hankinson, ed., *The Cambridge Companion to Galen* (Cambridge: Cambridge University Press, 2008), pp. 49-65; B. Morison, 'Logic', in Hankinson, *Cambridge Companion to Galen*, pp. 66-115.

253. Tieleman, 'Methodology', p. 49.

254. Text in Galen, *Institutio Logica*, ed. by C. Kalbfleisch (Leipzig: Teubner,

Justin's argument does not satisfy the form of a Greek philosophical proof, however, for, although he uses a term which has a specific meaning in logic, he does not employ it in that technical sense. Proofs in Aristotelian and Stoic logic each have a particular structure, but the Proof from Prophecy does not conform to either. The classic Aristotelian argument,[255] the syllogism, with two premises and a conclusion, takes the form: (i) if *a* is the case; and (ii) *b* is the case; then (iii) it necessarily follows that *c* is the case. A classic Stoic argument[256] of propositional logic also has three (different) stages, taking the form: (i) if *a*, then *b*; (ii) *a* is the case; (iii) therefore, *b* is the case. Justin's argument also has three stages: (i) the ancient prophets, inspired by the Prophetic Spirit, foretold events that would happen; (ii) those events have now occurred; (iii) therefore, both the prophecy and the fulfilment should be accepted as divinely ordained. This may look like an argument consisting of two premises and a conclusion, possibly either Aristotelian or Stoic in form, but it cannot actually be regarded as such. For, even if it is accepted (implicitly) that the future can be foretold and (i) is therefore a valid premise (which is problematic in itself), point (iii) is not a conclusion which follows necessarily from (i) and (ii). Justin's argument depends both on the way he reads the original prophecy and on his contention that a particular event fulfils that prophecy. Furthermore, a prophecy

1896), trans. in Galen, *Institutio Logica, English Translation, Introduction and Commentary*, by J.S. Kieffer (Baltimore: John Hopkins Press, 1964). Galen presents the Peripatetic and Stoic approaches to logic and then also a third which he terms 'relational syllogism'. In Chapter 1 of *Institutio Logica* Galen establishes ἀπόδειξις as the key term for discussion.

255. This has been extensively discussed in the secondary literature. See J.L. Ackrill, *Aristotle the Philosopher* (Oxford: Oxford University Press, 1981), pp. 79-93; W.K.C. Guthrie, *A History of Greek Philosophy: Volume 6, Aristotle: An Encounter* (Cambridge: Cambridge University Press, 1981), pp. 156-78; J. Barnes, *Aristotle* (Oxford: Oxford University Press, Oxford, 1982), pp. 27-36; P. Crivelli, 'Aristotle's Logic', in C. Shields, ed., *The Oxford Handbook of Aristotle* (Oxford: Oxford University Press, 2012), pp. 113-49; C. Shields, *Aristotle* (Abingdon: Routledge, 2007), pp. 106-25; R. Smith, 'Aristotle's Theory of Demonstration', in G. Anagnostopoulos, ed., *A Companion to Aristotle* (Chichester: Wiley-Blackwell, 2009), pp. 51-65; R. Smith, 'Logic', in J. Barnes, ed., *The Cambridge Companion to Aristotle* (Cambridge: Cambridge University Press, 1995), pp. 27-65.

256. For Stoic logic, see I. Mueller, 'An Introduction to Stoic Logic', in J.M. Rist, *The Stoics* (Berkeley: University of California Press, 1978), pp. 1-26; F.H. Sandbach, *The Stoics* (London: Chatto & Windus, 1975), pp. 95-100; J. Sellars, *Stoicism* (Chesham: Acumen, 2006), pp. 55-79; S. Bobzien, 'Logic', in B. Inwood, ed., *The Cambridge Companion to the Stoics* (Cambridge: Cambridge University Press, 2003), pp. 85-123.

could be interpreted differently, in which case it would have a different meaning; it could be fulfilled by a different event; or it might not be fulfilled at all. These are matters of judgement and a variety of different conclusions could be reached, so Justin's argument is not one of logical necessity.

Justin is not explicit about what he means by ἀπόδειξις. It is a term that need not be philosophical and can be used in a non-technical sense to mean that an argument should be accepted because there are good reasons for it.[257] An example is found in Plutarch's treatise on *The Study of Poetry*[258] where he quotes lines from Euripides which extol the superiority of virtue over wealth and goes on to comment: 'Is not this a proof [ἀπόδειξις] of what philosophers say regarding wealth and external advantages, that without virtue they are useless and unprofitable for their owners?'[259] There is no question that Euripides has provided a proof in a strictly logical sense; rather he has persuasively asserted a point which Plutarch regards as a good one and wishes to endorse.

When Justin criticises Marcionites in the *First Apology*, he equates the absence of proof with irrationality,[260] suggesting that the term 'proof' should mean making a convincing rational argument. He clearly regards his demonstration that prophecies made long ago have been fulfilled in Jesus as a rational argument for the truth of Christianity and he contrasts this proof with the mere assertions of others. Thus, in referring to ἀπόδειξις, he employs a term which has philosophical overtones but he uses it in an everyday sense and not as a term of philosophical logic.[261]

The Proof from Prophecy and Graeco-Roman Mythological Religion
Justin's argument is best seen not as the expression of a philosophical school, putting itself forward to rival – and, indeed, replace – those of the Greek tradition, but rather as a justification for Justin's preferred alternative to the mythological religion of Greece and Rome[262] for the

---

257. LSJ entry for ἀπόδειξις.
258. Plutarch, *Quomodo Adolescens Poetas Audire Debeat*, in *Moralia: Volume 1*, ed. by F.C. Babbitt, LCL 197 (Cambridge, MA: Harvard University Press, 1927).
259. Plutarch, *Quomodo Adolescens*, 36D.1-2.
260. *1A* 58.2.
261. These issues are touched on in H.G. Snyder, 'The Classroom in the Text: Exegetical Practices in Justin and Galen', in S.E. Porter and A.W. Pitts, eds, *Christian Origins and Greco-Roman Culture: Social and Literary Contexts for the New Testament* (Leiden: Brill, 2013), pp. 663-85, 676-85.
262. For criticism of Graeco-Roman religion as a theme in early Christian apologetic literature, see G. Dorival, 'L'apologétique chrétienne et la culture greque', in Pouderon and Doré, *Les apologistes chrétiens*, pp. 423-65, 424-25 and 441-47.

comparisons drawn in the *First Apology* are between Jesus Christ and figures from the Greek mythological tradition. Pretila has shown how, in Chapters 21 and 22, Justin highlights similarities between stories about Jesus and the stories in Greek myths as a way of making the story of Jesus comprehensible (he describes this as 'Incorporation of Myth')[263] and then how, from Chapter 53 onwards, Justin draws attention to dissimilarities between the Greek myths and the story of Jesus in order to place distance between the two (he describes this as 'Separation from Myth').[264]

In the first group of references, in Chapters 21 and 22, Justin describes how Jesus was crucified, died, rose again and was taken up into heaven but comments that 'we introduce nothing stranger than those you call the sons of Zeus'.[265] Individual gods are referred to – Hermes, Asclepius, Dionysus, Heracles, the Dioscuri, Perseus, Bellerophon and Ariadne – who also, like Jesus, ascended to heaven.[266] Justin refers to the crucifixion of Jesus but points out that the sons of Zeus also suffered: 'But if someone should object that he was crucified, this too is the same as your sons of Zeus who suffered and whom we have enumerated'.[267] Justin also cites parallels between Jesus and Perseus (the virgin birth) and between Jesus and Asclepius (healing the sick and raising the dead).[268]

Comparisons of this kind are inadequate for Justin, however, and he signals that, in due course, he will demonstrate the superiority of Jesus over the gods of the Greek myths: 'But as we promised, as the discourse proceeds, we will prove that he [Jesus] is in fact superior'.[269] He returns to this theme in Chapter 53 after he has laid out his Proof from Prophecy and then compares stories about Jesus with stories about Graeco-Roman mythological figures in ways that are critical of the latter. He says that prophecies he has shown to be about Jesus have been interpreted as relating

---

263. Pretila, *Re-appropriating 'Marvellous Fables'*, pp. 52-78.

264. Ibid., pp. 79-123.

265. *1A* 21.1.

266. *1A* 21.2-21.3. Minns and Parvis, *Apologies*, p. 133, n. 1, exclude Hermes and Bellerophon as later additions to the text, although other editors leave them in: Marcovich, *Apologiae*; Munier, *Apologie*; Barnard, trans., *Apologies*.

267. *1A* 22.3.

268. *1A* 22.5-22.6.

269. *1A* 22.4. Justin goes on to say: 'Or rather it has been proved, for superiority is shown by deeds'. Commentators, no doubt rightly, have taken this to be a reference back to Justin's comments about the teachings of Jesus in *1A* 15-17 (Munier, *Apologie*, p. 191, n. 9; Marcovich, *Apologiae*, p. 65, n. 13; Barnard, trans., *Apologies*, p. 130, n. 162). However, in spite of having shown the superiority of Jesus 'through deeds', Justin looks forward to the further (at this point unspecified) proof of superiority that in due course he provides.

to Greek mythological figures such as Dionysus, Bellepheron, Perseus, Heracles and Asclepius.[270] He rejects any such connections as false and criticises the myths themselves which, he says, 'have been told at the instigation of evil demons to deceive and lead astray the human race'.[271]

There is thus a very clear contrast between Justin's earlier and later references to Graeco-Roman mythology. What has led to the change is the intervening section on the Proof from Prophecy, which provides proof of the true status of Jesus, giving Justin the basis for critical comparisons with the divine figures of Greek mythology. Thus, Justin is able to say 'it is also not true of us, as it is of those who invent myths about the supposed sons of Zeus, that we only make assertions and do not show proofs';[272] and he contrasts his arguments for Christianity, the subject of proof deriving from prophecy, with mere assertions put forward in support of mythological stories about the Graeco-Roman gods. He has demonstrated that the ancient prophecies are fulfilled in Jesus Christ and can now refute counter-arguments that they should be interpreted as referring to Graeco-Roman myths.

Justin does not claim that there are opponents of Christianity who *have* argued that the prophecies were fulfilled in mythological stories; his contention is that evil demons created myths paralleling the life of Jesus that *could* be interpreted as fulfilling Justin's prophecies. It is possible that such a case was being made and that this is why Justin seeks to refute it, although there are reasons for regarding this as improbable. First, it was noted in Chapter 1 that the Jewish scriptures were not well-known outside Jewish and Christian circles and, if the prophecies were unfamiliar, debate in Graeco-Roman circles over their interpretation was scarcely likely. Second, no other texts of the time suggest that this case was being put (although the low rate of textual survival means that such an argument should be treated with caution). Third, Justin never specifically refers to anyone advocating the fulfilment of prophecies through Greek myths, even though he does name other intellectual opponents, such as Simon and Menander[273] and Marcion.[274]

---

270. *1A* 54.6-54.10.
271. *1A* 54.1. Criticisms of Greek gods and their mythological stories were a feature of Graeco-Roman culture itself (J. Pépin, *Mythe et allégorie: les origines grecques et les contestations judéo-chrétiennes* [Paris: Aubier-Montaigne, Paris 1958] and D.C. Feeney, *The Gods in Epic: Poets and Critics of the Classical Tradition* [Oxford: Clarendon Press, 1991], pp. 5-56) and not the creation of Christian polemic.
272. *1A* 53.1.
273. *1A* 26 and 56.
274. *1A* 26 and 58.

The more probable interpretation is that Justin posits an alternative reading to his own to demonstrate its shortcomings and to show that his own reading is to be preferred. Interpreting the prophecies as fulfilled in Greek mythological stories lacks the kind of proof which Justin has been able to deploy to demonstrate their fulfilment in the life of Jesus and the early history of Christianity. The contrast between the two therefore highlights the value of the evidential proof which Justin has brought to bear in support of his interpretations of the prophecies.

Justin's Approach to the Interpretation of Prophecy

Discussion of whether prophecies should be read as referring to Jesus or to figures from Greek mythology points up the importance of interpreting prophecies correctly. This issue now needs to be probed further, first, to clarify Justin's approach to the interpretation of prophecy in general, then, to show how in practical terms he matches individual prophecies with their fulfilments and, finally, to explore some of the specific connections between Justin's approach to interpretation and what is found in the Graeco-Roman literary tradition.

Justin wants to do more than bring prophecies to his audience's attention; he wants to explain how they should be understood and expose the dangers of misinterpretation. Text and interpretation are inseparable to Justin and correct links need to be made between what was foretold long ago and what has now occurred, or will occur, if the prophecies are to be interpreted rightly. Interpretation is problematic, however, because prophecies can be ambiguous or enigmatic; Justin refers to the way a prophecy may be 'unintelligible'[275] until its fulfilment has revealed its meaning.

For Justin, there is only ever one correct reading for each prophecy – the one he provides – and he does not recognise at any point that a text could have two different readings, both of which could be valid. Justin concedes that prophecies can be – and have been – interpreted incorrectly, however, and their fulfilments have not always been recognised when they have occurred. One case of incorrect interpretation of prophecies has already been discussed: relating them to mythological deities rather than to Jesus. Justin gives a more literary example of misinterpretation when he refers to Plato's *Timaeus*, saying: 'He arranged him as an X in the whole.'[276] Plato's error was that, while he recognised that the passage

---

275. *1A* 32.2.
276. *1A* 60.1. The reference is to *Timaeus* 36B, although some commentators think that this should be read in conjunction with 34A-B: Marcovich, *Apologiae*, p.

in the scriptural Book of Numbers should be read symbolically, he did so in terms of an incorrect symbol, the X, rather than the correct symbol, the cross.[277] This was due to ignorance since Plato lived well before the coming of Christ. It was only after the crucifixion that the importance of the cross as a symbol was apparent and references to it in earlier prophetic sayings could be recognised for what they were. Justin provides other examples of the significance of the cross as a symbol, such as, 'Diggers do not do their work, nor craftsmen likewise, unless by means of tools having this pattern',[278] and comments more generally that: 'This [the cross], as the prophet said beforehand, is the greatest symbol of his [God's] power and rule.'[279]

If Plato's flaw was, through ignorance, not to understand the symbolic significance of the cross, the Jews' failure, collectively, was not to recognise the fulfilment of the prophecies in Jesus Christ. They knew the prophecies and saw the coming of Jesus but did not match the two. So, their failure could not be put down to ignorance; rather it was due to a hermeneutical deficiency, an inability, or refusal, to read prophecies correctly, even when the necessary information was to hand. Justin refers several times to the Jews' rejection of Jesus, saying, for example: 'the Jews, who have the prophecies and who were always expecting the Christ to come, did not recognize him when he came'.[280] In Justin's view, this was because the Jews did not appreciate that the prophets sometimes spoke 'as though from a character'.[281] Addressing his Graeco-Roman audience in the second person he observes:

> This kind of thing [speaking through characters] is also to be seen amongst your own writers; there is one author of the whole and he sets out the speaking characters. Since they did not understand this, the Jews who have the books of the prophets did not recognize the Christ even when he came.[282]

---

116 n.; Barnard, trans., *Apologies*, p. 169, n. 357; Minns and Parvis, *Apologies*, p. 235, n. 2.

277. Minns and Parvis, *Apologies*, p. 235, n. 3, point out that the passage from Numbers 21:6-9 referred to here does not actually mention a cross or an X.

278. *1A* 55.3.

279. *1A* 55.2.

280. *1A* 49.5: see also 31.5, 36.3 and 53.6. Justin acknowledges that 'a few' Jews accepted Jesus as the Christ (53.6).

281. The phrase is from *1A* 36.1.

282. *1A* 36.2-36.3. Speaking through characters is discussed further below.

Plato and the Jews are criticised because, in different ways, they have misread the prophecies. Justin argues that his own interpretations should be accepted instead because they have an authority which stems from their *source*. He lays down a clear trail of authority for his interpretations, back to the Apostles, who preached the gospel to the gentiles and who received their understanding from Christ himself.[283]

In the *Dialogue with Trypho* the old man who reveals the prophecies to Justin says that they should be read with 'proper faith'[284] and he continues: 'Above all, beseech God to open to you the gates of light, for no one can perceive or understand these truths unless he has been enlightened by God and his Christ.'[285] Thus, it is faith in Christ that here enables readers to interpret prophecies correctly.

There is no old man figure in the *First Apology*. Justin says it was the Apostles who took Christ's message to the gentiles,[286] who preached Christianity and 'handed over the prophecies'.[287] He is no doubt referring here not just to the physical transfer of scrolls, but to the transfer of the understanding of the prophecies, since for him text and interpretation are inseparable. The Apostles were taught directly by Jesus and, as part of the teaching given to them after the Resurrection, Christ revealed how the prophecies should be read:

> when he had risen from the dead and had appeared to them
> and had taught them to read the prophecies in which all these
> things were foretold as going to happen, and when they had
> seen him ascending into heaven and had believed and had
> received the power he had sent from there to them and had
> gone to every race of human beings, they taught these things
> and were called apostles.[288]

Justin refers to Jesus Christ as 'our teacher and interpreter of unintelligible prophecies'.[289] Jesus is therefore not only the figure through whom the prophecies are fulfilled; he also provides the correct interpretations of them. The understanding and interpretation of the prophecies is part of Christ's teaching to the Apostles, which the latter passed on to their

---

283. Skarsaune, *Proof from Prophecy*, pp. 11-13.
284. *DT* 7.2.
285. *DT* 7.3.
286. *1A* 45.5 and 49.5.
287. *1A* 49.5.
288. *1A* 50.12.
289. *1A* 32.2.

gentile converts when they 'handed over the prophecies'. Indeed, the Apostles have an important role and a high status, since the prophecies foretold not just the events in the life of Christ but the missionary work of the Apostles too.[290]

There is a certain circularity to Justin's argument. It began with claims for Christianity that depended on the person of Jesus Christ, but this begged the question: why should the status and authority of Jesus be accepted? The answer was found in the Books of the Prophecies. However, these ancient, enigmatic texts required interpretation to be properly understood. Justin's understanding of the texts' meaning came from the Apostles who derived their understanding from Jesus. So, the claims made for the status and authority of Jesus, and therefore of Christianity, are shown not to be independent at all; they come from the teaching of Christ himself.[291]

Placing Christ's teaching on the interpretation of prophecies after the Resurrection is an interesting move, because by that stage some prophecies have been fulfilled in the first coming of Jesus, while others still remain unfulfilled. This is not because they are false prophecies; the unfulfilled prophecies relate to the second coming of Christ which will occur in the future. An example of a prophecy Justin reads in this way is: 'And how he was going to come from heaven with glory, hear also the things said in this regard through Jeremiah the prophet. They are these: "Behold one like the Son of Man comes upon the clouds of heaven, and his angels with him."'[292]

Justin describes how after the Resurrection Christ explained the meaning of the prophecies *collectively* to the Apostles and he himself adopts a similar approach. Prophecies are interpreted one at a time, but it is only when they are brought together and read as a group that their full meaning emerges. A prophecy may, for instance, foretell the entry of Jesus into Jerusalem but it is only when it is linked to other prophecies foretelling other events in Jesus' life that its significance becomes clear. An individual prophecy is therefore not to be viewed in isolation. Each can only be properly understood as part of a sequence foretelling a connected narrative of events and the meaning of each prophecy therefore depends on the meaning of them all. Justin's method is to extract individual prophecies from different books written by different authors at different

---

290. J. Behr, *The Formation of Christian Theology: Volume 1: The Way to Nicaea* (New York: St Vladimir's Seminary Press, 2001), p. 98.
291. Ibid., p. 96, also refers to the circularity of Justin's proof.
292. *1A* 51.8-51.9, although Justin attributes the quotation to Jeremiah it is actually from Daniel 7:13.

times, to interpret each of them and then to amalgamate them to create an account of events that has a coherent overall meaning. This then enhances the meaning of the individual prophecies, since each of them is seen to be a component of the larger sequence.

Matching Individual Prophecies with Their Fulfilments

The interpretation of prophetic texts requires the matching of individual prophecies with their fulfilments and the way Justin does this will now be examined. His basic method is to quote a prophecy verbatim and, either before or after, to specify how it should be interpreted. This is typically done by identifying the event which the prophecy foretold and it can be a simple process. Micah's prophecy that the Messiah would be born in Bethlehem and its fulfilment in the birth of Jesus are described quite straightforwardly, with just enough information to link prophecy and fulfilment:

> And he [Micah] spoke thus: 'And you Bethlehem, land of Judah, are by no means least among the rulers of Judah, for from you will come forth a leader who will shepherd my people.' And this is a village in the country of the Jews which is thirty-five stadia from Jerusalem in which Jesus Christ was born.[293]

Similarly, prophecies foretelling specific elements of the crucifixion narrative, such as the nailing of the hands and feet of Jesus to the cross and the casting of lots for his clothing, are matched with their fulfilments: 'And the phrase, "They pierced my hands and feet", was a description of the nails fixed to the cross in his hands and his feet. And after crucifying him those who crucified him cast lots for his clothing and divided it among themselves.'[294]

A prophecy may require a fuller explanation, however, and Isaiah 2:3-4 is a case in point:

> For a law will go forth from Sion and the word of the Lord from Jerusalem, and it will judge between nations and correct a great people, and they will beat their swords into ploughs and their spears into pruning-hooks and nation shall not take up sword against nation and they will no longer learn to make war.[295]

---

293. *1A* 34.1-34.2.
294. *1A* 35.7-35.8.
295. *1A* 39.1.

This prophecy is fulfilled in the Apostles' preaching of the gospel to the gentiles.[296] Justin identifies three moves in the Isaiah text: (i) the going out from Jerusalem, (ii) the 'correcting a great people' and (iii) the vision of a state of peace; and he equates these steps with a sequence of events: (i) the Apostles' going out from Jerusalem, (ii) their preaching of the Gospel to the gentile world and (iii) the absence of conflict among Christian converts, who are now prepared to be martyred. Justin's reading of the prophecy and its fulfilment may appear unexpected and may not be obvious from the wording of the text, but it is an example of Justin understanding an ancient prophecy in terms of recent historical events.

Interpreting a prophecy can be much more complex, however. The relatively short passage, Genesis 49:11, 'Tethering his colt at the vine and washing his robe in the blood of the grape,'[297] is enigmatic and ambiguous. Justin's first move is to identify the text as a prophecy foretelling the life and death of Jesus: 'a symbol making plain the things that would happen to Christ and would be done by him'.[298] He then splits the text into two, with each part interpreted separately and linked to different events in Christ's life. Of 'Tethering his colt at the vine' Justin says: 'For an ass's colt, tethered to a vine, stood at the entrance to a village. This he [Jesus] then commanded his associates to bring to him, and when it had been brought he mounted it, and sitting on it he made his entry into Jerusalem.'[299] The prophecy is related to a precise event in Christ's life, with the description expanded to provide a fuller picture linking the small event of tethering the colt to the larger and more significant one of Christ's entry into Jerusalem.

The second part of the text is interpreted as follows: 'For "washing his robe in the blood of the grape" heralded beforehand the suffering he was going to endure cleansing through his blood those who believed in him.'[300] This is enigmatic and, indeed, paradoxical. Why does the 'washing' herald the 'suffering'? Justin explains that the 'robe' represents 'the human beings who believe in him, in whom dwells the seed from God, which is the Logos,'[301] while the 'blood of the grape':

> indicates that the one who was going to appear would indeed have blood, but not from human seed, but from divine power. . . . For just as a human being has not made the blood

---

296. *1A* 39.2-39.3.
297. *1A* 32.5.
298. *1A* 32.5.
299. *1A* 32.6.
300. *1A* 32.7.
301. *1A* 32.8.

of the vine, but God has, just so this blood was revealed as not going to come from human seed, but from the power of God.[302]

Thus, it is the suffering of Christ's passion which cleanses believers. Using symbolic readings of blood and grape, the text foretells, not a small detail in the narrative of Christ's life, as was the case with the first part of the prophecy, but the whole of Christ's passion and its significance.

As well as interpreting each part of the prophecy separately, the two are brought together. Thus, after explaining the first part and before dealing with the second, Justin adds: 'And afterwards he was crucified, in order that the rest of the prophecy might be accomplished.'[303] This narrative link explains how the entry into Jerusalem connects with the subsequent passion of Christ, for, after entering Jerusalem, Jesus was crucified and this event led to salvation for Christian believers. The crucifixion – not actually mentioned in the prophecy – is, therefore, the connection which unites the two parts of the prophecy.

Most of the quotations in the chapters on Proof from Prophecy are relatively short[304] and are explained quite briefly. A longer instance is the citation of the whole of Psalms 1 and 2.[305] Before quoting the text, Justin describes what the reader should expect to find there:

> it is possible for you to learn how the Prophetic Spirit encourages human beings to live; and how he signifies that there was a banding together against Christ of Herod, the king of the Jews and the Jews themselves, and Pilate who was your procurator among them, together with the soldiers; and that he would be believed in by human beings from every race; and that God calls him Son and has promised to make all his enemies subject to him; and how the demons, as far as they are able, attempt to escape from the authority of the Lord God and Father of all and that of his Christ; and that God calls everyone to repentance before the coming of the day of judgment.[306]

302. *1A* 32.9 and 32.11.
303. *1A* 32.6.
304. A clear contrast with the *Dialogue with Trypho* where many of the quotations are much longer.
305. *1A* 40.5-40.19. Minns and Parvis, *Apologies*, p. 189, n. 1, note that the two psalms are often treated as one; S. Gillingham, *A Journey of Two Psalms: The Reception of Psalms 1 and 2 in Jewish and Christian Tradition* (Oxford: Oxford University Press, 2013).
306. *1A* 40.5-40.7.

No fewer than six different messages are identified here, and Justin's method is to link each of them with a portion of the psalmic text. First, the statement that the Prophetic Spirit encourages human beings to live is matched with the descriptions of the blessed and the ungodly:

> Blessed is the man who did not walk in the counsel of the ungodly and did not stand in the path of sinners . . . but his will is in the law of the Lord and on his law he will meditate day and night . . . and all that he does shall prosper. Not so are the ungodly, not so, but they are like dust which the wind blows from the face of the earth . . . and the way of the ungodly will perish.[307]

Next, the prophecy foretelling the conspiracy against Jesus, involving Herod, the Jews, Pilate and the soldiers, is matched with the description of kings and the rulers banding together: 'The kings of the earth were at hand and the rulers gathered together against the Lord and against his Christ.'[308] The following statement foretells that Jesus would be believed in by people of all races, although there is nothing in the text of Psalms 1 and 2 which obviously matches this. The statement prophesying that God calls Jesus his Son and promises to make his enemies subject to him is matched with the pronouncements attributed to God the Father: 'You are my Son. Today I have begotten you. Ask of me and I will give you nations as your inheritance and the ends of the earth as your possession.'[309] Next, the statement which describes how the demons attempt to escape from the authority of God and Christ is matched to the saying attributed to kings and rulers: 'Let us burst their bonds and throw off their yoke from us.'[310] Finally, the statement that God calls all to repent before the last judgement is matched to the exhortations addressed to the kings: 'And now O kings, understand, be instructed all judges of the earth. Serve the Lord in fear and exalt in him with trembling. Seize instruction, lest the Lord become angry, and you perish from the right way, when his anger suddenly blazes.'[311]

Justin's general strategy is clear; he breaks down the text of Psalms 1 and 2 and matches each component with one of a number of disparate messages. No attempt is made to attribute an overall meaning to the text; it is split into small sections whose separate meanings are then explained.

---

307. *1A* 40.8-40.10.
308. *1A* 40.11.
309. *1A* 40.14-15.
310. *1A* 40.11.
311. *1A* 40.16-18.

This example shows Justin presenting a prophetic text as particularly complex, one that contains a series of none too obvious messages on different themes. Explanations may precede texts, as here, or they may follow them, but, either way, the quotation and the explanation are inseparable; both are necessary to Justin's argument. Texts do not simply stand by themselves; they need to be interpreted, because their meanings are not straightforward. Thus, interpretation is critical to the reading of texts and Justin's audience can only understand the Books of the Prophecies when he explains them.

Justin's approach to textual interpretation fits best with short passages and it is noteworthy that, faced with a longer text, his response is to break it down into small sections and interpret each separately. He, therefore, does not provide a reading of any of the individual Books of the Prophecies as a whole. The body of texts from which Justin quotes is a quarry from which he extracts nuggets that he then explains piece by piece. Whether this is because he is accessing *testimonia* in which the texts are presented as discrete individual prophecies, or simply because this is the interpretative approach which he prefers, is difficult to know for sure, but his treatment of Psalms 1 and 2 suggests that the latter is very likely.

Justin's Interpretation of Texts and the Graeco-Roman Literary Tradition

Interpreting the scriptures correctly is thus critical for Justin and his use of short quotations from authoritative texts to support an argument has parallels in the approach sometimes taken in works in the Greek tradition. In his treatise on the study of poetry, for instance, Plutarch advances his argument by drawing on brief extracts from literary classics.[312] Justin's approach to the interpretation of prophecy reflects the Graeco-Roman literary environment in a number of more specific respects, however, and three in particular will now be considered: how Justin applies rationality to his reading of prophecies;[313] how prophecies are sometimes concerned with issues other than foretelling the future; and how symbolic readings are applied to the interpretation of difficult texts.

An emphasis on rationality has already been noted in Justin's discussion of proof. It is also found in his analysis of the phenomenon of prophecy in the section of the Proof from Prophecy that Minns and

---

312. Plutarch, *Quomodo Adolescens*.

313. Plutarch argued that prophecies were basically rational, even though their mode of presentation involved ambiguity, and interpretation was required to discern their meanings: Plutarch, *De E Apud Delphos*, 386E.

Parvis describe as a 'Treatise on different kinds of prophecy'.[314] Justin says here that prophecies uttered as if by someone other than the prophet can be spoken by one of three characters he identifies: God the Father, Christ or the people answering God:

> For at one time as heralding beforehand it [the divine Logos] says the things that are going to happen, at another time it speaks out as from the character of the Lord of all and Father God, and at another time as from the character of Christ, and at another time as from the character of the peoples answering the Lord or his Father.[315]

Justin highlights connections between this and the Graeco-Roman literary tradition when he says: 'This kind of thing is also to be seen amongst your own writers',[316] a reference perhaps to the practices of Greek drama, as suggested by Osborn,[317] or to the philosophical dialogue form popularised by Plato with its multiple characters. Moreover, the division of prophecy into different types reflects the fondness for classification frequently found in the Greek literary tradition, for example, in the analysis of literary styles[318] or types or oratory.[319]

Justin provides examples of the different characters. He describes sayings as from the character of God the Father, such as: '"What sort of house will you build for me?" says the Lord. The heaven is my throne and the earth the footstool of my feet',[320] sayings from the character of Christ, such as: 'I stretched out my hands to a disobedient and gainsaying people, to those walking in a way that is not good'[321] and prophecies from the character of the people answering God, one of which, foretelling the plundering of the land of the Jews, concludes: 'And with all these things, O Lord, you were content, and you were silent, and you humbled us exceedingly.'[322]

---

314. *1A* 36-44; Minns and Parvis, *Apologies*, p. 52.
315. *1A* 36.2.
316. *1A* 36.2.
317. Osborn, *Justin Martyr*, p. 89.
318. E.g. the four styles in Demetrius, *On Style*, section 36, trans. by D.C. Innes, in Russell and Winterbottom, eds, *Ancient Literary Criticism*, pp. 171-215, 181.
319. E.g. Quintilian, *Institutio Oratorica*, ed. by D.A. Russell, LCL 494 (Cambridge, MA: Harvard University Press, 2002), 12.10.
320. *1A* 37.3-37.4.
321. *1A* 38.1. Such prophecies provide opportunities for Justin to show the pre-existent Christ present and active in prophetic texts.
322. *1A* 47.3.

Emphasis on rationality in the interpretation of prophecy is also evident in the discussion of fate already referred to, in which Justin seeks to refute the idea that 'the things which happen happen through the necessity of fate'.[323] A similar emphasis is found when he explains paradoxical elements in prophetic texts and shows how they can be read rationally. Thus, while in straightforward cases prophecies uttered centuries ago have been fulfilled in events which have now occurred, such as the birth of Jesus in Bethlehem[324] or the healing of the sick and raising of the dead by Jesus,[325] other ancient prophecies describe as *past* events occurrences which will take place in the *future*, which at first sight appears nonsensical. Justin seeks to explain the paradox, making his general point as follows: 'he [the prophet David] foretells as having already happened things which are assuredly known as going to happen',[326] providing as an example a prophecy attributed to David which concludes by referring to the crucifixion in the past tense: 'let them rejoice among the nations: the Lord has reigned from the tree'.[327]

Rational explanation of the paradoxical is also found when a prophecy appears to change over time. What appears to be incredible or impossible when first uttered is made to seem coherent when the fulfilling event occurs and it is then shown to be explicable and true. Thus, referring to the virgin birth, Justin says: 'For God disclosed beforehand through the Prophetic Spirit that things were going to happen which were thought by people to be incredible and impossible, so that when they did happen they should not be disbelieved but should rather be believed because they had been foretold'.[328]

Prophecy is not, however, confined to foretelling the future. Barton's examination of what constituted prophecy in Jewish and early Christian thought in the period from the third century BCE to the mid-second century CE is helpful for understanding this. He identified four modes for reading prophecy: giving ethical instruction; providing foreknowledge of the present day; prognostication of future events; and revelation of mystical or theological truth.[329] Thus, prophecy covers a broad spectrum and in practice is seen rather loosely to include anything uttered by

323. *1A* 43.1.
324. *1A* 34.1-34.2.
325. *1A* 48.1-48.2.
326. *1A* 42.2.
327. *1A* 41.4. Minns and Parvis, *Apologies*, p. 189, n. 2; note Skarsaune's argument that the text is actually a composite of Psalm 96 and 1 Chronicles 16.
328. *1A* 33.2.
329. J. Barton, *Oracles of God: Perceptions of Ancient Prophecy in Israel after the Exile* (London: Darton, Longman & Todd, 1986), pp. 154-265.

someone who is identified as a prophet; as Barton puts it: 'Once a book is classified as a "Prophet", then anything it contains can easily come to be thought characteristic of "prophecy".'[330] The second and third of Barton's modes of reading concern foretelling the future and Justin's use of these has already been discussed. The first and fourth, ethical instruction and revelation of mystical or theological truth, are, however, also in evidence in the *First Apology*.

Prophecies are used by Justin to provide ethical instruction. This is not surprising, since issues of morality were of live concern in the debates of the Greek philosophical schools in the early Empire,[331] although Justin's prophetic mode of expression is quite different from that of Greek philosophy. In the preamble to the text of Psalms 1 and 2, already discussed, Justin's comment explicitly shows that for him prophecies have a moral dimension; he says that the text is one: 'from which it is possible for you to learn how the Prophetic Spirit encourages human beings to live.'[332] Later, a saying of Moses is described as dealing with the choice of good over evil[333] and a saying of Isaiah as containing an exhortation to behave rightly: 'Wash! Make yourselves clean! Take away iniquities from your souls. Learn to do good. Judge for the orphan, and give judgment for the widow.'[334] Another text from Isaiah, which rejects the cult of animal sacrifice and advocates right moral behaviour, reads:

> Even if you offer fine flour, incense, it is abomination to me. I do not want the fat of lambs and the blood of bulls. For who demanded this of your hands? But undo every bond of wickedness; break the knots of violent dealings, cover the homeless and the naked and share your bread with the hungry.[335]

Using prophecies to reveal, in Barton's phrase, mystical or theological truth, is also in evidence in the *Apology*. In the first instance, ancient prophecies can be significant because they comment in a deep sense on

---

330. Ibid., p. 7.
331. M. Trapp, *Philosophy in the Roman Empire: Ethics, Politics and Society* (Aldershot: Ashgate, 2007), pp. 1-62; and J. Dillon, *The Middle Platonists: A Study of Platonism 80 BC to AD 220* (London: Duckworth, 1977).
332. *1A* 40.5.
333. *1A* 44.1. This is preceded by: 'And the holy Prophetic Spirit taught us these things through Moses.'
334. *1A* 44.3.
335. *1A* 37.7-37.8. This is followed by the comment: 'So you are able to know of what kinds are the things that are being taught through the prophets as though from God' (37.9).

the meaning of divinely ordained events and explain their significance to an audience from outside Judaism and Christianity. While some prophecies concerning the death of Jesus forecast detailed points in the passion narrative, such as Christ being nailed to the cross or the casting of lots for his clothing,[336] others explain its overall soteriological significance.[337] The audience knows that Jesus was crucified but Justin invokes a text from Isaiah to explain the meaning of his death, part of which reads:

> This one bears our sins and suffers for us, and we reckoned him to be in suffering and in calamity and in distress. But he was wounded on account of our crimes and he was made weak on account of our sins. The discipline of peace is upon him, by his bruises we were healed. We were all led away like sheep, a human being was led astray in his way, and he gave him for our sins.[338]

A second instance of the use of prophecy to reveal mystical or theological truth is found in Justin's discussion of primal Creation, a subject much debated in the Graeco-Roman philosophical tradition.[339] Justin describes how the prophet Moses gives an account of events in the distant past beginning with the creation of the world and prefaces a quotation from Genesis 1 with the words: 'listen to what was said in so many words by Moses . . . through whom the Prophetic Spirit revealed how God created the world in the beginning and out of what'.[340] It is only because Moses is a prophet who has a direct connection to the Prophetic Spirit that he possesses such knowledge and can prophesy in this way.

Finally, in this review of links between Justin's approach to the interpretation of prophecies and the Graeco-Roman literary context, mention should be made of symbolic readings.[341] These had become established as one of the tools for interpreting literary texts in the Graeco-Roman tradition, by the Stoics in particular, and they were especially important for reading passages in Homer which appeared

---

336. *1A* 35.5.

337. E.g. *1A* 50.2, 50.8-50.10 and 51.5.

338. *1A* 50.8-50.10.

339. For Graeco-Roman interest in Creation, see D. Sedley, *Creationism and Its Critics in Antiquity* (Berkeley: University of California Press, 2007).

340. *1A* 59.1.

341. The term 'symbolism' is preferred to allegory here on the grounds that allegorical interpretations require a narrative dimension: Dawson, *Allegorical Readers*, pp. 3-4.

problematic.[342] In the Greek tradition of literary criticism the symbolic reading of a text was hidden, but it was a reading that was always intended by the author.[343] Justin takes this approach in his Proof from Prophecy: prophecies ultimately come from God who has determined their meanings, whether these are immediately apparent or are initially concealed and have to be revealed subsequently. In the *First Apology* symbolic readings have already been encountered in the discussion of blood and grape in Genesis 49:11; a further example is Justin's reading of Isaiah 1:19-20: 'And if you will it and if you heed me, you shall eat the good things of the earth, but if you do not heed me, a sword will devour you: for the mouth of the Lord spoke these things.'[344] This text is paradoxical since a sword cannot literally devour, so a non-literal interpretation is needed to explain it. Justin rejects the obvious reading that 'devour' is a figurative way of saying 'slain' and contends that it is the 'sword', not 'devour', which should be treated symbolically; thus, he describes how the sword represents the fire which consumes evildoers: 'But the aforesaid phrase, "a sword will devour you", does not say that those who do not listen will be slain by the sword, but the sword of God is the fire, of which those who choose to do evil things become food.'[345]

The Proof from Prophecy as Dependent Literature

Justin reveals how the Jewish scriptures support his argument in the Proof from Prophecy and he explains how these ancient texts should be read, often using methods of interpretation that would resonate with a Graeco-Roman audience. In the process, he creates within the *First Apology* his own literary work, which is more than a collection of quotations from the writings of others. It is a text in its own right, which uses interpretations of quoted texts to underpin his arguments. Justin's Proof from Prophecy will now be examined against the background of

---

342. F. Buffière, *Les mythes d'Homère et la pensée greque* (Paris: University of Paris, 1956); G.W. Most, 'Hellenistic Allegory and Early Imperial Rhetoric', in R. Copeland and P.T. Struck, eds, *The Cambridge Companion to Allegory* (Cambridge: Cambridge University Press, 2010), pp. 26-38. See also Héraclite, *Allégories d'Homère*, ed. and trans. by F. Buffière (Paris: Les Belles Lettres, 1962) (*HP*); and Heraclitus, *Homeric Problems*, ed. and trans. by D.A. Russell and D. Konstan (Atlanta: SBL, 2005) discussed further below.

343. Russell, *Criticism in Antiquity*, p. 97.

344. *1A* 44.4.

345. *1A* 44.5. For Christian inheritance of the Graeco-Roman practice of reading difficult texts symbolically, see E. Hatch, *The Influence of Greek Ideas on Christianity* (New York: Harper & Row, 1957), pp. 50-85.

contemporary literary practice and, specifically, the kind of handbooks, commentaries and treatises produced at the time. The texts selected for comparison are the *Handbook of Platonism* by Alcinous, the *Anonymous Commentary on Plato's* Theaetetus, *Homeric Problems* by Heraclitus, *On Fate* by Alexander of Aphrodisias and *On the Elements according to Hippocrates* by Galen. Comparisons will show that the Proof from Prophecy does not follow closely any single form of literature current at the time but that it is possible to identify similarities with a number of the types of writing then prevalent in literary culture.

In Chapter 1 it was noted that increased interest in the original founders of the Greek philosophical schools was a feature of the late Hellenistic period and that renewed attention was being given to study of the actual writings of these revered ancient authors. One consequence of this was the production of dependent literature related to those ancient works: that is, literature that depends for its existence on the text or texts to which it relates. The Proof from Prophecy can be described as a dependent text since it depends on the prophecies it cites and interprets, and its arguments could not stand on their own without those prophetic texts. Dependent literature could take several forms at the time – handbooks, commentaries and treatises – and Justin's work has characteristics in common with each of them.

A handbook summarises the ideas attached to a philosophical position. It may simplify, or attempt to systematise, ideas to make them more comprehensible, but its intention is essentially to enable its audience, typically in an educational context, to understand the doctrines concerned. A surviving example, broadly contemporary with Justin, is the *Handbook of Platonism* by Alcinous,[346] which summarises Platonic philosophy, quite briefly but systematically, under a series of standard headings: logic, physics and ethics. Like Justin's Proof from Prophecy

---

346. Editions of the text with, respectively, German and French translations: Alkinoos, *Didaskalikos Lehrbuch der Grundsätze Platons: Einleitung, Text, Übersetzung und Anmerkungen*, ed. by O.F. Summerell and T. Zimmer eds (Berlin: de Gruyter, 2007); and Alcinoos, *Enseignement des doctrines de Platon: Introduction, texte établi et commenté* by J. Whittaker, trans. by P. Louis (Paris: Les Belles Lettres, 1990). An English translation is Alcinous, *The Handbook of Platonism*, trans. with Introduction and Commentary by J. Dillon (Oxford: Clarendon Press, 1993). Authorship of the text is uncertain; attribution to Albinus, a second-century CE Middle Platonist, which used to be current among scholars (following the nineteenth-century German scholar, Freudenthal) is now largely rejected. The work is still thought to date from the second century CE (Whittaker in his edition places it at around 150), although this remains uncertain.

it seeks to explain to its audience the ideas of an ancient and revered tradition, although the similarity largely ends there. The *Handbook* does not quote extensively from Plato's original works – albeit that some short extracts are included[347] – but rather summarises Platonic arguments. It is thus some distance from Plato's actual words,[348] by contrast with Justin's work, which makes extensive use of verbatim quotations from the Books of the Prophecies. The *Handbook* expounds ideas but a critical difference is that, unlike Justin, the author does not use quotations from Plato as a basis for mounting his own arguments.

A commentary supports the work to which it relates and will typically progress through the original text, quoting from it and clarifying its meaning. Hellenistic philosophy spawned many commentaries, especially on the works of Plato and Aristotle;[349] indeed, the commentary form underwent a revival from the late first century BCE.[350] Few examples survive from before Late Antiquity,[351] however; one which does is *Commentarium in Platonis Theaetetum*, the *Anonymous Commentary on Plato's* Theaetetus,[352] thought to date from the late first century CE.[353] There are similarities between the *First Apology's* Proof from Prophecy and the *Commentary*, although it would be misleading to press the parallels too far, for the Proof is not simply a commentary on the Books of the Prophecies. The structure of the *Anonymous Commentary* consists typically of an extract from Plato's text – sometimes quite long – followed by paraphrase and then exegesis, although the transition from paraphrase

---

347. E.g. Alcinous, *The Handbook of Platonism*, Chapter 28 includes brief quotations from the *Theaetetus*, the *Republic*, the *Phaedo*, the *Laws* and the *Phaedrus*.

348. Dillon in his Introduction suggests that Alcinous is actually seeking 'to *avoid* direct quotation' (original italics), Alcinous, *Handbook of Platonism*, p. xxx.

349. M. Tuominen, *The Ancient Commentators on Plato and Aristotle* (Stocksfield: Acumen, 2009). Platonic texts are discussed in Dillon, *The Middle Platonists*. Stoic and Epicurean texts did not attract commentaries in the same way: Snyder, *Teachers and Texts*, pp. 14-121.

350. D. Sedley, 'Plato's *Auctoritas* and the Rebirth of the Commentary Tradition', in J. Barnes and M. Griffin, eds, *Philosophia Togata II: Plato and Aristotle at Rome* (Oxford: Clarendon Press, 1997), pp. 110-29.

351. Tuominen, *Ancient Commentators*, pp. 18-27. The term Late Antiquity is used to refer to the period between the third and the eighth centuries CE.

352. *Commentarium in Platonis* Theaetetum (*AC*), ed. by G. Bastianini and D. Sedley, in F. Adorno et al., eds, *Corpus dei papiri filosofici greci e latini: Testi e lessico nei papiri di cultura greca e latina: Parte III: Commentari* (Florence: Olschki, 1995), pp. 227-562. For the provenance of the text: pp. 235-36. The editors provide an excellent introductory analysis of the text (pp. 227-60) which is drawn on here.

353. *AC*, pp. 254-56.

to exegesis may not be clearly marked.[354] Exegesis can cover a number of issues: first, clarifying obscure points, particularly linguistic ones; second, highlighting points which support the commentator's interpretation of the text or refute the interpretations of others; third, pointing up a difficulty in understanding Plato's text and offering a solution; fourth, introducing qualifications; and, finally, comparison of Plato's thought with that of others.[355] Critical views of the quality of the *Commentary* vary considerably. Dillon's verdict is that it 'in general maintains a level of stupefying banality',[356] while its modern editors, Bastianini and Sedley, recognising a certain unevenness of quality, comment that, nevertheless, 'at its best it can be extraordinarily subtle'.[357]

Like the anonymous author of the *Commentary*, Justin pays close attention to the precise wording of the ancient text, although without considering the sort of detailed linguistic points which sometimes preoccupy the anonymous author. Justin shares his view that ancient texts require interpretation to be properly understood, that text and interpretation go together and that, although different readings may be canvassed, one is to be preferred. The Proof from Prophecy differs significantly from the *Anonymous Commentary*, however, in that the latter is concerned almost exclusively with clarifying the text and expounding its meaning. The *Theaetetus* is not used in the *Commentary* as a basis for mounting an argument separate from Plato's text, as Justin seeks to do in the Proof from Prophecy.

It was also possible for a commentary to have a theme of its own. Such a text could betray similarities with the Proof from Prophecy, although these are likely to be outweighed by the differences. An example is *Homeric Problems* by Heraclitus,[358] dated (speculatively) to the end of the first century CE or the beginning of the second.[359] *Homeric Problems* has the definite apologetic objective of showing how apparent difficulties in Homer's text can be satisfactorily explained and their meaning properly understood. This is done in the interests of preserving the reputation of the texts; but rather than progressing through the text and commenting on points requiring interpretation, Heraclitus adopts a different methodology better suited to his aims. First, he selects passages for comment, on the grounds that they are problematic because Homer

---

354. *AC*, p. 257.
355. *AC*, pp. 257-59.
356. Dillon, *The Middle Platonists*, p. 270.
357. *AC*, p. 260.
358. Heraclitus, *Homeric Problems*.
359. *AH*, pp. xi-xiii.

appears to be speaking of the gods in an impious or blasphemous way and, second, a single method of interpretation, the allegorical, is used to show how they can be satisfactorily explained.[360] Making selective use of extracts from chosen texts and interpreting them in ways which support his own argument gives *Homeric Problems* affinities with the Proof from Prophecy. However, in another sense Heraclitus' approach is the reverse of Justin's. For, while Justin starts with the case he wants to make and then draws on ancient texts for support, the author of *Homeric Problems* starts with ancient texts and makes an argument that is essentially one of justification: that apparent problems in the texts can be resolved by finding the right way of reading them. *Homeric Problems* is therefore unlike the *First Apology's* Proof from Prophecy in that it does not advance an argument of its own which is separate from the arguments in the texts being discussed.

The final form to consider is the philosophical treatise, although again similarities with Justin's Proof from Prophecy tend to be outweighed by differences. Typically, a treatise examines an issue or an area of philosophy and presents an argument which is the author's own. When, however, it draws heavily on an earlier philosophical source – commonly a work by the founder of a philosophical school – it can be described as a dependent text. Survival of such texts from before Late Antiquity is rare but one example, *On Fate* by Alexander of Aphrodisias, dates from about half a century after Justin.[361] At the outset and again in the conclusion, Alexander describes his own work as an account of the opinions of Aristotle on the subject of fate, showing that his aim is to expound the ideas of one thinker.[362] In simple terms, Alexander's argument is in favour of a non-deterministic Aristotelian view and against the determinism characteristic of Stoicism. Chapters 2-6 explain Aristotle's position; Chapters 7-38 then refute the Stoic position. Alexander draws heavily on material from Aristotle, although he uses his own words rather than quotations; and, since there is no Aristotelian text dealing specifically with fate, his evidence is drawn from a number of Aristotle's works.[363]

---

360. Buffière distinguishes three types of allegorical exegesis in the text, physical, moral and historical: Héraclite, *Allégories d'Homère*, pp. xxi-xxvi.

361. It is dedicated to the Emperors Septimius Severus and Caracalla: Alexander of Aphrodisias, *On Fate*, Introduction, p. 15. The Introduction (pp. 3-32) provides useful background and discussion of the issues dealt with in the text. References to the text are to page and line numbers in Sharples' edition.

362. Alexander says that his book 'contains the opinion concerning fate and responsibility held by Aristotle, of whose philosophical teaching I am the principal exponent': *On Fate*, p. 41, ll. 15-17.

363. Ibid., Sharples, Introduction, p. 23, describes the text as 'an attempt to

Justin's Proof from Prophecy has some affinities with a treatise of this kind since he is making an argument on a theme of his choice and drawing heavily on the work of earlier authors. Moreover, he expounds and explains the thought of those ancient writers whose works he believes reveal divine truths. However, he builds his argument out of quotations from the prophetic texts, which Alexander does not, although he clearly has access to Aristotle's works. The interplay between text and interpretation and the integration of quotations into argument that are hallmarks of Justin's method, and which lead him into close discussion of particular words and phrases, is completely absent from Alexander's treatise.[364]

A closer fit can be found between Justin's work and the treatises of Galen.[365] The latter was Justin's younger contemporary who originated from Asia Minor and came to Rome towards the end of Justin's life.[366] He became a celebrated author of treatises in both medicine and philosophy,[367] which he regarded as closely-related fields.[368] There is no suggestion here that Galen and Justin knew each other or directly influenced each other's work. Like Justin, Galen engaged in debates in which he advanced his own views and attacked the positions of others.[369] He also drew heavily on the work of ancient thinkers and the title of one of his works, *On the Doctrines of Hippocrates and Plato*,[370] identifies

---

formulate, on the basis of Aristotle's writings, an opinion on a question which he had not himself considered'. According to a recent modern commentator, Frede, *A Free Will*, pp. 19-30, Aristotle did not actually have a doctrine of free will.

364. Alexander also wrote commentaries on Aristotle's works, such as the *Prior Analytics* and the *Metaphysics*, which adhere closely to the text, so he was familiar with that literary form: BNP article on Alexander of Aphrodisias by R.W. Sharples.

365. The starting point for the discussion here is the article by Snyder (cited above) comparing the methods of Justin and Galen: Snyder, 'The Classroom in the Text'.

366. Galen was born in Pergamum in 129 CE and lived probably into the second century. He first came to Rome in the early 160s: Hankinson, 'The Man and His Work'.

367. Ibid.

368. One of his works was entitled *The Best Doctor Is also a Philosopher*; G.E.R. Lloyd, 'Galen and His Contemporaries', in Hankinson, *The Cambridge Companion to Galen*, pp. 34-48, 42-43.

369. Notably in his discussion of the different medical sects known as Dogmatists, Empiricists and Methodists: Lloyd, 'Galen and his Contemporaries', pp. 41-42.

370. Galen, *On the Doctrines of Hippocrates and Plato*, ed. and trans. by P. de Lacy, 3 parts (Berlin: Akademie-Verlag, 1978-1984).

his two strongest influences. An examination of Galen's *On the Elements According to Hippocrates*,[371] will reveal parallels with the work of Justin in a number of respects: in the use of quotations from authoritative texts and in concern for their correct interpretation, in the location of authority in antiquity and in the significance of proof. Significant differences between the two writers are, however, also apparent.

On the Elements argues for the existence of four elements, earth, air, fire and water (and also four qualities and four humours) and puts forward doctrines which originated with Hippocrates.[372] Galen makes his own arguments but draws support from Hippocrates, with some thirty quotations from the latter's *On the Nature of Man*[373] being identified by the modern editor of *On the Elements* in what is a relatively short Greek text.[374] The passages from Hippocrates are brief and are woven into Galen's arguments.

As was the case with Justin's prophecies, it is not sufficient for Galen simply to quote from Hippocrates, since the texts cited do not speak for themselves. He interprets what Hippocrates says so that his words will be understood correctly. *On the Elements* is polemical and much of it is devoted to the refutation of ideas of thinkers with whom Galen disagrees.[375] One significant area of disagreement concerns the way in which Hippocrates should be interpreted, with Galen criticising his opponents for incorrectly understanding Hippocrates.[376] In Chapter 3, for instance, he contends, at a very detailed level, that the term ἐνεον 'eneon' should not be read as one word with a smooth breathing in Greek (meaning 'being in') 'as most followers of Hippocrates have done', but as two words ἐν ἑον 'en eon' with a rough breathing (meaning 'being one').[377] In Chapter 7 he attacks the position of 'those who do not

---

371. Galen, *On the Elements According to Hippocrates*, ed. and trans. by P. de Lacy (Berlin: Akademie-Verlag, 1996).
372. The author regards inclusion of the phrase 'according to Hippocrates' in the title as important: Galen, *Elements*, 9.30.
373. Ibid., Introduction, p. 50.
374. In de Lacy's edition the Greek text covers just over fifty pages, with each page typically between half and two thirds occupied by text.
375. Galen, *Elements*, Introduction, p. 45, lists the thinkers with whom Galen takes issue; in Chapters 6-9, for instance, which discusses the four qualities, Galen's main protagonist was Athenaeus, who held that the four qualities were in fact elements.
376. Some modern scholars criticise Galen for his misrepresentation of Hippocrates' ideas, e.g. G.E.R. Lloyd, 'Scholarship, Authority and Argument in Galen's *Quod Animi Mores*', in P. Manuli and M. Vegetti, eds, *Le opere psicologiche di Galeno* (Naples: Bibliopolis, 1988), pp. 11-42, 30-31.
377. Galen, *Elements*, 3.50.

understand Hippocrates correctly'[378] and in Chapter 8, arguing that Hippocrates uses the terms 'hot', 'cold', 'wet' and 'dry' to refer to elements and not to qualities, says that: 'the majority of those who call themselves Hippocrateans overlook this, and in addition they think that by wet, dry, hot, and cold he refers to something else, not to the common elements of all things'.[379]

Questions must arise as to why Galen cites Hippocrates and the nature of the authority he considers Hippocrates to have. There are no equivalents of the Septuagint legend or of Justin's Prophetic Spirit to explain the special status of *On the Nature of Man* or its author. Indeed, very little is said about Hippocrates at all; Galen refers to him without explanation, no doubt because he expects his audience to know who he was. In two respects, however, Galen's references to Hippocrates suggest something about how he perceives his authority, both of which betray affinities with Justin.

The first is that Galen refers to Hippocrates' antiquity and, more specifically, to the fact that he was the first to advance the doctrine of the four elements. In Chapter 5 of *On the Elements* Galen says that not only did Hippocrates 'lead the way by affirming in his book "On the Nature of Man" that they [earth, fire, air and water] are the elements of all things in the cosmos, but he was also the first to define the qualities that they [the elements] have by virtue of which they can mutually act and be acted upon'.[380] In Chapter 9 he refers to 'Hippocrates as one who employed the *ancient* brevity of expression' (italics added)[381] and a little later speaks of him as: 'the very first to have discovered the elements of the nature of existing things and the first to have given an adequate proof'.[382] To Galen, being ancient and being the first are important attributes.

The second point which is striking in Galen's references to Hippocrates is that he uses the term 'proof', as has already been seen in the last quotation. In Chapter 2, having quoted Hippocrates, Galen comments that: 'He seems to me to give most excellently and at the same time in the fewest possible words the essential point of his proof that the element cannot be one in form and power';[383] and in Chapter 3 he

---

378. Galen, *Elements*, 7.12; again, at 5.14, he says: 'It appears, then, that Aristotle and Hippocrates have ordered their arguments in the same way but that the commentators do not understand them.'
379. Ibid., 8.8.
380. Ibid., 5.32.
381. Ibid., 9.11.
382. Ibid., 9.25.
383. Ibid., 2.4.

says that: 'The speed with which the men of former times expressed their thoughts is admirable. Hippocrates in the fewest possible words indicated all these things and provided a valid proof [ἀπόδειξις] that the element is not one.'[384] That Galen attached importance to logical proof generally has already been noted, so it not surprising that for him it is one of the significant features of the arguments in Hippocrates' *On the Nature of Man*.[385]

As well as these similarities, however, comparison between Justin and Galen also reveals significant differences. There is no sense in Galen that the authoritative texts are prophetic, or that they are enigmatic or ambiguous, even though he contends that other commentators have misinterpreted them. Galen draws on a text which is clearly part of the received literary heritage[386] but, for him, its value is primarily that Hippocrates advances arguments which are *correct* and that he can demonstrate that they are valid and logical.[387] For Justin, the prophecies were authoritative because they were the accurate words of ancient prophets inspired by the Prophetic Spirit. Logical proof was not a quality Justin found in the authoritative texts themselves. It was, however, a quality he prized and one he considered he brought to bear himself in his explanations of the prophecies and, particularly, in the way he showed how ancient prophecies had been fulfilled. Galen writes as a philosopher seeking out correct arguments through the use of logical reasoning and finds that very often the arguments of Hippocrates are persuasive.[388] Justin's writings, by contrast, are ultimately dependent on divine revelation, firstly, through the prophecies revealed by the Prophetic Spirit and, subsequently, through his demonstration that those prophecies have now been fulfilled through God's revelation in Jesus Christ.

Justin's text, therefore, does not fit very closely with any of the models of dependent literature current in the early Imperial period, although it has some features in common with each of those examined here. It has greater affinity with Galen's treatise, *On the Elements*, than with any of the others, since both Galen and Justin keep closely to the words of their authoritative texts, quote them frequently and exactly, and use them as

---

384. Galen, *Elements*, 3.30.
385. A comparison between Galen and Justin's uses of the term 'proof' would be valuable but cannot be pursued here.
386. For the high regard in which Hippocrates was held, see O. Temkin, *Hippocrates in a World of Pagans and Christians* (Baltimore: Johns Hopkins University Press, 1991), pp. 49-75.
387. Snyder, 'The Classroom in the Text', pp. 678-80.
388. Ibid., p. 680.

a basis for their own arguments. Perhaps the most critical difference between the Proof from Prophecy and the other types of dependent literature is that all the others deal with texts which were already established classics by revered authors. The audience would either have had prior acquaintance with the texts, or at least would have known them by reputation and recognised their authority. Justin, by contrast, quotes from and interprets texts, with which his audience will be unfamiliar, and he knows this. So, he has the significant additional task of acquainting his audience with the texts and of demonstrating why they should be regarded as authoritative.

Conclusion

Justin shows that the Jewish scriptures can be used as evidence in apologetic arguments directed towards a non-Jewish Graeco-Roman audience. He does this even though the Jewish scriptures are unfamiliar to the audience and he has to explain their provenance, the basis of their authority and how they should be interpreted. Justin selects particular texts and interprets them in particular ways and he also presents the Jewish scriptures as essentially prophetic in nature. He reads the scriptures as a collection of texts with a single overall message. However, it is not an obvious one and the texts must first be broken down to locate individual messages contained in particular passages, which are then amalgamated to create a coherent argument out of the pieces. It is this argument which is presented by Justin as the truth to be discerned from the Books of the Prophecies.

Justin does not disguise the fact that the Books of the Prophecies originated with the Jews but he re-interprets them in a Christian light. The key point for Justin is that the Jews (or most of them) misinterpreted the prophecies contained in the ancient scriptures they preserved and consequently rejected Jesus Christ. Indeed, Justin takes a distinctive stance towards the Jews; in the circumstances of dialogue with a Graeco-Roman audience, he recognises that they have now been defeated and humiliated by their Roman conquerors. He expresses neither criticism nor regret at this for he is aware that the Jews' rejection of Jesus Christ will lead to their condemnation at the last judgement, as was also foretold in those same ancient prophecies.

Perhaps Justin could have based his argument for the status of Jesus on recent works of Christian literature rather than on ancient prophetic texts. In the *First Apology* Chapters 15-17, he draws on the teachings of Jesus, including quotations which modern scholars recognise to be from the Synoptic tradition, and he extols their virtues; but he does not characterise them as derived from textual sources. The same applies when a reference is made – again, recognisably from the Synoptic tradition – to the birth of Jesus as the fulfilment of the prophecy in Isaiah 7:14; no textual source is specified.[389] In the *Apology* authoritative texts are ancient and are inspired by the Prophetic Spirit; recent Christian writings do not have these characteristics.

Justin positions himself partly within and partly outside the prevailing culture of his time. He links his argument based on prophecy to strains of prophetic thought which would be familiar to a Graeco-Roman audience from their own traditions. He employs a number of literary strategies that the Graeco-Roman tradition applied to highly regarded ancient texts and his own work betrays similarities to some of the forms of writing prevalent at the time. There are, however, limits to his use of these strategies since they are adapted to meet his apologetic objective of advancing a case for Christianity. Although asked to accept the texts he is promoting as authoritative, Justin's audience is not invited to treat them as part of the Graeco-Roman literary tradition; Justin always maintains clear water between the Books of the Prophecies and the mainstream Graeco-Roman literary corpus. Moreover, he does not compromise on his presentation of these sacred texts of Christianity in order that they should be seen as compatible with the traditions of Graeco-Roman culture; indeed, if his audience accepts what he says, they must necessarily reject their own tradition of mythological religion.

One of the most significant features of the way Justin's argument draws on Graeco-Roman traditions is the emphasis he places on rationality, for he asserts that his argument from prophecy is rational and, indeed, that it is a proof. His claims could, however, also be described as the result of revelation, first, on the part of the Prophetic Spirit in giving out the prophecies and, second, through the divinely ordained events of the life of Jesus and the growth of Christianity which fulfil them. If Justin's audience is to accept his arguments, it will need to recognise that matching ancient prophecies with their recent fulfilments demonstrates both that the original prophecies are ultimately from God and that the fulfilling events are part of divine purpose. Further, it must acknowledge that this is a rational stance to take. The audience would also have to assent to something that was not part of the tradition of Graeco-Roman literary culture – that ancient prophecies can be drawn on as evidence in support of a rational argument – and this might have been difficult for them to accept.

389. *1A* 33.5: references to Luke 1:31-32; and Matthew 1:20-21.

Chapter 3

Tatian's *Oratio* and the 'Barbarian Writings'

The *Oratio ad Graecos* is Tatian's only surviving work.[1] It is a problematic text, couched in the form of a classical oration, and in style and presentation very much a product of its Graeco-Roman milieu; at the same time, it is an apologetic work rooted in the Jewish traditions from which Christianity emerged and fiercely critical of Graeco-Roman culture.

On first examination, the *Oratio* appears to make very little use of the Jewish scriptures. For Tatian, as for Justin, the scriptures are, however, critically important, although in somewhat different ways; to Justin the scriptures are essentially prophetic texts, while for Tatian they are a source of philosophical ideas; Justin quotes extensively from the scriptures, Tatian hardly at all.

Before looking in detail at Tatian's use of the scriptures, what is known about the author will be considered and the nature of the text discussed: its contents and form, its original audience and the historical circumstances which produced it. These remain matters of speculation on which there is much less certainty than was the case with Justin's *First Apology*. Previous scholarship on the *Oratio* will then be reviewed and the approach to the text which is taken here will be described.

---

1. Referred to hereafter as *Oratio*. References to the text are to chapter and paragraph numbers in *Tatiani Oratio ad Graecos*, ed. by M. Marcovich (Berlin: de Gruyter, 1995). Translations are from *Tatian: Oratio ad Graecos and Fragments*, ed. by M. Whittaker (Oxford: Clarendon Press, 1982), adapted where appropriate. Other modern editions consulted: *Tatianos: Oratio ad Graecos: Rede an die Griechen*, ed. by J. Trelenberg (Tübingen: Mohr Siebeck, 2012); and *Gegen falsche Götter und falsche Bildung: Tatian, Rede an die Griechen*, ed. by H.-G. Nesselrath (Tübingen: Mohr Siebeck, 2016). There is no *Sources Chrétiennes* edition.

Background

Very limited information is available about Tatian's life – much of it deriving from the *Oratio* itself – and his biography can only be sketched tentatively and in outline.[2] His birth is dated by scholars to around the 120s. He says in the *Oratio* that he was 'born in the land of the Assyrians'[3] – thought to be a reference to Syria[4] – and that he received a Greek education. At some stage, he moved to Rome. He was converted to Christianity and became acquainted with certain texts,[5] encountering, and being influenced by, Justin.[6] Tatian represents his conversion to Christianity as the desertion of Greek culture in favour of barbarian, saying (to Greeks) that 'we abandoned your wisdom even though I myself was very distinguished in it'[7] and also that 'having said farewell to Roman arrogance, Athenian cold cleverness and the unintelligible dogmas of the Greeks, I sought out the philosophy which according to you is barbarous.'[8]

Tatian became a Christian teacher and subsequently moved from Rome back to the eastern Mediterranean, where he disappears from view. He compiled a harmonisation of the Gospels, known as the *Diatessaron*, which exerted considerable influence over several centuries, although only fragments survive in their original form.[9] He acquired a reputation for heretical views from an early stage, as the late second-century, Christian writer Irenaeus records.[10] However, his *Oratio* was

---

2. For Tatian's biography: Whittaker, *Oratio*, pp. ix-x; Trelenberg, *Oratio*, pp. 1-8; M. Elze, *Tatian und seine Theologie* (Göttingen: Vandenhoeck & Ruprecht, 1960), pp. 16-19; W.L. Petersen, 'Tatian the Assyrian', in A. Marjanen and P. Luomanen, eds, *A Companion to Second-century 'Heretics'* (Leiden: Brill, 2005), pp. 125-58, 129-34. Nesselrath, *Gegen falsche Götter*, p. 5, comments aptly that little is known of Tatian's life and that little is not certain.

3. *Oratio* 42.1.

4. F. Millar, *The Roman Near East 31 BC-AD 337* (Cambridge, MA: Harvard University Press, 1993), p. 227; Grant, *Greek Apologists*, p. 115.

5. *Oratio* 29.2.

6. He is twice named in the *Oratio* at 18.6 and 19.2.

7. *Oratio* 1.5.

8. *Oratio* 35.2. The translation here follows Marcovich's emendation of the text to add καὶ τοῖς Ἑλλήνων (of the Greeks) before δόγμασιν (dogmas) and follows Whittaker's καθ'ὑμᾶς (according to you), which follows the most reliable manuscripts and is supported by Trelenberg and Nesselrath, over the conjectural emendation to καθ' ἡμᾶς (according to us) favoured by Marcovich.

9. W.L. Petersen, *Tatian's Diatessaron: Its Creation, Dissemination, Significance, and History in Scholarship* (Leiden: Brill, 1994).

10. Irénée, *Contre les hérésies: Livre 1*, ed. by A. Rousseau and L. Doutreleau, 2 vols (Paris: Éditions du Cerf, 1979), 1.28.1.

copied and preserved by Christians and in the early fourth century the Christian historian Eusebius refers to it with approval.[11] The oldest surviving manuscripts (copies of a lost tenth-century original) date from the early eleventh century and so, while somewhat older than the earliest manuscript of Justin's *First Apology*, were still produced many centuries after the original composition.[12]

Issues concerning the *Oratio*'s structure and contents have prompted considerable discussion among commentators. Of the recent editors, Whittaker comments that 'it is difficult to trace an ordered scheme'[13] and Marcovich that the structure of the *Oratio* 'is rather loose and ill-organised'.[14] The analyses of the contents of the text, which these two editors provide, list the topics covered, without identifying any very clear progression, although they group the chapters in similar ways.[15] Trelenberg, by contrast, presents the text as having a clearer and more coherent structure; he identifies an introduction (Chapters 1-4) and a conclusion (Chapter 42), framing the two main sections whose themes are the basic teachings of the Christian faith (Chapters 5-20) and a comparison between Christianity and Paganism (Chapters 21-41), each of them neatly divided into four sub-sections.[16] Nesselrath adopts a position somewhere between Whittaker and Marcovich, on the one hand, and Trelenberg, on the other;[17] his description of the structure of the text has the introduction (Chapters 1-4) and epilogue (Chapter 42), in between which are two main sections (although in his case the split is between Chapters 5-30 and 31-41). In Nesselrath's view, Tatian presents the contents of the *Oratio* more arbitrarily, its arrangement lacking the neatness of structure identified by Trelenberg.[18]

It is not a critical issue which of these approaches has the most validity since it is the contents of the text which are the concern here rather than its structure. The *Oratio* contains two types of material: sections criticising Greek culture – such as Chapters 1-3, 8-11, 16-19 and 21-28 – where a hostile and vituperative tone is frequently adopted; and passages

---

11. Eusebius, *HE* 4.29.
12. Marcovich, *Oratio*, pp. 3-4.
13. Whittaker, *Oratio*, p. xx.
14. Marcovich, *Oratio*, p. 5.
15. Whittaker, *Oratio*, pp. xviii-xx; Marcovich, *Oratio*, pp. 5-6.
16. Trelenberg, *Oratio*, pp. 28-29. The sub-divisions of the first section are: creation and eschatology, demonology, psychology and anthropology; those of the second are: the inferiority of pagan culture, the questionable value of pagan educational activities, pagan and Christian ethics, and the proof of antiquity.
17. Nesselrath, *Gegen falsche Götter*, pp. 11-14.
18. Ibid., p. 11.

in which Christian ideas are presented – such as Chapters 4-7, 12-15, 20, 29-30 and 36-41 – that are more measured in tone. These latter passages address a range of issues which Tatian clearly regards as significant in debates between Christians and non-Christians.

Considerable uncertainties surround the date and location of the composition of the *Oratio* – greater than in the case of the *First Apology* – and they remain essentially unresolved. It is therefore not possible to establish the particular circumstances which prompted Tatian to write it. Various proposals regarding the original location and date of the text have been put forward but none has yet commanded general assent.[19] For location, Rome, Greece and Antioch have all been suggested.[20] Proposals for dating range from the early 150s by Harnack[21] to the late 170s by Grant.[22] Some scholars, such as Barnard and Hunt,[23] date the *Oratio* to before Justin's death in about 165, while Marcovich argues that it was written after that date, on the basis that Tatian's references to Justin indicate that he was already dead.[24] Dating issues are complicated by suggestions that the text may not all have been written at the same time; Karadimas argues that three pre-existing speeches were incorporated into the *Oratio*,[25] while Osborne divides the text into two parts, one prepared for oral delivery and the other not.[26] Such complications render datings which depend on a single reference in the text, such as those of

19. For a recent summary of the main contributions to this debate, see Trelenberg, *Oratio*, pp. 8-15.
20. 'Probably' Rome by Whittaker and Greece by Harnack (Whittaker, *Oratio*, p. x), prepared for delivery in Athens by Grant, *Greek Apologists*, pp. 117-18, and Antioch by J. Lössl, 'Date and Location of Tatian's *Ad Graecos*: Some Old and New Thoughts', in M. Vinzent and A. Brent, eds, *SP*, vol. 74 (Leuven: Peeters, 2016), pp. 43-55.
21. Trelenberg, *Oratio*, p. 9.
22. R.M. Grant, 'The Date of Tatian's Oration', *HTR*, vol. 46 (1953), pp. 99-101. G.W. Clarke, 'The Date of the Oration of Tatian', *HTR*, vol. 60 (1967), pp. 123-26, successfully demolishes Grant's arguments.
23. L.W. Barnard, 'The Heresy of Tatian – Once Again', *JEH*, vol. 19 (1968), pp. 1-10; and E.J. Hunt, *Christianity in the Second Century: The Case of Tatian* (London: Routledge, 2003), p. 3.
24. Marcovich, *Oratio*, pp. 1-3. Edwards' suggestion that the composition of the *Oratio* was actually prompted by the death of Justin lacks convincing support: Edwards, 'Apologetics', p. 553.
25. D. Karadimas, *Tatian's* Oratio ad Graecos: *Rhetoric and Philosophy/Theology* (Stockholm: Almquist & Wiksell International, 2003): the speeches occupy Chapters 8-11, 32-35 and 22-30.
26. A.E. Osborne, 'Tatian's Discourse to the Greeks: A Literary Analysis and Essay in Interpretation' (PhD, University of Cincinnati, 1969), pp. 4-28; Chapters 1-30 and 42 comprise the first part and Chapters 31-41 the second.

Harnack and Hunt,[27] problematic. Two of the most recent contributors to the debate, Trelenberg and Lössl, favour a date after 172 for the finalisation of the work, with Trelenberg referring to what he calls the unmistakable portfolio character of the text,[28] and Lössl (who favours Antioch for location) suggesting that certain sections, 'pre-Antiochene' in character, had been written earlier.[29]

The text presents itself as a dialogue between the author and his audience, with first and second persons used extensively.[30] The arguments in the text are clearly relevant to interactions between Christians and non-Christians and appear to be part of an ongoing debate in which the audience has some prior acquaintance with Christianity but is hostile to the author. There are allusions to earlier exchanges between Tatian and his real or imagined audience;[31] the text imputes views to them,[32] attributes to them opinions about the author[33] and reports (or puts into their mouths) criticisms of Christian beliefs and practices.[34] The debate is a binary one in which Christianity is presented favourably, while Greek ideas and Greek culture are heavily criticised and, indeed, ridiculed.

Tatian, like Justin, was a Greek-educated convert to Christianity; and the contents of the *Oratio* concern debates between Christians and Greek-educated non-Christians, which he himself had once been. The audience is described as 'men of Greece'[35] and the number of allusions to Greek literature[36] suggests that Tatian is targeting, and seeking to

---

27. A. Harnack, *Die Überlieferung der griechischen Apologeten des zweiten Jahr-hunderts in der alten Kirche und im Mittelalter*, 2 vols (Leipzig: Hinrichs, 1882), 1, pp. 196-98, relies on the reference to Peregrinus Proteus in 25.1; and Hunt, *Christianity in the Second Century*, p. 3, on the reference to Justin in 19.2.
28. Trelenberg, *Oratio*, pp. 15 and 230-40.
29. Lössl, 'Date and Location', p. 52.
30. E.g. Chapter 1 is written largely in the second-person plural and Chapter 11 largely in the first-person singular.
31. E.g. *Oratio* 21.1: 'You who abuse us should compare your myths with our narratives.'
32. E.g. *Oratio* 26.1: 'Stop leading foreign words in triumph'; 26.2: 'You ask who God is'; 26.3: 'Tell me, why do you divide up time?'
33. E.g. *Oratio* 35.3: 'Tatian . . . is innovating with his barbarian doctrines'.
34. For views, e.g. *Oratio* 6.3 and 33.1 (talking nonsense) and for practices, e.g. 25.5 (cannibalism).
35. *Oratio* 1.1: the phrase is repeated later, e.g. 12.6, 13.1 and 21.1.
36. Whittaker, *Oratio*, p. 87, lists classical quotations from twenty-six authors (excluding Justin), five of whom she says are not named by Tatian. Marcovich, *Oratio*, p. 84, lists twenty-five authors (excluding Justin); there are, however, only seventeen names common to the two lists. Other references to classical authors do not involve quotations: e.g. in Chapters 2 and 3, in which Tatian

impress, an audience from the πεπαιδευμένοι (the educational elite).[37] Author and audience are presented as sharing a common Greek educational background[38] and Tatian includes references to the Greek literary tradition without explanation, a sign that he expects his audience to recognise them. There is, however, no indication that he expects his audience – who are presented as having some knowledge of Christianity – to be familiar with the Jewish literary tradition.

The style of presentation of the *Oratio* is that of a text composed for oral delivery. Some commentators have taken this at face value, treating it as a real speech actually delivered,[39] while others are sceptical about this.[40] Some of the same issues arise with Tatian's *Oratio* as with Justin's *First Apology*. The audience at which the text was directed could be located in a number of places, one possibility being that the external audience suggested by the text's presentation was the actual audience,[41] and another that the audience was wholly internal to Christianity.[42] The text could record the terms of a debate or debates that actually took place, or it could be an imaginative presentation by a Christian writer of issues and arguments he considers likely to arise in debates with non-Christians but still in reality aimed at an internal audience. As with Justin, it may be too simple to treat the *Oratio* as directed towards *either* an internal *or* an external audience, since it could have

attacks philosophers, he mentions Diogenes, Aristippus, Plato, Aristotle, Heraclitus, Zeno, Empedocles, Pherecydes, Pythagoras and Crates, albeit only briefly in each case. See N. Zeegers-Vander Vorst, *Les citations des poètes grecs chez les apologistes chrétiens du IIe siècle* (Louvain: Université de Louvain, 1972), pp. 302-3, for Tatian's Homeric quotations.

37. The word appears at *Oratio* 25.5: see J.E. Fojtik, 'Tatian the Barbarian: Language, Education and Identity in the *Oratio ad Graecos*', in J. Ulrich, A.-C. Jacobsen and M. Kahlos, eds, *Continuity and Discontinuity in Early Christian Apologetics* (Frankfurt am Main: Peter Lang, 2009), pp. 23-34.

38. M. Whittaker, 'Tatian's Educational Background', in E.A. Livingstone, ed., *SP*, vol. 13, no. 2 (Berlin: Akademie-Verlag, 1975), pp. 57-59.

39. E.g. R.C. Kukula, *Tatians sogenannte Apologie: Exegetisch-Chronologische Studie* (Leipzig: Teubner, 1900), pp. 15-16; and A. Puech, *Recherches sur le Discours aux grecs de Tatien* (Paris: F. Alcan, 1903), p. 5.

40. E.g. Young, 'Greek Apologists', p. 85: 'the artificiality of such a generalised address is evident – this can never have been literally an oration to a specific audience'.

41. The suggestion of Droge, *Homer or Moses?*, pp. 97-101, that Tatian may have written in response to Celsus is, like the argument referred to in Chapter 2 that Celsus wrote in response to Justin, based on similarities of argument between the two authors rather than close textual connections and it remains speculative at best.

42. *E.g. Nesselrath, Gegen falsche Götter, p. 19.*

been both; alternatively, audiences for the text could have been located on the margins of Christianity and consisted of new or prospective converts.

One suggestion canvassed in the scholarly literature, which has much to commend it, is that the *Oratio* should be regarded as a *protrepticus*, part of a textual tradition going back to the early Greeks[43] and associated particularly with Aristotle.[44] Such a text aimed to encourage students to undertake philosophical instruction with a particular teacher, without, however, spelling out his teachings in detail. Reading the text as a *logos protrepticus* was proposed many years ago by Puech[45] and, subsequently, supported by Grant who describes the sections expounding Christian ideas as 'properly a "protreptic" inviting the reader to follow Tatian and become a convert'.[46] A recent and powerful advocate of such an interpretation is McGehee[47] who highlights a number of reasons why a protreptic reading helps to explain notable features of the text: its vituperative style, its ridicule of other philosophies, its random references to unexplored ideas – which will be followed up in later instruction – and its offer to answer questions.[48]

These arguments for the *Oratio* having the form of a *protrepticus* are strong and tend to tip the balance towards the audience being a real external one; it seems much less likely that a Christian author would present the text as he does if he was addressing a purely internal Christian audience, since he would have no good reason not to expose

---

43.   For the origins of protreptic: J.H. Collins II, *Exhortations to Philosophy: The Protreptics of Plato, Isocrates and Aristotle* (New York, Oxford University Press, 2015).

44.   Aristotle's *Protrepticus* survives only in fragments: Aristotle, *Protrepticus: An Attempt at Reconstruction*, by I. Düring (Göteborg: Acta Universitatis Gothoburgensis, 1961). For its influence in antiquity: W. Jaeger, *Aristotle: Fundamentals of the History of His Development*, trans. by R. Robinson, 2nd edn (Oxford: Oxford University Press, 1948), pp. 60-79; for influence on Christian writers: G. Lazzati, *L'Aristotele perduto e gli scrittori cristiani* (Milano: Società Editrice, 1938). For protreptic texts in epistolary form (Christian and non-Christian): S.K. Stowers, *Letter Writing in Greco-Roman Antiquity* (Philadelphia: Westminster Press, 1986), pp. 112-25.

45.   A Puech, *Les apologistes grecs du IIe siècle de notre ère* (Paris: Libraire Hachette, 1912), pp. 153-54 and 169-70 (which links the protreptic quality of the text with the absence of scriptural quotations); and Puech, *Recherches*, pp. 41-42 and 97-102: 'A work like the Discourse to the Greeks is not an exposition of faith, it is a preparation for faith' (p. 99).

46.   Grant, 'Forms and Occasions', p. 222. For the *Oratio* as a protreptic text: Pellegrino, *Studi su l'antica apologetica*, pp. 43-45.

47.   M. McGehee, 'Why Tatian Never "Apologized" to the Greeks', *JECS*, vol. 1 (1993), pp. 143-58.

48.   Ibid., p. 152.

scriptural texts to them openly. On this reading, Tatian's aim is to capture his readers' interest in his ideas and to offer them the prospect of further instruction at a later stage. As he himself says, 'if you wish to examine our teachings I will give you an easily understood and full account'[49] and 'I offer myself to you, ready for an examination of teachings.'[50] Thus, his intention is to whet his audience's appetite for his teachings by outlining some of his ideas but holding back on a detailed exposition.[51]

The Scholarly Context

Previous scholarship on Tatian has been concerned with the theological material to be found in the *Oratio*: on his place in the development of Christian thought and on the influences which shaped his ideas. Two monographs – by Elze and Hunt – have examined his thinking in some depth;[52] they advance different views but share a common concern to position Tatian in the philosophical debates of his contemporaries. Elze locates Tatian within the Middle Platonism current in the second century, identifying connections with particular thinkers, notably, Alcinous and Atticus. Hunt is concerned to rebut the contention of Grant that Tatian had significant links with Valentinianism[53] and presents him as a Christian philosopher in a tradition derived from Justin; thus, in her view, influences from Hellenistic philosophy, including Middle Platonism, were mediated through Justin. There has been continuing scholarly interest in understanding Tatian's ideas, examples being articles by Lössl[54] and Koltun-Fromm[55] and, most recently, the collection of essays covering a range of issues (by Prostmeier, Strutwolf and Lakmann, Gemeinhardt, Timotin and Ritter) in Nesselrath's edition of the text.[56]

---

49. *Oratio* 30.4.
50. *Oratio* 42.2.
51. A point made by Puech, *Les apologistes grecs*, pp. 169-70. Lössl has recently commented on the increasing support among scholars for the idea that the *Oratio* is a *proptrepticus*: J. Lössl, 'Zwischen Christologie und Rhetorik: Zum Ausdruck "Kraft des Wortes" (λόγου δύναμις) in Tatians "Rede an die Griechen"', in F.R. Prostmeier and H.E. Lona, eds, *Logos der Vernunft – Logos des Glaubens* (Berlin: de Gruyter, 2010), pp. 129-47, 130.
52. Elze, *Tatian und seine Theologie*; Hunt, *Christianity in the Second Century*.
53. R.M. Grant, 'The Heresy of Tatian', *JTS*, vol. 5 (1954), pp. 62-68.
54. J. Lössl, 'Hermeneutics and the Doctrine of God in Tatian's *Ad Graecos*', in J. Baun, A. Cameron, M. Edwards and M. Vinzent, eds, *SP*, vol. 45 (Leuven: Peeters, 2010), pp. 409-12.
55. N. Koltun-Fromm, 'Re-imagining Tatian: The Damaging Effects of Polemical Rhetoric', *JECS*, vol. 16 (2008), pp. 1-30.
56. Nesselrath, *Gegen falsche Götter*, pp. 193-303.

Tatian's approach to and use of the Jewish scriptures has, however, not been a particular interest of either Elze or Hunt, or of more recent scholars. This is evidenced by the absence of any discussion of the issue in the extensive introduction to Trelenberg's edition of the text[57] and in the introduction and essays contained in Nesselrath's edition.[58]

Going back in time, however, two scholars who, in their different ways, discussed Tatian and the Jewish scriptures are Harnack in the late nineteenth century and Grant in the mid-twentieth, although neither comments at length. In a discussion of the Old Testament's importance for early Christianity, Harnack stresses the significance of the Jewish scriptures for Tatian and provides some analysis of Chapter 29 of the *Oratio* where Tatian discusses the texts he calls the 'Barbarian Writings'.[59] Harnack highlights features of the contents of these texts as Tatian characterises them – the Creation narrative, prophecies, the moral code and rigid monotheism – and emphasises Tatian's positive view of the style of the scriptures as marked by 'vigour coupled with simplicity'.[60] This passage of Tatian's and these issues will be considered further below; suffice it to say at this stage that Harnack's comments, briefly sketched rather than fully-developed, provide one starting point for an examination of Tatian's work.

Given Harnack's massive influence on later scholarship, it is perhaps surprising that the issues he highlights here have not been more extensively developed by other scholars. A short article by Grant[61] has, however, examined Tatian's use of the Jewish scriptures. Grant writes of a Bible which consists of an Old Testament and a New Testament and he concludes that 'Tatian found the New Testament much more congenial than the Old'.[62] The terms 'Old Testament' and 'New Testament' are arguably anachronistic in this context – they do not appear in the *Oratio* or in other apologetic texts of the time – and one consequence is that Grant ignores the role of extra-canonical Jewish texts; as will be shown below, this leads him to misrepresent Tatian in some respects.

Nevertheless, Grant's article is valuable, not least for his classification of scriptural references. Some of his conclusions are questionable, such as the identification of allusions to Genesis 2-3, where the references are

---

57. Trelenberg, *Oratio*, pp. 1-80. There are only three entries against Old Testament in Trelenberg's Index.
58. Nesselrath, *Gegen falsche Götter*, pp. 3-36 and 193-303.
59. Harnack, *The Expansion of Christianity*, 1, pp. 279-89; for Tatian, pp. 281-82.
60. Ibid., p. 282.
61. R.M. Grant, 'Tatian and the Bible', in K. Aland and F.L. Cross, eds, *SP*, vol. 1, no. 1 (Berlin: Akademie-Verlag, 1957), pp. 297-306.
62. Ibid., p. 303.

much more likely to be to the Enoch tradition;[63] he also suggests that there are references to Pauline texts, such as Galatians and Philippians, which may not survive close scrutiny.[64] Grant does, however, make some pertinent comments in the course of the article, pointing, for instance, to Tatian's use of allusions rather than quotations,[65] although some of his other observations, such as the identification of strong Gnostic influences, may be questioned.[66] Most important in the present context, however, is that Grant does not consider how scriptural references impact on Tatian's arguments.

The Approach Taken Here

Thus previous Tatian scholarship leaves room for a more extended examination of the use Tatian makes of the Jewish scriptures in his arguments and this book seeks to provide it. Given the uncertainties already highlighted concerning the circumstances in which the *Oratio* was produced, however, it is not possible to examine the text against its own particular background; it can only be read and interpreted as a work originating somewhere in the Roman Empire in the mid- to late second century.

As with Justin's *First Apology*, Barclay's analysis of the different categories of apologetic audience helps to provide clarity. The declared audience for the *Oratio* is the very generalised 'men of Greece' invoked in the text. The intended audience, as noted above, is more problematic and could have been either external to Christianity or internal or somewhere on the borderland between the two, although the attractions of a protreptic reading of the text noted above mean that a genuine external audience is a real possibility. The implied audience is, however, broadly defined as those from a Graeco-Roman cultural background.

---

63. Ibid., pp. 304-5. He, for instance, takes the phrase 'one who was cleverer than the rest' in *Oratio* 7.4 to allude to the description of the serpent in Genesis 3:1 and the words 'and men and angels followed him and proclaimed as god this rebel against God's law' again in *Oratio* 7.4 to refer to Adam's disobedience in Genesis 2-3. The influence of 1 Enoch on the *Oratio* is discussed below.

64. They are not included in the list of 'Biblical Quotations and Allusions' in Whittaker, *Oratio*, p. xvii, or in the corresponding list in Marcovich, *Oratio*, p. 83. Even Grant himself, 'Tatian and the Bible', p. 303, comments that not all his Pauline references are equally convincing.

65. Grant, 'Tatian and the Bible', p. 297.

66. Grant, 'Tatian and the Bible', p. 297. Hunt, *Christianity in the Second Century*, pp. 20-51, has effectively undermined Grant's argument here.

The approach adopted here will in essence be the same as was the case with Justin's *First Apology*: that the arguments put forward in favour of Christianity are considered and analysed without reference to whom the intended audience might have been or to precisely when and where the text was written, but rather to its implied audience and to a Graeco-Roman context more generally conceived. Like Justin's *First Apology*, Tatian's *Oratio* will be treated as a repository of arguments which a Christian writer in a Graeco-Roman literary environment of the mid- to late second century portrays as significant in potential or actual debates with non-Christians. References here to the audience of the text are to the implied audience. As was the case with Justin, however, in order to avoid unnecessarily convoluted phraseology, and in accordance with the way the text presents itself, the audience of the *Oratio* will be referred to in what follows as if it is external to Christianity.

Tatian engages with his audience on a number of issues and uses the Barbarian Writings – through quotations and references – to support his arguments. The issues he deals with will be reviewed in turn but, before doing this, the character of the Barbarian Writings as presented by Tatian will be considered, starting with his perspective on the texts' authority. From there, discussion will move on to the nature of the Barbarian Writings, which texts they comprise, the kind of texts they are and the tradition from which they come.

The Authority of the Barbarian Writings

For Tatian the authority of the Barbarian Writings centres on three characteristics: their antiquity, which is linked with their authorship, their status as divine texts and their content and style. The starting point for examination of these issues is 29.2, which appears surprisingly late in the *Oratio*. This important passage contains Tatian's overall appraisal of the Barbarian Writings in terms of their contents, their value and significance, and their authority:

> While I was engaged in serious thought I happened to read some Barbarian Writings, older by comparison with the doctrines of the Greeks and more divine by comparison with their errors. The outcome was that I was persuaded by them because of the lack of arrogance in the wording, the artlessness of the speakers, the easily intelligible account of the creation of the world, the foreknowledge of the future, the remarkable quality of the precepts and the idea of a single ruler of the universe.

Tatian does not say here how he came to read the texts, except that he was 'by myself'[67] and 'engaged in serious thought'.[68] However, he claims that his encounter with them was crucial for his conversion to Christianity. Tatian's comments are presented as personal experience, although it is impossible to know how literally to take them as autobiography;[69] he may simply be using this form to present his material. In the previous chapter it was noted that, in the *Dialogue with Trypho*, Justin claims to have learned about the Jewish scriptures from an old man whom he met and that this led to his conversion to Christianity.[70] Early Christian apologetic texts commonly include an account of the author's conversion, which may or may not be historically accurate, and such texts are written with apologetic intent.[71]

The antiquity of the Barbarian Writings is essential to Tatian's concept of their authority and he follows Justin in describing the texts as ancient and, more particularly, as 'older by comparison with the doctrines of the Greeks'.[72] He later acknowledges that describing his ideas as innovative could attract criticism, attributing to his adversaries the comment that: 'Tatian is innovating with his barbarian doctrines, beyond the Greeks and the countless hordes of philosophers.'[73] The argument from antiquity is Tatian's defence against such criticism and, although mentioned only briefly in 29.2, it is developed later at considerable length. There is no reference to the Septuagint legend but in Chapters 31 and 35-41 Tatian puts forward his chronological argument to demonstrate that the Barbarian Writings are older than Greek literature. The argument depends on identifying who the authors of texts are and establishing their relative antiquity. Tatian describes how historical sources show that the most ancient author of the Barbarian Writings is Moses, 'the originator (ἀρχηγός) of all barbarian wisdom', and that he pre-dates the most ancient author in the Greek tradition, Homer, 'the oldest of poets and historians'.[74]

---

67. *Oratio* 29.1.
68. *Oratio* 29.2.
69. Whittaker, *Oratio*, p. xv, reads Tatian's words at face value: 'His own conversion was an intellectual one; he was won over by reading Scriptures.'
70. Justin, *DT* 7-8.
71. J. Engberg, '"From among You Are We. Made, not Born Are Christians": Apologists' Accounts of Conversion before 310 AD', in Ulrich, Jacobsen and Kahlos, eds, *Continuity and Discontinuity*, pp. 49-77: 'the apologists used their accounts of conversion to construct their own identities as converts and Christians and they used them in a deliberate way to make new Christians' (p. 77).
72. *Oratio* 29.2.
73. *Oratio* 35.3.
74. *Oratio* 31.1.

Moses is significant for Tatian's argument because he can be dated from reliable Egyptian sources:

> Egyptian chronological registers are accurate and their records were translated by Ptolemy – not the king but a priest of Mendes. In his account of the acts of the kings, he says that in the time of Amosis king of Egypt the journey took place of the Jews from Egypt to the lands which they entered under the leadership of Moses.[75]

The Exodus therefore took place during the reign of Amosis king of Egypt. Tatian quotes Ptolemy of Mendes as saying that 'Amosis lived at the time of king Inachus'.[76] He says that Inachus was king of Argos and provides a list of the Argive kings to show that he considerably pre-dated Agamemnon, in whose reign Troy was taken.[77] He concludes from this that, 'if Moses lived in the time of Inachus he is four hundred years older than the Trojan War'.[78] The earliest possible date for Homer is that he was contemporary with the Trojan War (the subject of the *Iliad*),[79] so Moses must therefore have pre-dated Homer by a sizeable margin.[80]

Support for this chronological argument does not come from the Barbarian Writings. Tatian uses Greek, Chaldean, Phoenician and Egyptian sources,[81] commenting that such evidence will be the more compelling for his audience: 'As witnesses I will not cite our own people, but will rather make use of Greek supporters. . . . I shall resist you with your own weapons and take from you proofs that are above suspicion.'[82]

Tatian cites a large number of authors, not only as support for his case, but also to press a more general argument for the superiority of the barbarian over the Greek.[83] No fewer than sixteen Greek writers are

---

75. *Oratio* 38.1.
76. Ibid.
77. *Oratio* 39.1.
78. *Oratio* 39.2.
79. *Oratio* 36.1.
80. Tatian draws on the well-established scholarly tradition of synchronising chronologies of different peoples, notably the Jewish, Egyptian and Greek: B.Z. Wacholder, 'Biblical Chronology in the Hellenistic World Chronicles', *HTR*, vol. 61 (1968), pp. 451-81.
81. *Oratio* 31 and 36-38.
82. *Oratio* 31.2.
83. Tatian follows Greek grammarians' practice of quoting lists, in this case of authors, and in Chapter 1 of inventions (discussed below): R.M. Grant, 'Studies in the Apologists', *HTR*, vol. 51 (1958), pp. 123-34, 124.

named in connection with the dating of Homer,[84] all but one of whom[85] are familiar to modern scholarship from other sources[86] and, although for the most part their writings have not survived in anything more than fragments,[87] a number of them are known to have written works relevant to the points at issue, concerned either with Homer[88] or with history.[89] Scholars such as Grant and Droge may well be right in maintaining that Tatian did not consult the works of these writers directly but rather took his information from handbooks.[90] He says nothing about the named writers individually but reference to multiple authorities is no doubt designed to strengthen support for his conclusion. He is, however, highly critical of the Greek writers collectively and the large number of the sources becomes a problematic issue when Tatian asserts that their widely divergent views show that they are both inconsistent and inaccurate.[91] Such criticism of Greek literature notwithstanding, he is still able to use the sources he cites to establish his case for the priority of Moses, since, even though they may disagree with one another, they all concur in the view that Homer considerably postdates the Trojan War and this is the essential first stage of his argument.

Among barbarian sources, Tatian cites Berossus (Chaldean), Theodotus, Hypsicrates and Mochus (Phoenician) and Ptolemy of Mendes (Egyptian). He says Berossus is drawn on as a source by Juba, that Menander of Pergamum wrote on the same subject as the three

---

84. *Oratio* 31.3-4. A first group of five are Theagenes of Rhegium, Stesimbrotus of Thasos, Antimachus of Colophon, Herodotus of Halicarnassus and Dionysius of Olynthus; a second group of four are Ephorus of Cumae, Philochorus of Athens and the Peripatetics, Megaclides and Chameleon; and a final group of seven are Zenodotus, Aristophanes (of Byzantium), Callistratus, Crates (of Mallus), Eratosthenes (of Cyrene), Aristarchus (of Samothrace) and Apollodorus (of Athens).

85. The exception is Dionysius of Olynthus.

86. BNP articles on Theagenes by S. Matthaios, Stesimbrotus and Zenodotus by M. Baumbach, Antimachus by M. Fantuzzi, Herodotus, Ephorus and Philochorus by K. Meister, Megaclides by G. Damaschen, Chameleon by H. Gottschalk, Aristophanes and Callistratus by F. Montanari, Crates by M. Broggiato and Eratosthenes by F. Zaminer and R. Tosi.

87. The historian Herodotus is the notable exception.

88. E.g. BNP for Theagenes and Megaclides.

89. E.g. BNP for Eratosthenes and Herodotus.

90. 'Naturally he took his authorities on the subject from schoolbooks' (Grant, *Greek Apologists*, p. 125); and 'In all probability he put together his list of writers on the date of Homer on the basis of some handbook which dealt with this question' (Droge, *Homer or Moses?*, p. 92).

91. *Oratio* 31.6.

Phoenicians (and so perhaps used them as sources) and that Ptolemy
is used by Apion. It is therefore likely that Tatian only knew the original
writers named through the intermediate sources, Juba, Menander and
Apion.[92] The barbarian authors are praised by Tatian in a way that
those from the Greek tradition are not; Berossus is described as 'a very
able man',[93] the Egyptian chronological records translated by Ptolemy
of Mendes are 'accurate'[94] and Apion is 'a man of high repute'.[95] Thus,
Tatian's account of historical sources enables him to reinforce one of his
main themes – the superiority of the barbarian over the Greek – and to
do so with reference to written sources.

Tatian's argument for the chronological priority of Moses has
inevitably entailed the identification of Moses as an individual; otherwise,
unlike Justin, he refers to none of the authors of the Barbarian Writings
by name. Moses is, however, clearly not the only barbarian author, since
he is described as the leader of a group of 'those who philosophised like
him [Moses]',[96] although the other members of the group are not named.
In the way he describes the antiquity and authorship of the Barbarian
Writings, Tatian follows Justin in echoing the tradition of Ancient
Wisdom, according to which the very earliest thinkers, who flourished
before the advent of the Greek philosophical schools, possessed the
highest level of wisdom.

As well as arguing for the antiquity of the Barbarian Writings, Tatian
maintains that these texts are, in some sense, divine, although there is
nothing in the *Oratio* to parallel Justin's Prophetic Spirit. Tatian does not
give the same emphasis as Justin to the divine nature of the texts. However,
there are echoes of the same sentiment in his – admittedly occasional –
use of forms of the term '$\theta\varepsilon\tilde{\iota}o\varsigma$' (divine). In the important passage in 29.2
referred to above he describes the Barbarian Writings as 'more divine'
($\theta\varepsilon\iota o\tau\acute{\varepsilon}\rho\alpha\iota\varsigma$) than the errors of Greek thought. This theme is not specifically
developed in the *Oratio* and what is meant by labelling texts as divine is
not discussed but allusions to it are found in two other places.

First, Tatian says at one point that: 'It is possible to understand the
details if one does not conceitedly reject the most divinely inspired
[$\theta\varepsilon\iota o\tau\acute{\alpha}\tau\alpha\varsigma$] interpretations, which from time to time have been expressed
in writing and have made those who study them real lovers of God.'[97] The

---

92. Grant, *Greek Apologists*, p. 127.
93. *Oratio* 36.4.
94. *Oratio* 38.1.
95. *Oratio* 38.2.
96. *Oratio* 40.2.
97. *Oratio* 12.4.

Barbarian Writings are not specifically mentioned here, but the passage clearly refers to written texts as divinely inspired and it is most probably the Barbarian Writings that Tatian has in mind. Second, he refers a little later to 'using words of more divine [θειοτέρας] significance'[98] just before he criticises those who decline to take instruction from followers of a 'Barbarian Code of Law'. This last phrase should be taken as a reference to the Barbarian Writings (as will be discussed later), so the term 'divine' used here in relation to 'words' again refers most probably to the Barbarian Writings.

The third source of the authority of the Barbarian Writings, in addition to their antiquity and their divine nature, lies in their general qualities: in the contents of the texts and their style of presentation. Tatian describes what he has learned from his experience as a reader; it is not only the ideas and doctrines in the texts which are significant, but also the way they are written: their simplicity, readability and lack of pretension.

In 29.2 Tatian says that he was persuaded by: 'the lack of arrogance in the wording, the artlessness of the speakers, the easily intelligible account of the creation of the world, the foreknowledge of the future, the remarkable quality of the precepts and the idea of a single ruler of the universe'. The qualities here attributed to the Barbarian Writings are not purely descriptive, but also normative: he says he is *persuaded* by them (μοι πεισθῆναι ταύταις συνέβη). This passage performs several functions: it conveys something about the content of the texts, it provides some evaluation of those contents through the terms of approbation used and it comments, approvingly, on the style of the texts. Tatian describes how the Barbarian Writings deal with 'the creation of the world', they contain prophecies, 'foreknowledge of the future', and moral 'precepts' and they promote the concept of monotheism, 'the idea of a single ruler of the universe'. He uses evaluative terms to express his approbation: the precepts are of 'remarkable quality' and the account of Creation is 'easily intelligible'. He also draws attention to the style of the Barbarian Writings and does so positively, referring to 'the lack of arrogance in the wording' and 'the artlessness of the speakers'. By contrast, Justin did not discuss the style of his authoritative texts, although the fact that his Septuagint legend has them lodged in a prestigious Greek royal library suggests that he regarded them as possessing literary as well as prophetic value.

In his discussion of the Barbarian Writings Tatian echoes some aspects of the way texts are considered in the Greek tradition of literary criticism which was briefly referred to in Chapter 1 above. Some classical literary theorists, notably, Demetrius, Cicero and Quintilian, analysed

---

98.   *Oratio* 12.9.

types of style appropriate to different kinds of literature.[99] Somewhat in contrast to the Second Sophistic emphasis on sophistication and complexity in literary style, these writers all speak approvingly of the Plain Style, when it is used in appropriate circumstances. Demetrius, for instance, describes ordinary diction and clarity of expression as commendable features of the Plain Style; he also highlights these qualities as characteristics of persuasiveness,[100] which suggests that the Plain Style might be particularly apt for apologetic discourse. Tatian's approbation of the simplicity of the Barbarian Writings' style fits well with this strand of literary criticism.

Tatian's comments on the style of the Barbarian Writings reflect in other respects what is found in works of Greek literary criticism. The surviving *oeuvre* of ancient Greek texts is richer in works of theory than in the discussion of specific texts[101] but there are some extant instances of the latter. One is *Oration 52* by the first-century-CE, Greek sophist Dio Chrysostom[102] which compares the three tragedians of ancient Athens, Aeschylus, Euripides and Sophocles. Dio provides a succinct summary of each tragedian's style, contrasting it with the other two; his verdicts on Aeschylus and Euripides are as follows:

> Aeschylus' grandeur and archaic splendour, and the originality of his thought and expression, seemed appropriate to tragedy and the antique manner of heroes; it had nothing subtle, nothing facile, nothing undignified.
>
> Euripides' intelligence and care for every detail – nothing unconvincing or negligent is allowed to pass, and instead of bare facts he gives us the whole force of his eloquence – is the

---

99. Demetrius, *On Style*, in Russell and Winterbottom, *Ancient Literary Criticism*, pp. 171-215, with the Plain Style discussed at pp. 206-8; also in *Ancient Literary Criticism*, extracts from Cicero's works, notably *Brutus* and *De Oratore*, trans. by M. Winterbottom, pp. 216-64, with the Plain Style considered at pp. 240-43, and extracts from Quintilian, *Institutio Oratoria*, trans. by M. Winterbottom, pp. 372-423, with the Plain Style featuring at pp. 413-15.
100. *Ancient Literary Criticism*, Russell and Winterbottom, eds, pp. 210-11.
101. Translations of texts in *Ancient Literary Criticism*, Russell and Winterbottom, eds.
102. Text in Dio Chrysostom, *Discourses 37-60*, trans. by H.L. Crosby, LCL 376 (Cambridge, MA: Harvard University Press, 1946), pp. 338-52; translation in *Ancient Literary Criticism*, Russell and Winterbottom, eds, pp. 504-7. For Dio: G.M.A. Grube, *The Greek and Roman Critics* (London: Methuen, 1965), pp. 327-32. Lampe, *From Paul to Valentinus*, pp. 287-88 and 429, argues for influences from Dio on the *Oratio*.

opposite of Aeschylus' simplicity. This is the style of the man of affairs and the orator; the reader can learn many valuable lessons from it.[103]

Another example of such criticism is the essay on Thucydides by Dionysius of Halicarnassus[104] which examines at length the style of a single writer.[105] Although largely devoted to detailed comments on particular passages, Dionysius also makes more general appraisals of Thucydides, for instance, in describing his diction: 'Its qualities are solidity and compactness, pungency and harshness, gravity, tendency to inspire awe and fear, and above all these the power of stirring the emotions.'[106]

Tatian's description of the style of the Barbarian Writings echoes the kind of succinct appraisal of the qualities of a literary text found in such works. He is discussing the Barbarian Writings as if they were classic texts in the Greek tradition, even though, as will be shown later, he seeks to position them outside, rather than within, that tradition.

The Nature of the Barbarian Writings

Having shown where Tatian locates the authority of the Barbarian Writings, his view of the nature of the texts themselves will now be examined. This involves three issues: which texts comprise the writings; the kind of texts they are; and how the literary tradition of the Barbarian Writings contrasts with that of the Greeks.

Tatian does not present the writings as a clearly defined set of texts. The phrase 'certain Barbarian Writings' (γραφαῖς τισιν βαρβαρικαῖς) in 29.2 is imprecise, particularly with the adjective 'certain' (τισιν) included. No further definition is given and Tatian does not discuss there or elsewhere which texts the term includes. Scholars have tended to treat the term 'Barbarian Writings' as synonymous with the Jewish scriptures – as that phrase is understood today[107] – but it is too simple to assume

---

103. *Ancient Literary Criticism*, Russell and Winterbottom, eds, pp. 505-6.
104. Dating from the first century BCE: BNP article on Dionysius of Halicarnassus by S. Fornaro.
105. Text in Dionysius of Halicarnassus, *Critical Essays: Volume I: Ancient Orators*, ed. by S. Usher, LCL (Cambridge, MA: Harvard University Press, 1974), pp. 462-632: trans. in *Dionysius of Halicarnassus: On Thucydides*, by W.K. Pritchett (Berkeley: University of California, 1975).
106. Pritchett, *Dionysius*, 18 (Chapter 24) (transliterations of Greek words omitted).
107. Grant, 'Tatian and the Bible', pp. 303-5 (using the phrase 'Old Testament'); Droge, *Homer or Moses?*, p. 82 (using the phrase 'Jewish scriptures'); Hunt, *Christianity in the Second Century*, p. 181 (using the phrase 'Hebrew scriptures').

that the two are coterminous. The phrase is perhaps best regarded, not so much as a precise description of a defined set of texts, but rather as a reference to a tradition of writing which contains a number of texts, while lacking clear boundaries.

Even when a reference to a specific scriptural text can be identified, the form in which Tatian accessed it remains unclear. In previous chapters, the prevalence of collections of extracts from texts has been highlighted and, if Tatian was drawing on sources of this kind, they could have contained a mix of material culled from different texts. He may not have been aware himself of the ultimate origin of the material he was using and, indeed, issues of this kind may not have concerned him. What was important may have been that texts emanated from a tradition whose doctrines he had come to accept; and the fact that he does not identify the specific sources of particular ideas may be because it was much more significantly the tradition and not the individual text that mattered to him.

As noted above, the literary tradition of the Barbarian Writings, according to Tatian, originated with Moses, although other, later writers also contributed to it. The origins of the tradition were ancient, but this was not necessarily so of all its components; other writers followed Moses and contributed texts over time. It remained a single tradition, however, and essentially an anonymous one, in which, apart from Moses, authors are not individually identified. Thus, Tatian's presentation differs from that of Justin, in which a number of the prophetic authors are named. Indeed, Tatian's identification of Moses may only have been necessary because the chronological comparison with Homer required it as part of the argument demonstrating the Barbarian Writings' antiquity.

Tatian's very general description in *Oratio* 29.2 of the themes he encountered in the Barbarian Writings provides limited clues to the identity of the texts. He refers to the creation of the world, the foretelling of the future, some precepts of high quality and the doctrine of monotheism. Tatian's description is much broader than Justin's, which was concerned with the authoritative texts as a source of prophecies. Creation indicates the early chapters of Genesis and foretelling the future suggests prophetic texts, although it is not apparent which ones. High-quality precepts and monotheism are both strong themes in the Jewish scriptures but characteristic of a wide range of texts. They could refer, for example, to texts from the Pentateuch, such as the Decalogue, to the Psalms or to those texts which modern scholars classify as prophetic books.

Tatian's use of references to the Barbarian Writings will be considered below and that discussion will provide pointers to the scope of the term. The particular texts which feature in the *Oratio* are determined by the arguments that Tatian presents, so it is apologetic intentions that shape his portrayal of the Barbarian Writings. To anticipate, Tatian will be shown to make clear references to the early chapters of Genesis and to one of the Psalms, to refer to historical texts, prophets and Jewish law codes and also to make allusions to 1 Enoch and to traditions which include works such as Jubilees and 4 Ezra. None of the texts Tatian quotes from or alludes to is, however, considered in detail in the *Oratio* and he does not identify any of the references he makes to specific books.

Tatian's use of the term 'barbarian' in the phrase 'Barbarian Writings' is novel. It was noted in Chapter 2 above that 'barbarian' only appears a few times in Justin's *First Apology* and never in relation to the Books of the Prophecies. While Justin's phrase emphasises the prophetic contents of the texts, Tatian's phrase, 'Barbarian Writings', draws attention to their provenance. The writings are not identified as Jewish; indeed, the terms 'Jew' or 'Jewish' are nowhere used in connection with them;[108] they are attributed simply to barbarians and then not to any particular barbarian people.[109]

There are a number of indications in the *Oratio* which suggest the kind of texts that Tatian considers the Barbarian Writings to be. It is the philosophical that predominates, in contrast to Justin's account of his authoritative texts as prophetic in nature. There are, however, indications that other vocabularies can be applied to the texts – the prophetic, the historical and the legal – and these will be considered first.

Prophecy generally has a very low profile in the *Oratio*, even though in 29.2 Tatian referred to the Barbarian Writings as providing 'foreknowledge of the future'. There are only two other references to texts as prophetic, or at least as having been written by prophets, both very general and difficult to link with particular texts. One is Tatian's description of events as recounted by 'our prophets';[110] the other is where prophets are referred to as providing teaching on the future prospects of humankind: they 'used to foretell the things that the rest of the souls did not know'.[111]

---

108. The only references to the Jews are when Tatian refers to historical events (Nebuchadnezzar's campaigns [*Oratio* 36.3], Solomon's marriage [*Oratio* 37.2] and the Exodus [*Oratio* 38.1]).

109. As happens with the inventions attributed to particular barbarian peoples in *Oratio* 1.

110. *Oratio* 36.3. This probably alludes to Jeremiah (see below).

111. *Oratio* 20.6.

Tatian also suggests on occasion that the Barbarian Writings are historical texts. His chronological argument depends on historical sources that are Chaldean, Phoenician and Egyptian, rather than Jewish, but he does recognise that the latter exist, even though he does not use them: 'As witnesses I will not cite our own people.'[112] There is also a brief reference to Jewish historical writings when Tatian mentions the campaigns of Nebuchadnezzar:

> Berossus, a Babylonian, . . . set out the details of their kings, starting with one of them called Nebuchadnezzar, who campaigned against the Phoenicians and the Jews. We know that these events have been recounted by our prophets and that they occurred much later than the time of Moses, seventy years before the rule of the Persians.[113]

The reference is not specific – Tatian says only that texts exist which were written by 'our prophets' – but probably alludes to the Book of Jeremiah which, while largely comprising prophetic material, also contains some narrative, including an account of the campaign of Nebuchadnezzar against the Jews.[114]

There is a single – extremely unspecific – reference to the Barbarian Writings as legal in character: 'You who do not reject the Scythian Anacharsis even now must not think it beneath you to take instruction from those who adhere to a Barbarian Code of Law [νομοθεσία].'[115] Tatian does not specify the writings he is alluding to here, but the reference is probably to texts from the Pentateuch which contain the Jewish law.[116]

The dominant impression to emerge from the *Oratio* is, however, that the Barbarian Writings are philosophical works. In Tatian's eyes, they are a set of texts which rival, and should supplant, the writings of the Greek philosophical tradition. This is evidenced in two ways. Firstly, the terms Tatian uses to describe both the authors and the contents of the Writings indicate that he regards them as philosophical in nature. Thus, the description of Moses as 'the originator of all barbarian wisdom' (σοφία),[117]

---

112. *Oratio* 31.2.
113. *Oratio* 36.3. The final phrase here no doubt refers to the exile of the Jews to Babylon which according to the Jewish scriptures lasted seventy years: 2 Chronicles 36:21 and Jeremiah 25:11-12.
114. Jeremiah 52.
115. *Oratio* 12.10.
116. The term νομοθεσία appears in the Septuagint at 2 Maccabees 6:23 where it refers to Jewish dietary laws.
117. *Oratio* 31.1.

identifies him as a philosopher and other authors of the Barbarian Writings who followed Moses are described as 'those who philosophised like him'.[118] Philosophical terms are also used to describe ideas: Tatian refers to 'the philosophy which according to you is barbarous',[119] to 'barbarian doctrines [δόγματα]'[120] and, at one point, says that: 'All who wish to philosophise with us are welcome.'[121]

Second, it will be shown below that the Barbarian Writings are used to support Tatian's philosophical arguments, for instance, concerning the creation of the world and the nature of humankind. Tatian uses the Writings to advance his own preferred philosophy as an alternative to those of the Greek schools. This contrasts with Justin's *First Apology* which, although it sometimes criticised Greek philosophy, did not use the ancient prophecies as a tool in philosophical debates, but rather to confront the Graeco-Roman myth-based religion. Tatian does not bring evidence or arguments from the Barbarian Writings to bear when he is criticising the Greeks; they are not mentioned in the passages in which he is attacking Greek philosophy, such as Chapters 2 and 3 where he denigrates philosophers as individuals and ridicules both their behaviour[122] and their ideas.[123] Indeed, the only point at which the Barbarian Writings intersect with Greek philosophy is when Tatian alludes to the theft theory discussed in the previous chapter. Following Justin, he describes how the Greeks imitated, but distorted, what they read in the Barbarian Writings, leading their philosophical schools into erroneous doctrines:

> For with great care their sophists tried to counterfeit all they learned from the teaching of Moses and those who philosophised like him, first in order to be thought to speak with originality, and second in order that, in concealing through rhetorical artifice the things they did not understand, they might distort the truth as mythology.[124]

118. *Oratio* 40.2.
119. *Oratio* 35.2.
120. *Oratio* 35.3.
121. *Oratio* 32.7. Translation here follows Marcovich's admittedly speculative addition of φίλοι which is accepted by Trelenberg but rejected by Nesselrath.
122. E.g. Plato 'was sold by Dionysius because of his gluttony' (*Oratio* 2.1) and Aristotle 'used to fawn in a very uncultured way on that wild young man Alexander' (*Oratio* 2.2).
123. E.g. the way in which 'God is portrayed [by Zeno] as the creator of evil, who lives in sewers and worms and in those who do unmentionable things' (*Oratio* 3.3); and 'I laugh at the old wives' tales of Pherecydes, Pythagoras' takeover of his doctrines . . . and Plato's copying of them' (*Oratio* 3.5).
124. *Oratio* 40.2.

Quotations from the Barbarian Writings

Turning now to the way Tatian makes reference to the Barbarian Writings in the *Oratio*, it is quickly apparent from a reading of the text that he makes very limited use of direct quotations. This is in clear contrast to the way Justin cites prophetic texts. The one clear quotation – 'since they were made for a little while lower than the angels'[125] – is from Psalm 8:5[126] and is introduced in a discussion on the nature of humankind. It is described as a 'saying' (κατὰ τὸν εἰπόντα λόγον),[127] so it is a conscious quotation, although the source is not disclosed. This is the only instance in which Tatian refers to a text from the Jewish scriptures in this way. (On one other occasion a text is described as a 'saying' [τό εἰρημένον]: a Christian text, John 1:5, is cited, 'the darkness does not comprehend the light', but, again, the source of the quotation is not specified.)[128]

The paucity of quotations from the Barbarian Writings is at first sight surprising. Given Tatian's general comments on the nature and qualities of the texts, he might be expected to quote from them extensively.[129] Tatian is known to have been the author of the *Diatessaron*, a harmonisation of the four canonical Gospels, and to have written a work of that kind he must have had a strong interest in the close reading of texts. Moreover, according to Eusebius, Rhodon, a disciple of Tatian, recorded that his teacher produced a book on *Problems*, in which 'he had promised to set out what was obscure and puzzling in Holy Writ',[130] and this also suggests an interest in expounding scriptural texts at a detailed level.

---

125. *Oratio* 15.10.
126. The quotation from Psalm 8 appears in Hebrews 2 so this could be Tatian's source. Hunt's contention (*Christianity in the Second Century*, pp. 43 and 193) that Tatian must have been quoting from the latter since he uses the term 'angels' rather than the 'God' of the original is, however, fallacious because the Septuagint translation of Psalm 8:5 uses the term 'angels'; the Hebrew original (*elohim*) is ambiguous and has been translated both by 'God'/'gods' and by 'angels', but Tatian quotes the Greek text. (For the debate on this, see A.A. Anderson, *The Book of Psalms: Volume 1: Introduction and Psalms 1-72* [London: Oliphants, 1972], p. 103; P.C. Craigie, *Psalms 1-50*, with supplement by M.E. Tate, 2nd edn [Nashville: Thomas Nelson, 2004], p. 108).
127. *Oratio* 15.9.
128. *Oratio* 13.2.
129. Hunt, *Christianity in the Second Century*, p. 54, comments 'despite the reverence Tatian expresses for the Hebrew Scriptures in his conversion account, his allusions to the Old Testament are very sparse'. She does not explore why this is the case.
130. Eusebius, *HE* 5.13.

There are, however, two specific factors that explain the absence of quotations, both of which concern issues touched on already; one is the protreptic character of Tatian's *Oratio* and the other is the Second Sophistic context in which he was writing.

As has been noted, a protreptic work introduces a new philosophy without giving a full account of it. While such a text may contain short references and brief allusions to the foundational texts of the philosophy in question, there are unlikely to be extensive quotations, since detailed consideration of authoritative texts is left for a later occasion. This absence of quotations accords with what is found in Tatian's *Oratio*.

In Chapter 1 above reference was made to the cultural phenomenon known as the Second Sophistic. This did not feature as a significant issue in discussion of Justin's Proof from Prophecy but it is relevant to Tatian's *Oratio*, not least with respect to the use of quotations. Second Sophistic authors are fond of including quotations from and allusions to well-established classic texts, especially the works of Homer, and of treating them in a distinctive way.[131] References are employed for display purposes, to show the author's knowledge and erudition and to give his audience the satisfaction of recognising them. They are not included primarily to advance the author's argument;[132] rather the subject under discussion is used as a prompt to refer to a classic text. Examples of this can be found in the work of Philostratus and Lucian. In his *Lives of the Sophists*, the third-century author Philostratus on a number of occasions cites lines from the classical canon of Greek poetry; he writes, for instance, about Isaeus, the Assyrian sophist, saying:

> He had to represent the Lacedaemonians debating whether they should fortify themselves by building a wall, and he condensed his argument into a few words from Homer: 'And thus shield pressed on shield, helm on helm, man on man. Thus stand fast, Lacedaemonians, these are our fortifications!' (*Iliad* 16.215)[133]

131. For the pervasive influence of Homer: F. Buffière, *Les mythes d'Homère*. For the importance of Homer in elite Roman literary culture: J. Farrell, 'Roman Homer', in R. Fowler, ed., *The Cambridge Companion to Homer* (Cambridge: Cambridge University Press, 2004), pp. 263-69.

132. This was not completely new with the Second Sophistic; Quintilian at the end of the first century CE describes how orators introduce quotations from established classics, both to demonstrate their own erudition and to delight their audiences: Quintilian, *Institutio Oratoria*, 1.8:11-12.

133. Philostratus, *Lives of the Sophists*, ed. by W.C. Wright, LCL 134 (Cambridge, MA: Harvard University Press, 1921), 1.514. Other examples are at 1.521 (*Iliad*

Something similar is found in the work of Tatian's Second Sophistic contemporary, Lucian. Bompaire[134] describes his use of ornamental quotation to confer authority and provide enrichment: 'Their common characteristic is to have no usefulness at all for the narrative development . . . they simply embellish the discourse.'[135] This general observation is supported by Householder's detailed work on Lucian's use of quotations[136] and by Bouquiaux-Simon's analysis of Lucian's Homeric references[137] which are often used merely 'to adorn and enrich the prose of the author'.[138]

The dearth of citations from the Barbarian Writings notwithstanding, Tatian follows Second Sophistic practice in quoting from or alluding to Greek literature on a number of occasions. References to Homer are the commonest; indeed, there are more quotations in the *Oratio* from Homer than from Jewish and Christian writings.[139] Tatian's Homeric references are typically very brief – often only allusions[140] – and they operate as verbal embellishments or rhetorical flourishes which, because of their source, would be recognisable to Tatian's classically-educated audience.

An example is Tatian's quotation of a line from Homer which appears both in the *Iliad* (1.599) and the *Odyssey* (8.326) and describes the laughter of the gods.[141] In both cases the laughter is prompted by the actions of Hephaestus, the god of fire, but these Homeric circumstances bear no relation to the subject matter of the *Oratio* at the point the reference is made, where Tatian is describing the delight taken by demons in the destructive impact of fate on humankind. Homer's reference is not

---

16.40), 1.539 (*Iliad* 10.535), 1.542 (*Iliad* 9.312), 1.544 (Hesiod, *Works and Days* 25), 2.558 (*Odyssey* 4.498) and 2.580 (*Odyssey* 3.1).

134. J. Bompaire, *Lucien écrivain: imitation et création* (Paris: de Bocard, 1958), pp. 382-404.

135. Ibid., p. 389.

136. F.W. Householder, *Literary Quotation and Allusion in Lucian* (New York: Columbia University Press, 1941), pp. 41-55, for summary tables.

137. O. Bouquiaux-Simon, *Les lectures homériques de Lucien* (Bruxelles: Palais des Académies, 1968), especially pp. 352-74.

138. Ibid., p. 358.

139. Whittaker, *Oratio*, p. 87, lists fourteen quotations from the Iliad and two from the Odyssey, one line appearing identically in both.

140. S. Freund, '"Und wunderbar sind auch eure Dichter, die da lügen . . ." (Tat., orat. 22,7): Beobachtungen zu Gestalt, Auswahl und Funktion von Dichterzitaten in der griechischen Apologetik am Beispiel Tatians', in C. Schubert and A. von Stockhausen, eds, *Ad veram religionem reformare: frühchristliche Apologetik zwischen Anspruch und Wirklichkeit* (Erlangen: Erlangen Forschungen, 2006), pp. 97-121.

141. *Oratio* 8.1.

concerned with fate; it is not relevant to Tatian's argument and is only included for reasons of rhetorical display. The same can be said of one clear allusion to Plato in the *Oratio*: 'The soul's wings are the perfect spirit, but the soul cast it away because of sin, fluttered like a nestling and fell to the ground',[142] which uses a metaphor from a passage in the *Phaedrus*,[143] where Plato is discussing the nature of the soul. This colourful image is introduced for the same rhetorical reasons as the Homeric quotations; there is no connection between Tatian's argument and the argument in *Phaedrus* at this point and, indeed, there cannot be, since Plato is arguing for the immortality of the soul, which is not a doctrine Tatian shares.

Tatian's quotations from classical authors depend, like those of Second Sophistic writers, on the audience's prior familiarity with the texts from which the quotations are drawn. He does not, however, quote similarly from the Barbarian Writings; indeed, there would be no point in doing so since these texts were unfamiliar to his audience; they were not part of the common culture of educated Greeks, so any references would fall on deaf ears.

Tatian's Use of the Barbarian Writings

The Barbarian Writings are, however, far from irrelevant to Tatian's arguments and in sections such as Chapters 4-7 and 12-15, where he is putting forward his own philosophical ideas, they are an important source on which he draws. He uses the Barbarian Writings in a number of ways: by including brief phrases from the texts, too short to be termed quotations, by alluding to ideas that can be traced to specific sources and by using less precise references which can only be related more generally to a textual tradition. Tatian's use of these techniques will be examined with reference to the main issues addressed in the *Oratio*: the nature of Creation, the nature of humankind, the fall of angels and humankind and the Eschaton (unlike Justin, he is not concerned with demonstrating the status of Jesus Christ). Tatian's references may be brief and their sources may never be identified or acknowledged, but they play an important part in the *Oratio*.

Two brief phrases from Genesis 1 are especially important to Tatian: 'in the beginning' (ἐν ἀρχῇ) (Genesis 1:1); and 'the image and likeness of God' (εἰκών καὶ ὁμοίωσις τοῦ θεοῦ) (Genesis 1:26-27).[144]

---

142. *Oratio* 20.2. Identified in Marcovich, *Oratio*, p. 41, n., and Hunt, *Christianity in the Second Century*, p. 214.
143. Plato, *Phaedrus*, 246C.
144. Tatian uses slightly different formulations at different points; the quotation

The Nature of Creation

'In the beginning', and Genesis 1, more generally, are central to Tatian's account of Creation. The nature of primal Creation was a much-discussed topic in the Greek philosophical tradition with differing accounts put forward by the various schools, such as the Platonists, the Peripatetics and the Stoics. The debates on this issue cannot be considered in detail here[145] but one perspective which the Greek schools all shared was that the process of creation entailed the ordering of pre-existing matter. As Sedley puts it: 'That even a divine creator would, like any craftsman, have to use pre-existing materials is an assumption that the ancient Greeks apparently never questioned.'[146] Tatian's doctrine, which was at variance with this, can be characterised as *Creatio ex nihilo* (creation out of nothing):[147] in other words, before Creation matter did not exist at all. His use of the phrase 'in the beginning' therefore serves to stress that divine creation of the cosmos was the beginning and that matter did not have any existence before that.

Tatian describes in *Oratio* 4.3 how the monotheistic God is the sole existing being prior to Creation, forming the universe out of nothing: 'Our God has no origin in time; he alone is without beginning and is himself the beginning of all things.' The phrase 'in the beginning' is then quoted explicitly and prominently at the commencement of 5.1 where Tatian states that 'God was in the beginning' and this is soon followed by 'The Lord of all things, himself the foundation of the whole, was alone in relation to the creation which had not yet come into being.' Shortly afterwards, at 5.6, the Word is described as begotten 'in the beginning'. Thus, the phrase from Genesis 1:1 is used to support Tatian's argument

here is from *Oratio* 15.3. The standard Septuagint text has 'καὶ εἶπεν ὁ Θεός, ποιήσωμεν ἄνθρωπον κατ' εἰκόνα ἡμετέραν καὶ καθ' ὁμοίωσιν': *Septuaginta, Vetus Testamentum Graecum: Vol. I: Genesis*, ed. by J.W. Wevers (Göttingen: Vandenhoeck & Ruprecht, 1974) ('And God said: "Let us make humankind according to our image and according to likeness"', *NETS*).

145. Sedley, *Creationism*, surveys the field. In Tatian's own time the issue of creation was actively debated by philosophers, with contributions from prominent figures such as Calvernus Taurus and Atticus, who both wrote commentaries on Plato's *Timaeus*: Dillon, *Middle Platonists*, pp. 242-46 and 252-57.

146. Sedley, *Creationism*, p. xvii.

147. Tatian is credited with being the first Christian writer explicitly to adopt the *creatio ex nihilo* position: May, *Creatio ex Nihilo*, pp. 148-54. May acknowledges that Basilides had previously advanced a *creatio ex nihilo* argument but regards him as a Gnostic and so not (in his terms) a Christian theologian (*Creatio ex Nihilo*, pp. 62-84). It was not inevitable that Christian writers would interpret Genesis 1 along *creatio ex nihilo* lines; others, e.g. Justin, took a different view: May, *Creatio ex Nihilo*, pp. 120-33.

that the act of Creation was the beginning of the existence of the cosmos, that matter did not have any form of existence before that and is critical for distinguishing his view from those of the Greek philosophical schools.[148]

Tatian's Creation account is not in the form of a narrative and, therefore, is unlike Genesis 1 in which the process of creation takes place over six days. His ideas are expressed through abstract argument, so it is less obvious that Genesis is a source than if he had referred to actual events in the Creation narrative. Two factors pointing to the importance of Genesis for Tatian are, first, references to the concept of separation and, second, a close semantic connection between *Oratio* 4 and Genesis 1. First, he describes how God originally created matter as raw and formless and, then, by a process of separation, formed it into heavens, stars and earth: 'it [matter] should be thought of partly as raw and formless before its separation [using διάκρῖσις] and partly as organised and orderly after its division. So by this process of division [using διαίρεσις], the heavens are created from matter, and also the stars in the heavens'.[149] The concept of separation also appears in Tatian's description of the creation of the Word by God: 'He [the Word] came into being by separation [using μερισμός], not by section'.[150] These references reflect the way Genesis 1 describes the creation of the cosmos as a series of acts of separation, of light from darkness, of waters below from waters above, and of earth from seas; Tatian does not, however, use the Septuagint verb for 'to separate', διαχωρίζειν,[151] so the connection between his *Oratio* and Genesis 1 is one of ideas, not semantics.

The second link which can be detected between the *Oratio* and Genesis 1 is a semantic one, however, and this is the similarity between Tatian's adjacent use of two terms, the comparatively rare 'κατασκευαστής' (constructor) and 'ἀόρατος' (invisible),[152] and the Septuagint wording of Genesis 1:2: 'ἀόρατος καὶ ἀκατασκεύαστος'.[153] In both cases these terms occur together at a point where Creation is being discussed. In *Oratio* 4.3 the sentence which follows begins: 'We know him [God] through his creation'; while in Genesis the phrase occurs in the description of

148. The phrase ἐν ἀρχῇ appears only once in the *Timaeus* (28B 5), the key Platonic text on the creation of the cosmos, and then not with reference to primal creation (TLG search).

149. *Oratio* 12.2.

150. *Oratio* 5.3.

151. Genesis 1:4, 7, 14 and 18.

152. *Oratio* 4.3. There are only 24 other occurrences of κατασκευαστής in the whole TLG Corpus (TLG search).

153. Translated as 'invisible and unformed' in *NETS*.

the state of the earth at the outset of primal Creation. The similarity of theme here strengthens the suggestion that in 4.3 Tatian was echoing – consciously or not – the wording of Genesis 1:2.

In view of the points made here, Hunt's contention that 'The cosmology that Tatian presents in his *Oration* displays no direct dependence upon the Biblical account'[154] cannot be upheld. She further maintains that allusions which have been read here as references to Genesis 1 refer instead to John 1, which also commences with the phrase 'in the beginning'. [155] It would probably be wrong to treat this as a binary issue – either Genesis or John – since Tatian may be referring simultaneously to both texts. He is discussing primal Creation – highlighted as a key theme of the Barbarian Writings in *Oratio* 29.2 – and then moves on to consider the Creation and the Fall – also themes in the early chapters of Genesis – but the incarnation of the Word which is a prime concern of John 1 is not discussed or alluded to by Tatian. All of this strongly suggests that it is much more Genesis than John that he has in mind.

The Nature of Humankind

The phrase 'image and likeness of God' from Genesis 1:26-27 is central to Tatian's account of humankind. The nature of the human soul and psyche was a long-established issue of debate in Greek philosophy, with different traditions – such as the Platonic, the Stoic and the Epicurean – advancing diverse views.[156] In the second century CE these issues were still the subject of lively discussion and disagreement (which cannot be considered in detail here)[157] and Tatian presents his view of the human soul against this contemporary philosophical background.

---

154. Hunt, *Christianity in the Second Century*, p. 71.
155. Hunt, *Christianity in the Second Century*, pp. 126-27.
156. The classic Platonist account of the tripartite soul is found in Plato's *Republic*: Plato, *Republic*, ed. by C. Emlyn-Jones and W. Preddy, LCL, 2 vols (Cambridge, MA: Harvard University Press, 2013); a second-century CE textbook view of Platonism is Alcinous, *The Handbook of Platonism*, especially Chapters 23-25. For brief summaries of the Stoic position: Sellars, *Stoicism*, pp. 81-106; and the Epicurean: C. Gill, 'Psychology', in J. Warren, ed., *The Cambridge Companion to Epicureanism* (Cambridge: Cambridge University Press, 2009), pp. 125-41.
157. Trapp, *Philosophy in the Roman Empire*, pp. 98-133. At the risk of over-simplification, the Platonist tradition held to a tripartite soul and the Stoic tradition to a unitary soul, so in advancing a doctrine of a bipartite soul, Tatian was at variance with both. An example of a second-century-CE philosopher discussing the nature of the soul is Albinus: Dillon, *Middle Platonists*, pp. 290-98.

Tatian argues that humankind was originally created with two kinds of spirit, a soul and a higher spirit, and that the higher spirit accorded human beings immortality; after primal Creation this was lost and they became merely mortal. 'Image and likeness of God' is Tatian's description of the original higher spirit and is critical to his account;[158] he refers to it no fewer than four times. In the first instance, humankind is described as a spiritual being originally endowed with 'two different kinds of spirits, one of which is called the soul, and the other is greater than the soul; it is the image and likeness of God. The first men were endowed with both.'[159] In the second case, Tatian employs a compressed form of the phrase, 'image and likeness of God', to make the point that, when the more powerful, or higher, spirit departed from humankind, it became mortal: 'The creature who was made in the image of God, when the more powerful spirit left him, became mortal.'[160] In the third instance, when Tatian is again describing the nature of humankind, he says that 'humankind alone is "the image and likeness of God"', adding that the human being is 'not one who behaves like the animals, but who has advanced far beyond his humanity towards God himself'.[161] In the fourth reference, Tatian poses the question, what does the phrase 'divine image and likeness' mean? His long explanation demonstrates the importance of the phrase for him:

> What is not capable of comparison is Being itself, but what is capable of comparison is nothing other than what is similar. The perfect God is fleshless, but humankind is flesh. The bond of the flesh is the soul, but it is the flesh which contains the soul. If such a structure is like a temple, God is willing to dwell in it through his representative, the spirit.[162]

The Fall of Humankind and the Fall of the Rebel Angels
Other than when discussing Creation and the nature of humankind, Tatian's references to the Barbarian Writings are less direct and better described as allusions. In two instances, the allusions are sufficiently explicit to be traceable to specific texts: the fall of humankind and the fall

---

158. Hunt, *Christianity in the Second Century*, p. 136, acknowledges that 'Tatian's understanding of the creation of man is clearly influenced by *Genesis*, since he states that the Word made man "in the likeness of the Father"' but she does not discuss the issue further.
159. *Oratio* 12.1.
160. *Oratio* 7.5.
161. *Oratio* 15.3.
162. *Oratio* 15.4-5.

of the rebel angels; in two other cases, however, the allusions are more generally to literary traditions rather than specific texts: the creation of angels and the Eschaton. Greek philosophical schools did not address issues such as these and the sources for Tatian's ideas must therefore be sought within the Jewish tradition.

The two traceable allusions are found in *Oratio* 7 where the fall of humankind and the fall of angels are discussed. The second and third chapters of Genesis are a source for the fall of humankind, although not an explicit one; Tatian does not refer to the Genesis narrative and there is no mention of Adam and Eve. The fall of angels is not mentioned in Genesis and Tatian's source for this is most likely 1 Enoch.[163]

In discussing the fall of humankind, Tatian includes two key ideas which can be traced back to Genesis 2-3. The first is his assertion that, as originally created, humankind possessed free will[164] and that this was an essential contributory factor leading to the Fall: 'Now the Word before he made humankind created angels, and each of the two forms of creation has free will. . . . This was in order that the one who was bad might be justly punished, since he had become wicked through his own fault.'[165] A connection can be detected here with the narrative in Genesis 3, which describes how acts of disobedience, first, by Eve and, then, by Adam, in both cases freely undertaken, lead to their expulsion by God from the Garden of Eden. Genesis does not use the language of free will but Tatian's comment can be read as a second-century Christian interpretation of the underlying meaning of the narrative in Genesis 3, echoing the notion (also found in Philo[166]) that the exercise of human free will was responsible for the Fall.

The second key idea traceable to Genesis 2-3 is Tatian's contention that the Fall led to the loss of the higher spirit which was originally present in humankind and so to the loss of primal human immortality; he says that: 'The creature who was made in the image of God, when the more powerful spirit left him, became mortal.'[167] This echoes Genesis

---

163. As noted above, Grant's contention that there are explicit references to Genesis 2-3 is hard to credit, particularly as the allusions can be read more plausibly as referring to 1 Enoch (see below).

164. Hunt, *Christianity in the Second Century*, p. 137, identifies free will as an essential component of Tatian's account of 'Man' but does not point to any link with Genesis 2-3.

165. *Oratio* 7.2.

166. Philo, *Questions on Genesis*, 1.55, commentary on Genesis 3:22 (Hunt, *Christianity in the Second Century*, p. 214, n. 177). This is not to suggest that Tatian knew Philo's work.

167. *Oratio* 7.5.

3:3, in which, although the concept of the loss of the higher spirit is not present, the loss of immortality is described as the consequence of disobedience in the Garden of Eden: 'but of the fruit of the tree that is in the middle of the orchard, God said, "You shall not eat of it nor shall you even touch it, lest you die."'[168]

The fall of the rebel angels is briefly described by Tatian in the passage translated by Whittaker as: 'The demons had to move house, and those created first were banished, the former were cast down from heaven, the latter from not this earth, but one better ordered than here.'[169] The meaning of this passage has generated controversy; Hunt argued against Whittaker that οἱ μὲν and οἱ δὲ should be rendered by 'some' and 'others' rather than 'the former' and 'the latter',[170] a reading supported by the two most recent translators of the text, Trelenberg and Nesselrath.[171] Thus, Hunt's rendering is: 'The demons had to move house, for those who were created first have been banished; some have been cast down from heaven, whilst others [have been cast down] not from this earth, but from [one] better ordered than here.'[172] Although the meaning of the passage remains ambiguous, Hunt's translation is, on balance, to be preferred. VanderKam's comment that 'all is not pellucid' here is therefore well-judged. He is also perceptive in maintaining that the first part of the sentence is a clear reference to the contents of 1 Enoch: 'the parallelism – the demons driven to another abode which is then equated with being cast from heaven – shows that the beings whom Tatian called demons are the angels of 1 Enoch 6-16'.[173]

The fall of the rebel angels is not part of the Genesis narrative but an account of it is found in 1 Enoch 6-11,[174] a text related to Genesis 6-9 – and, more specifically, to Genesis 6:1-4[175] – although containing much additional material. In brief, 1 Enoch 6-11 describes two myths: first, how fallen angels led by Shemihazah came down from heaven to

---

168. *NETS*.
169. *Oratio* 20.3.
170. Hunt, *Christianity in the Second Century*, p. 134.
171. Trelenberg, *Oratio*, p. 139; Nesselrath, *Gegen falsche Götter*, p. 77 (both using the phrases '*die einen*' and '*die anderen*').
172. Hunt, *Christianity in the Second Century*, p. 134.
173. J.C. VanderKam, '1 Enoch, Enochic Motifs, and Enoch in Early Christian Literature', in J.C. VanderKam and W. Adler, eds, *The Jewish Apocalyptic Heritage in Early Christianity* (Assen: Van Gorcum, 1996), pp. 33-101, 65.
174. *1 Enoch 1: A Commentary on the Book of 1 Enoch, Chapters 1-36, 81-108*, by G.W. Nickelsburg, ed. by K. Baltzer (Minneapolis: Fortress Press, 2001), pp. 165-228.
175. Ibid., p. 166.

earth and married human women and how their offspring then brought
sin and evil to the world; and, second, how Asael brought knowledge
from heaven down to earth and again how this brought evil into the
world. Both Shemihazah and Asael are banished and imprisoned until,
at God's command, archangels intervene. Tatian does not follow the 1
Enoch narrative and his reference is brief and allusive. The importance
of Enoch for early Christianity has, however, long been appreciated,[176]
although its significance for Tatian has not generally been recognised,[177]
but VanderKam's contention that the reference in the *Oratio* is to 1 Enoch
makes for a powerful case.

   Tatian alludes here to a source outside Genesis but from elsewhere in
the Jewish literary tradition.[178] Modern scholarship regards Chapters 1-36
of 1 Enoch as a Hellenistic work completed by the third century BCE.[179]
However, the text presents itself as the work of an ancient figure, Enoch,
who also appears in Genesis 5.[180] The named author is prominent in the
narrative of 1 Enoch, with Chapters 12-36 a first-person account of his
exploits. In the second century CE it is most likely that the text bearing
Enoch's name would have been regarded as of ancient provenance and so
it is unsurprising to find a Christian author such as Tatian treating it as
both ancient and authoritative.

The Creation of Angels and the Eschaton
In addition to these two traceable allusions – to the fall of humankind
and the fall of the rebel angels – the *Oratio* contains two allusions that
relate more generally to Jewish literary tradition, rather than to specific
texts. The first is the brief mention of the creation of angels: 'Now
the Word before he made humankind created angels.'[181] The creation
of angels does not appear in Genesis 1, although it features in later

---

176. H.J. Lawlor, 'Early Citations from the Book of Enoch', *Journal of Philology*, vol.
    25 (1897), pp. 164-225; J.C. VanderKam, *Enoch: A Man for All Generations*
    (Columbia: University of South Carolina Press, 1995); A.Y. Reed, *Fallen Angels
    and the History of Judaism and Christianity: The Reception of Enochic Literature*
    (Cambridge: Cambridge University Press, 2005). The New Testament letter of
    Jude, vv. 14-15, explicitly cites (and names) Enoch.
177. Lawlor, 'Early Citations from the Book of Enoch', and Nickelsburg, *1 Enoch 1*,
    pp. 82-108 (review of its influence on early Christian writings) do not mention
    Tatian.
178. Reed, *Fallen Angels*, p. 175, suggests that Tatian's knowledge of Enoch came via
    Justin rather than directly.
179. Nickelsburg, *1Enoch 1*, p. 7.
180. Nickelsburg, *1Enoch 1*, p. 71.
181. *Oratio* 7.2.

Jewish works. Reference was made in Chapter 1 to the 'Rewritten Bible' tradition which was a feature of Hellenistic-Jewish literature. It is not possible to know which texts Tatian knew but the Book of Jubilees, which retells the Genesis 1 Creation narrative and is an example of this tradition, adds the creation of angels on the first day to the Genesis account.[182] Tatian therefore probably refers here either to Jubilees or to some other Jewish development of the Genesis tradition.[183] Jubilees is regarded by modern scholarship as a Hellenistic-Jewish work, dated to the second century BCE.[184] However, it presents itself as the work of Moses, to whom the account of Creation is dictated by an angel at the behest of God on Mount Sinai.[185] The text emphasises Moses' authorship and, as with 1 Enoch, it seems most likely that in the second century CE it would have been regarded as of ancient provenance; so, again, it is unsurprising that a Christian author such as Tatian would treat it as authoritative.

Discussion of the fate of humankind at the end of the world is the other instance where Tatian appears to owe a debt to Jewish literary tradition, even if his sources cannot be precisely identified. His ideas are not expressed in sufficient detail to link them with specific Jewish texts. However, Tatian's use of 1 Enoch as a source has already been noted and, since it is primarily an eschatological text,[186] Tatian may well be drawing on it or, more generally, on texts from Jewish eschatological tradition.[187]

Tatian affirms his belief in a bodily resurrection and a last judgement, 'our examiner is God, the creator himself',[188] and he links the Eschaton to original Creation in two respects. First, he contends that bodily death will take human beings back to their state before birth, saying that: 'it was through my birth that I, previously non-existent, came to believe that I did exist. In the same way, when I who was born cease to exist through death and am seen no more, I shall again be as in my

---

182. *The Book of Jubilees*, ed. J.C. VanderKam, 2 vols (Leuven: Peeters, 1989), 2, 2.2.

183. The practice of retelling the Genesis 1 account, but with changes, is found, e.g., in 4 Ezra: *Fourth Ezra: A Commentary on the Book of Fourth Ezra*, ed. by M.E. Stone (Minneapolis: Fortress Press, 1990), pp. 178-89.

184. VanderKam, ed., *Jubilees*, 2, V-VI.

185. Ibid., 2, 1.27 and 2.1.

186. Nickelsburg, *1 Enoch 1*, p. 37.

187. For discussion of this tradition: C. Rowland, *The Open Heaven: A Study of Apocalyptic in Judaism and Early Christianity* (London: SPCK, 1982); VanderKam and Adler, eds, *The Jewish Apocalyptic Heritage in Early Christianity*.

188. *Oratio* 6.2.

previous state of non-existence before birth.'[189] Second, he describes the immortal life which humankind can attain after death as a restoration of the union of soul and spirit which existed in humankind at the primordial stage before the Fall, arguing that: 'we have learned things we did not know through prophets who were convinced that the spirit together with the soul would obtain the heavenly garment of mortality – immortality – and used to foretell the things that the rest of the souls did not know'.[190]

Linking Creation to the Eschaton in this way is a feature of 1 Enoch and of other Jewish texts which influenced early Christianity.[191] The main theme of 1 Enoch is the coming judgement of God and it links the initiation of evil soon after Creation with its eradication at the end of the world.[192] Tatian's statements cannot be specifically linked with that text. However, another work, 4 Ezra 6, which connects Creation with the last judgement, also links the concept of God as creator with that of God as judge.[193] Like 1 Enoch, the influence of 4 Ezra on early Christian writings is well-attested and it could have been among Tatian's sources.[194] As with 1 Enoch and Jubilees, 4 Ezra is regarded by modern scholarship as a late Hellenistic-Jewish work, probably as late as the first century CE.[195] However, its putative author, Ezra, who features prominently in the text, presents himself as an ancient figure located in Babylon during the exile in the sixth century BCE[196] where he has a series of visions.[197] Thus, it seems likely that in the second-century-CE 4 Ezra would have been regarded as an ancient text. Tatian's direct dependence on particular works cannot be demonstrated but his discussion of the Eschaton appears to owe a debt to traditions that include texts such as 1 Enoch and 4 Ezra.

---

189. *Oratio* 6.3.

190. *Oratio* 20.6.

191. Rowland, *Open Heaven*, pp. 146-55.

192. Nickelsburg, *1 Enoch 1*, p. 37: 'The mythic materials conflated in chaps. 6-11 constitute a narrative that begins with an explanation of the origins of certain types of evil in the world and ends by anticipating its eradication on a purified earth among a righteous humanity.'

193. J.A. Moo, *Creation, Nature and Hope in 4 Ezra* (Göttingen: Vandenhoeck & Ruprecht, 2011), p. 45.

194. Stone, *Fourth Ezra*, pp. 1-2 and 43.

195. Dated between the fall of Jerusalem in 70 CE and a reference in a work of Clement of Alexandria c. 190 CE, the most likely date being the reign of Domitian 81-96 CE: Stone, *Fourth Ezra*, pp. 9-10.

196. 4 Ezra 3.1: 'In the thirtieth year after the destruction of our city, I Salathiel, who am also called Ezra, was in Babylon' (Stone, *Fourth Ezra*, p. 53).

197. Stone, *Fourth Ezra*, pp. 50-51.

Christian Texts

Tatian occasionally alludes to texts which have since become part of the Christian New Testament. As a general rule, such allusions are outside the scope of this book. They do, however, have some relevance since Tatian uses New Testament citations and allusions to support his Jewish scriptural references rather than to make separate and independent arguments. Thus, when describing God the creator, he adds, in explanation, the phrase 'God is spirit' from John 4:24 to support his contention that God existed before there was matter and that God was in fact the cause of the existence of matter: 'God is spirit, not pervading matter, but the maker of material spirits and of the forms that are in matter.'[198] Then, a little later, while making his argument that the invisible and impalpable God is known through his creation, he adds in support an allusion to Romans 1:20: 'what is invisible in his power we understand through what he has made.'[199] Later still, in his account of the nature of humankind in the divine image and likeness, Tatian claims that, while God is fleshless and humankind is flesh: 'the bond of the flesh is the soul, but it is the flesh which contains the soul.'[200] Here he draws support from allusions to 1 and 2 Corinthians and Ephesians, which refer to the human being as the temple of God:[201] 'If such a structure is like a temple [ναὸς], God is willing to dwell in it through his representative, the spirit.'[202]

Given the way that the Christian texts are used here in support of Jewish scriptural references, it is not impossible that they could, in Tatian's eyes, also fall within the scope of the term 'Barbarian Writings'. It was noted earlier that Tatian sets up a dichotomy between two competing cultures, the Greek and the barbarian, and, if the Christian writings are not part of Greek culture, which they are not in the way Tatian uses the term, then they would have to be part of the barbarian alternative. Arguments have also been made earlier for the prevalence of collections of extracts from authoritative texts in the second century and, if Tatian was accessing such sources, they could have contained not only material from a variety of Jewish texts, but also extracts from Christian writings which amplify or comment on the more ancient material. This contention is somewhat speculative. However, two factors lend some credence to the argument: first, the fluid nature of Tatian's presentation of the Barbarian Writings

---

198. *Oratio* 4.3.

199. *Oratio* 4.3.

200. *Oratio* 15.4.

201. 1 Corinthians 3:16 and 6:19, 2 Corinthians 6:16 and Ephesians 2:21-22: see Whittaker, *Oratio*, p. 30; Marcovich, *Oratio*, p. 33.

202. *Oratio* 15.5.

as lacking strict boundaries and, second, his citation of allusions from Christian texts to support points being made on the basis of the Jewish scriptures.

Tatian's Method for Using the Scriptures

Tatian's use of references to the Barbarian Writings leads him to adopt a particular method for presenting his arguments which is very different from that of Justin. Whereas in the *First Apology*'s Proof from Prophecy each text was set beside its explanatory interpretation, in the *Oratio* quotations and allusions are incorporated seamlessly into the text. There is an example of this in Chapter 15 where Tatian is giving an account of aspects of the nature of the human soul. At three points in the chapter, he injects a reference to substantiate his argument (italicised in the extracts below). First, discussing the nature of humankind in general, he claims: 'Humankind is not, as the croakers teach, a rational being capable of intelligence and understanding . . . but humankind alone is *the image and likeness of God*.'[203] Second, when explaining how the divine spirit can inhabit the human soul, he says: 'The perfect God is fleshless, but humankind is flesh. The bond of the flesh is the soul, but it is the flesh which contains the soul. If such a structure is like a *temple*, *God* is willing to *dwell* in it through his representative, the *spirit*.'[204] Third, when discussing the position of humankind after the Fall, Tatian says that:

> after their loss of immortality human beings have overcome death by death in faith, and through repentance they have been given a calling, according to the saying, *since they were made for a little while lower than the angels*. It is possible for everyone defeated to win another time, if he rejects the constitution making for death.[205]

The references are incorporated into the text, although differently in each case. In the first, a brief quotation from Genesis 1 is included to register the point Tatian wishes to make; in the second, words are added which allude to 1 Corinthians 3; while, in the third, a lengthier quotation, from Psalm 8, is melded into the text. In all three cases, however, the reference is used to bolster the argument and, indeed, is made part of it, and the text moves seamlessly from Tatian's words into

---

203. *Oratio* 15.3.
204. *Oratio* 15.4-5.
205. *Oratio* 15.9-10.

the scriptural reference and back out again into Tatian's words. There is an obvious contrast here with the Second Sophistic use of quotations described above.

Barbarian Writings and Barbarian Culture

The uses which Tatian makes of the Barbarian Writings have now been examined in detail. It has become clear that, despite initial appearances to the contrary, he does in fact refer to them extensively in his arguments. Stepping back from the detail focusses attention on the term 'barbarian' itself – part of the phrase 'Barbarian Writings' – which Tatian uses in a broader sense to refer not just to texts but to a whole culture. Discussion of the wider cultural issues involved here prompts examination of Tatian's *Oratio* in the context of the Graeco-Roman literary culture of the time.

In Greek culture, there was a dichotomy between Greek and barbarian, with the presumption that what was Greek was superior to what was barbarian.[206] The reality is, however, more complex, for in Greek literature attitudes towards barbarians were not necessarily characterised by simple opposition and antagonism.[207] Strong criticism of aspects of Greek culture is found within its own literary tradition, in the work of Lucian, for instance, who satirised particular individuals and cultural practices,[208] including philosophy,[209] while there could also be considerable admiration for aspects of barbarian culture, the so-called *laudatio barbarorum*.[210] Gruen's careful analysis of some key

---

206. A classic account of Graeco-Roman attitudes to barbarians is provided by Y.A. Dauge, *Le Barbare: Recherche sur la conception romaine de la barbarie et de la civilisation* (Brussels: Latomus, 1981).

207. An example of such complexity is found in the second-century Greek writer Lucian's 'True History': Lucian, *Selected Dialogues*, trans. by D. Costa (Oxford: Oxford University Press, Oxford 2005), pp. 203-33. The narrator meets Homer who reveals himself to be from Babylon and therefore a barbarian, which is ironical since he is the seminal figure in Greek literary culture; Lucian comments that barbarians may more perfectly acquire Greek *paedeia* than Greeks: H.-G. Nesselrath, 'Two Syrians and Greek Paideia: Lucian and Tatian', in G.A. Xenis, ed., *Literature, Scholarship, Philosophy and History: Classical Studies in Memory of Ioannis Taifacos* (Stuttgart: Franz Steiner Verlag, 2015), pp. 129-42, 131-33.

208. C.P. Jones, *Culture and Society in Lucian* (Cambridge, MA: Harvard University Press, 1986).

209. An example is 'Hermotimus or On the Philosophical Schools', Lucian's longest text, in which Lycinus persuades Hermotimus of the folly of following any philosophy (Lucian, *Selected Dialogues*, pp. 88-128). See also C. Robinson, *Lucian and His Influence in Europe* (London: Duckworth, 1979).

210. J.H. Waszink, 'Some Observations on the Appreciation of "The Philosophy of

texts has shown that Greek attitudes towards the 'other' – which includes barbarians – were far more nuanced than simple stereotyping of the concepts Greek and barbarian would suggest.[211]

The term 'barbarian' came to be applied to early Christianity by Graeco-Roman writers and early Christian authors responded to this accusation. Antonova has charted this phenomenon through a succession of authors (including Tatian) from the second to the fourth century[212] and has demonstrated how varied and complex were Christian authors' responses to the charge of barbarism. In the case of Tatian's *Oratio*, references to barbarian are wholly praiseworthy. He writes admiringly of barbarian culture and disparagingly of Greek, without equivocation. In the last chapter it was shown how Justin, in his *First Apology*, expressed some criticisms of Greek philosophy and used his citations of prophecies as a basis for attacking Graeco-Roman mythological religion; in the *Oratio* Tatian launches a much broader assault on Graeco-Roman culture as a whole, including its myth-based religion and its philosophical traditions, but extending far beyond them.

At the beginning of the *Oratio* Tatian argues that many important inventions and discoveries are actually barbarian rather than Greek innovations and these cover a wide range, including geometry, history, the alphabet, sculpture, music, astronomy and magic, divination and the cult of sacrifice.[213] Later in the text considerable space is devoted to hostile accounts of other aspects of Greek culture, including sorcery and medicine,[214] acting and mime,[215] drama and music[216] and gladiatorial shows.[217] In the early chapters of the *Oratio* aspects

---

     the Barbarians" in Early Christian Literature', in L.J. Engels et al., eds, *Mélanges offerts à Mademoiselle Christine Mohrmann* (Utrecht: Spectrum, 1963), pp. 41-56; and Droge, *Homer or Moses?*, pp. 88-91.

211. E.S. Gruen, *Rethinking the Other in Antiquity* (Princeton: Princeton University Press, 2010). For the complexity of the representation of barbarian in Graeco-Roman literature, see also S.E. Antonova, *Barbarian or Greek? The Charge of Barbarism and Early Christian Apologetics* (Leiden: Brill, 2019), pp. 58-128.

212. Antonova, *Barbarian or Greek?*

213. *Oratio* 1: the various inventions and discoveries are attributable to different barbarian peoples: e.g. geometry and history to the Egyptians, the alphabet to the Phoenicians, sculpture to the Etruscans, music to the Phrygians and Tyrrhenians, astronomy to the Babylonians, magic to the Persians, divination to the Telmessians and the cult of sacrifice to the Cyprians.

214. *Oratio* 16-18.

215. *Oratio* 22.

216. *Oratio* 24.

217. *Oratio* 23.

of Greek culture original to them, such as their language[218] and their philosophy,[219] are singled out for particular criticism. The language of the Greeks is their own and not derived from barbarians. However, it is a cause of dissension because the different Greek peoples – Dorians, Attics, Aeolians and Ionians – speak different forms of the language and the result is, in Tatian's words, that: 'I do not know whom to call Greek.'[220]

The philosophies of the Greeks are attacked through the wholesale denigration of philosophers and their characters, with Diogenes, Aristippus, Plato, Aristotle, Heraclitus, Zeno, Pherecydes, Pythagoras and Crates singled out for particular criticism.[221] Moreover, the quarrels among philosophers who advance different, and, indeed, contradictory, doctrines are criticised by Tatian.[222] In line with the theft theory referred to above, Tatian argues that the Greeks derived some of their philosophy from the Barbarian Writings and that, while they took over many inventions from barbarian peoples as they were, their inheritance from barbarian philosophy was subject to misunderstanding and distortion. Tatian therefore claims that Greek philosophy, as it is, should be rejected along with the rest of Greek culture.

Tatian presents his authoritative writings as the texts of a barbarian philosophy which challenges, and which should supplant, those of the Greek Schools he denigrates. His wish is to return to the uncorrupted original barbarian philosophy, with the Barbarian Writings as the core texts of barbarian culture and Christianity as the philosophy built upon those texts.[223] Tatian's advocacy of the Barbarian Writings is thus one part, but a crucial one, of his broader case for the superiority of barbarian culture over Greek.[224]

---

218. *Oratio* 1.4.
219. *Oratio* 2 and 3.
220. *Oratio* 1.4.
221. *Oratio* 2 and 3.
222. *Oratio* 25. Tatian uses the terms σύμφωνος and ἀσύμφονος, which are employed in a similar way (but more extensively) by Theophilus of Antioch and are discussed in Chapter 4 below.
223. For Tatian's presentation of Christianity as a barbarian philosophy: Malingrey, 'Philosophia', pp. 120-21.
224. Fojtik, 'Tatian the Barbarian', considers Tatian's arguments for the superiority of barbarian over Greek cultural identity but does not give the central place to the Jewish scriptures advocated here. Antonova's account of Tatian's response to the charge of barbarism (Antonova, *Barbarian or Greek?*, pp. 146-62) similarly does not recognise the importance of the Barbarian Writings for his presentation of barbarian culture.

This is a provocative stance to take. Wholesale attacks on the Greek philosophical tradition were not unfamiliar in Graeco-Roman culture, as is evident from the prevalence of sceptical traditions of thought.[225] Tatian's rejection of Greek culture is, however, accompanied by his positive promotion of the barbarian alternative. Reference was made earlier to the way in which the basically negative connotations surrounding the idea of the barbarian in Graeco-Roman culture could be ameliorated by more positive aspects; Droge argues that Tatian takes such a view and that he follows in the footsteps of *laudatio barbarorum*.[226] This, however, is to underplay Tatian's originality, since he breaks new ground in claiming that barbarian culture should actually be preferred to the Greek.[227]

Tatian's argument for the cultural positioning of the Barbarian Writings leads to the emergence of characters in the text. In Justin's *First Apology* three characters were identified, Romans, Jews and Christians, with Romans prominent as the addressees of the petition. In the *Oratio*, however, the delineation of character is more ambiguous; the Romans are absent and the two characters who emerge clearly are the addressees – the Greeks – and the barbarians. Tatian sets up an opposition between them, condemning the Greeks and lauding the barbarians. Christians (and Jews) are not explicitly mentioned in the *Oratio*, although the first-person plural is used by Tatian to refer to Christians,[228] so they have a presence in the text, if an unacknowledged one. The plural possessive pronoun 'our' is also used on a number of occasions to refer to barbarians[229] and this indicates at the minimum a very close affinity between the barbarians of ancient times and the Christians of Tatian's own day. It is possible that Tatian would actually include Christians within the scope of the term 'barbarian', although, if not, they are at least the current heirs and successors of ancient barbarian culture. The ancient texts of the barbarians are authoritative texts for Christians; indeed, they are the critical link between Tatian's new religion and the barbarian culture to which he aspires to attach himself and Christians generally.

---

225. R.J. Hankinson, *The Sceptics* (London: Routledge, 1995).

226. Droge, *Homer or Moses?*, pp. 88-91.

227. Gruen, *Rethinking the Other*, does not suggest that any writers of the time in the Graeco-Roman tradition expressed the wholesale preference for barbarian over Greek found in the *Oratio*.

228. There are numerous examples in the *Oratio*: e.g. 'We are convinced that there will be a bodily resurrection' (6.1), 'we, for whom death now comes easily' (14.5) and 'We are not foolish' (21.1).

229. E.g. 'our own people' (*Oratio* 31.2), 'our prophets' (36.3) and 'our way of life and history according to our laws' (40.3).

The Jews are absent as characters from the *Oratio*. In Justin's *First Apology*, it was found that the role of the Jews was played down and that they were barely acknowledged as the source for the Books of the Prophecies. Tatian, however, plays down the role of the Jews much further, to the point where, at least in relation to the Barbarian Writings, they are not referred to at all. It may be that in view of the Jews' defeat by the Romans and their humiliating expulsion from Jerusalem – referred to explicitly by Justin – Tatian does not wish to associate himself and his ideas directly with the Jews. Indeed, it is possible that Tatian describes his authoritative writings as barbarian precisely because he wishes to avoid referring to them as Jewish; it is noteworthy that he does not attribute the Barbarian Writings to any one barbarian people, as he does with all the inventions he describes in Chapter 1 of the *Oratio*; and, since the Jews are not mentioned in the text, it is also the case that there are no references to antagonism or conflict between Christians and Jews.

The *Oratio* and the Graeco-Roman Literary Context

The relationship between Tatian's *Oratio* and the Graeco-Roman literary context is an ambiguous one, since the text exhibits features which locate it firmly within its surroundings even though in many respects it is at odds with Greek culture. In Chapter 2 above, it was noted that Justin's Proof from Prophecy had affinities with a number of forms of writing from Greek literary traditions but that it did not fit precisely with any single model. In Tatian's case the position is different, in one sense, in that the *Oratio*[230] follows one of the commonest and longest-established forms in Graeco-Roman literature, the oration, a form which flourished in the era of the Second Sophistic.[231] There is, however, no obviously close parallel with Tatian's work in the extant classical writings of the time, although there are similarities to be noted with three different authors who were his contemporaries. Thus, Tatian's text has affinities with the *Orations* of the prominent, second-century Greek orator, Aelius Aristides;[232] in *Oration 33*,

---

230. The manuscript title is simply ΤΑΤΙΑΝΟΥ ΠΡΟΣ ΕΛΛΗΝΑΣ (Marcovich, *Oratio*, p. 7) with no term, such as 'ΛΟΓΟΣ', to indicate specifically the form of the work. It has all the characteristics of an oration, however. *Oratio ad Graecos* is the title commonly applied to the work by modern scholars and is used by most modern editors, e.g. Whittaker, Marcovich and Trelenberg.

231. For which, see Kennedy, *Art of Rhetoric*.

232. He came originally from Smyrna in Asia Minor, travelled extensively and spent time in Rome: BNP article on Aelius by E. Bowie. Forty-four of his orations survive: *Aelii Aristidis Smyrnaei quae supersunt omnia*, ed. by B. Keil, 2 vols (Berlin: Weidmann, 1893-98); and *Aelius Aristides: The Complete Works*, trans.

for instance, Aelius engages directly with his audience, citing attacks they have made, responding to them and expressing criticism of his own in ways which are reminiscent of Tatian.[233] In terms of subject matter, however, Tatian's work is closer to that of the second-century Greek writer, Maximus of Tyre.[234] Forty-one of his *Dissertations*, which discuss philosophical and religious issues, survive; *Dissertation 11*, entitled 'Plato on God', for instance, discusses themes which are also important to Tatian: the nature of the human soul (11.7) and the nature of God (11.8-11.12). The strongly vituperative tone adopted by Tatian is, however, not a feature of the work of either Aelius or Maximus. There was a strand of writing in the Graeco-Roman tradition which involved the use of diatribe and public denigration as modes of literary expression.[235] Tatian's *Oratio* can be viewed in that context[236] and there are close parallels to be found, in terms of tone, with works by his contemporary, Lucian, such as *The Death of Peregrinus*.[237]

Stylistically, scholars have noted Tatian's use of linguistic and rhetorical devices characteristic of Greek literature of the time. One feature, the use of quotations from and allusions to classic Greek literary works has already been discussed. Puech has identified other features of style characteristic of Second Sophistic writers in the *Oratio*, drawing attention in particular to Tatian's inclusion of asianisms.[238] The significant usage which Tatian makes of rhetorical devices has also been highlighted by scholars of ancient literary style, notably, Kennedy and Karadimas.[239]

C.A. Behr, 2 vols (Leiden: Brill, 1981-86). He is cited as a parallel with Tatian by E. Norelli, 'La critique du pluralisme grec dans le *Discours aux Grecs* de Tatian', in Pouderon and Doré, *Les Apologists Chrétiens*, pp. 81-120, 109-13.

233. Behr, ed., *Aelius Aristides*, 2, pp. 166-72: discussed in C.A. Behr, *Aelius Aristides and the Sacred Tales* (Amsterdam: Adolf M. Hakkert, 1968), pp. 102-3.

234. Text: Maximus of Tyre, *Dissertationes*, ed. by M.B. Trapp (Stuttgart: Teubner, 1994). Translation: Maximus of Tyre, *The Philosophical Orations*, trans. with an Introduction and Notes by M.B. Trapp (Oxford: Clarendon Press, 1997). Trapp, ed., *Philosophical Orations*, pp. xlix-li, notes points of comparison between Maximus and Christian apologists.

235. V. Arena, 'Roman Oratorical Invective', in Dominik and Hall, eds, *Companion to Roman Rhetoric*, pp. 149-60. The BNP article on 'Invective' by W.-L. Liebermann refers to a literary tradition going back to Plato of ψόγος (vituperation), a descriptive term cited in Grant, *Greek Apologists*, p. 116, with reference to the *Oratio*.

236. The description of a diatribe as 'an ethical lecture of a popular nature, often rather loosely put together out of commonplace arguments or examples', in Kennedy, *Art of Rhetoric*, p. 469, fits Tatian's *Oratio* rather well.

237. Lucian, *Selected Dialogues*, pp. 74-87.

238. Puech, *Recherches*, pp. 14-36, refers to 'asiatic eloquence' (p. 21).

239. G.A. Kennedy, *Classical Rhetoric and its Christian and Secular Tradition from*

As well as in questions of style, the influence on Tatian of Second Sophistic culture can be detected more broadly in two themes present in the *Oratio*, those of Greekness and of exile. Modern scholars have identified a preoccupation in Second Sophistic literature with the theme of Greek identity within the Roman Empire, as concerns about the preservation of 'Greekness' in the context of an Empire which had expanded to encompass the culturally Greek eastern Mediterranean were worked through. The theme of exile is also explicitly considered in a number of Second Sophistic texts, which explore not least how experience of exile relates to the articulation of identity, and Whitmarsh[240] has shown how Greek writers, such as Musonius Rufus,[241] Dio Chrysostom[242] and Favorinus,[243] used accounts of exile as a mechanism for reflecting on what it meant to be Greek.

The articulation of these ideas in the *Oratio* has unexpected consequences. For, while Second Sophistic writers examine the nature of their Greek identity, which they do not repudiate, Tatian turns matters on their head by rejecting altogether the Greek culture to which he originally belonged and promoting instead his newly discovered barbarian identity. Similarly, while the Second Sophistic writers considered the experience of exile and how it related to their Greek cultural identity, Tatian advocates voluntary self-exile, not as part of a process of articulating his Greekness, but as a route to the abandonment of his Greek heritage in favour of his new barbarian identity. Thus, he echoes, but at the same time contradicts, the concerns with Greek identity and with exile which were common themes in the literature of the time.

At the heart of the barbarian culture which Tatian seeks to promote in preference to the Greek, he places the Barbarian Writings. There is no suggestion in the *Oratio* that these texts were written in anything other than the Greek language – a Hebrew original is never mentioned – but, in spite of this, Tatian does not seek to position them within Greek literary culture and they are never referred to as if they belong to any of the conventional classifications of Greek literature; they are described only as barbarian. Thus, in some ways, Tatian's promotion of the Barbarian

---

Ancient to Modern Times Second edition rev & enlarged (University of North Carolina Press, Chapel Hill 1999) 153-155; Karadimas, *Tatian's* Oratio ad Graecos.

240. T. Whitmarsh, '"Greece is the World": Exile and Identity in the Second Sophistic', in Goldhill, ed., *Being Greek under Rome*, pp. 269-305.
241. Musonius Rufus, 'That exile is not an evil': ibid., pp. 276-85.
242. Dio Chrysostom, '13th Oration: On Exile': ibid., pp. 285-94.
243. Favorinus, 'On Exile': ibid., pp. 294-303.

Writings sets him at odds with the prevailing Greek culture, while in other ways it serves to connect him to it. How Tatian came to occupy the position he did must be a matter of speculation. He refers to criticisms made of him for embracing barbarian doctrines[244] and if, following his conversion to Christianity, he really was faced with reactions of this kind from non-Christians, then one possible response would have been to turn criticisms into virtues and argue that his newly-acquired barbarian heritage was actually a mark of superiority, rather than inferiority, when contrasted with the Greek cultural identity to which he was previously attached. He carries this point to an extreme, however, in arguing that the barbarian culture should actually supplant the Greek and this leads him to a paradoxical position, in which he is condemning Greek culture wholesale, while in many respects writing from inside the Greek tradition.

Such a response to criticism on Tatian's part may, however, contain an element of irony. Nasrallah,[245] in highlighting similarities of tone between Tatian and Second Sophistic writers, describes how Tatian 'draws upon satirical conventions of the second sophistic'[246] and characterises the *Oratio* as 'a piece of humor, a satire, a joke of sorts'.[247] Antonova describes as parody both Tatian's account of the accusations levelled at him and of his defence against criticism.[248] The *Oratio* can be read as a text which promotes a philosophy called Christianity in place of the existing philosophical schools, but a philosophy which is to be preferred to them because its antiquity and the doctrines to be found in its writings render it superior; however, it is a philosophy which is still located within the confines of the Greek cultural world. Faced with accusations that he has adopted barbarian ways, however, Tatian chooses to present his argument as one which provokes a clash between two cultures and to argue that Christianity is not Greek at all but barbarian and, furthermore, that what makes it distinctively and unavoidably barbarian is that its authoritative texts derive, not from Greek philosophical schools, but from an alien tradition which originated in the writings of one of the barbarian peoples.

---

244. *Oratio*, 35.3. For the *Oratio* as a response to accusations that Christianity was barbarian, see Antonova, *Barbarian or Greek?*, pp. 161-62.

245. L. Nasrallah, 'Mapping the World: Justin, Tatian, Lucian, and the Second Sophistic', *HTR* Vol. 98 (2005), pp. 283-314.

246. Ibid., p. 299.

247. Ibid., p. 300.

248. Antonova, *Barbarian or Greek?*, p. 162: 'In his response to the charge of barbarism and mimicry of it, Tatian is imitating and replicating the polemic language of his opponents. In this manner, it is a parody of accusation and a parody of defense that he achieves in his *Address to the Greeks*.'

Conclusion

Setting Tatian's *Oratio* alongside Justin's *First Apology* shows two Christian apologists making use of the Jewish scriptures but doing so in very different ways. The ancient texts can be viewed prophetically or philosophically and the apologist may cite exact quotations or invoke the scriptures in more general ways through the use of allusions. The scriptures can provide evidence to support an argument like the Proof from Prophecy and can also support a protreptic case promising further enlightenment on a later occasion. It is noteworthy, however, that neither Justin nor Tatian uses the scriptures as a source of historical material.

The *Oratio* form which Tatian used, together with modes of style and presentation culled from Greek literary culture, would have given the text a familiarity of appearance for a Graeco-Roman audience. Much of the work is, however, devoted to assaults on the Graeco-Roman way of life, not least its literary culture. Members of the audience might well have been accustomed to satire but the uncompromising character of Tatian's attack on Greek culture could have made his message a disconcerting one; for, although, like Justin, he presents a choice between Graeco-Roman culture and the Christian (barbarian) alternative, he does so much more starkly and the contrast – indeed, the conflict – between the two cultures emerges particularly strongly when he is discussing their literary texts and traditions.

Nevertheless, the Jewish scriptures play no part in Tatian's assaults on Graeco-Roman culture. Their role is to support arguments presented in the more measured sections of the work promoting Christian ideas. Tatian, in effect, presents himself as the model of someone who has become dissatisfied with Greek culture, including its literary heritage, and for whom exposure to the Jewish scriptures has opened up a new way forward. It may, however, be the case that only someone who is already sympathetic to Tatian's wholesale criticism of Greek culture – perhaps attracted by the satirical and ironical tone in which the criticisms are couched – would be prepared to consider the alternative which he offers. The Jewish scriptures do not have a high visibility in the *Oratio*, although the concrete evidence of antiquity they provide is important in bestowing on arguments for Christianity a credibility which in a Graeco-Roman context would otherwise be lacking. It is not clear, however, that in other respects reference to the scriptures would make the argument for Christianity any more convincing to Tatian's audience than would otherwise be the case; for it asks a great deal of that audience not only to reject their own cultural heritage completely, but to accept an alien literary culture as their alternative focus of allegiance, especially one whose name, barbarian, had such generally negative connotations.

Since Tatian makes very little use of scriptural quotations, there are limits to what can be said about his approach to scriptural interpretation and, especially, to the way that the reading of individual passages of text should be approached. It is, however, clear that he not only values the scriptures for their antiquity, their contents and their divine inspiration, but also regards them as works whose literary style should be admired. The scriptures are not used by Tatian to demonstrate the status of Jesus Christ as they are by Justin; they are, however, presented not only as fundamental for his own conversion to Christianity, but also, critically, as an important source of philosophical ideas and he discusses them with positive enthusiasm.

Chapter 4

The *Ad Autolycum* of Theophilus of Antioch: History and Commentary

The next, and final, text to be considered in this book is the *Ad Autolycum* of Theophilus of Antioch.[1] Of the three, it is the text which has received the least attention from modern scholarship. Engberg has suggested that this may in part be because Theophilus' interests do not align well with those of later scholars.[2] Be that as it may, *Ad Autolycum* remains one of only a small number of substantial Christian texts from the second century to have survived in their entirety and for that reason alone it merits serious consideration.

For this book, *Ad Autolycum* is a core text because the importance of the Jewish scriptures to its author is obvious. There are similarities with Justin's *First Apology* and Tatian's *Oratio* in its treatment of the scriptures, with prophecy and philosophy both being significant themes. Theophilus goes further, however, and extends the uses to which the Jewish scriptures are put into new areas: they are viewed as coherent and connected narratives; they are a source for accurate history; and they become the subject of a line-by-line commentary, the earliest example of such a form in extant Christian literature.

---

1. References to *Ad Autolycum* (*AA*) are to book, chapter and paragraph numbers in *Theophili Antiocheni ad Autolycum*, ed. by M. Marcovich (Berlin: de Gruyter, Berlin 1995). Translations are from *Theophilus of Antioch: Ad Autolycum*, ed. by R.M. Grant (Oxford: Clarendon Press, 1970), adapted where appropriate. The other modern edition consulted, one of the earliest volumes to be published in the *Sources Chrétiennes* series, is: *Théophile d'Antioche: Trois livres à Autolycus*, ed. G. Bardy and trans. by J. Sender (Paris: Éditions du Cerf, 1948).
2. J. Engberg, 'Conversion, Apologetic Argumentation and Polemic (Amongst Friends) in Second-Century Syria: Theophilus' *Ad Autolycum*', in M. Blömer, A. Lichtenberger and R. Raja, eds, *Religious Identities in the Levant from Alexander to Muhammed: Continuity and Change* (Turnhout: Brepols, 2015), pp. 83-94, 84: 'The otherwise comparative lack of interest in Theophilus can perhaps partly be explained by the fact that he was silent on matters that have tended to interest later scholars the most: Christ, the incarnation and atonement.'

Before examining these issues in detail, however, some background will be provided on Theophilus and on his *Ad Autolycum*. Previous scholarship and its relevance to the theme of this book will then be considered, before clarifying the approach to the text which will be adopted here.

Background

Ad Autolycum is the only text attributed to Theophilus of Antioch to survive. It presents itself as a work in three books addressed by Theophilus to an individual called Autolycus. Based primarily on references in later Christian writers, scholars are agreed that the author of the work was in all probability Theophilus, Bishop of Antioch in the 170s and 180s.[3] Its provenance is accepted as being Antioch,[4] although the city is not mentioned and the only geographical reference is to the rivers Tigris and Euphrates being 'on the edge of our regions'.[5] This is remarkably inexact and it is only identification of the author as bishop of Antioch in later Christian literature that links the work to that city.[6] Theophilus is recorded as having written other works, none of which survives.[7] The one extant manuscript of *Ad Autolycum* regarded as having independent value, *Venetus Marcianus graecus 496*, is dated to the eleventh century,[8] roughly contemporary with the oldest surviving manuscripts of Tatian's *Oratio*.

Ad Autolycum's three books have a degree of independence of theme and structure; they were probably written separately and later brought together.[9] Book 3 can be dated after 180 CE because it refers to the death of Marcus Aurelius in that year.[10] Books 1 and 2 are likely to have been written earlier.[11] References to earlier books in later books suggest that the author saw them as a single work.[12] Theophilus applies a different

3. Grant, *AA*, pp. ix-x; R. Rogers, *Theophilus of Antioch: The Life and Thought of a Second-Century Bishop* (Lanham: Lexington Books, 2000), pp. 4-6.
4. Grant, *AA*, p. ix; Rogers, *Theophilus*, pp. 4-6.
5. *AA* 2.24.4.
6. E.g. Eusebius, *HE* 4.24.
7. Rogers, *Theophilus*, pp. 4-6.
8. Marcovich, *AA*, p. 1. The section of the manuscript containing the text of this work is headed θεοφίλου πρὸς αὐτόλυκον (Marcovich, *AA*, p. 15, n.).
9. Rogers, *Theophilus*, p. 7.
10. *AA* 3.28.6: Grant, *AA*, p. ix; Rogers, *Theophilus*, p. 7.
11. Grant, *Greek Apologists*, p. 143; Marcovich, *AA*, p. 3; Rogers, *Theophilus*, p. 7.
12. Marcovich, *AA*, p. 3: 'that the author meant all three books to belong to the same work is witnessed by his references; e.g. at 3.3.5 to 1.9.5; at 3.19.4 to

descriptive term to each book,[13] with Book 1 a ὁμιλία,[14] Book 2 a σύγγραμμα[15] and Book 3 a ὑπόμνημα,[16] although it is doubtful whether sharp distinctions should be drawn on the basis of these terms; Grant translates them as 'discourse', 'treatise' and 'memorandum', none of which is a very precise term.

The structure of *Ad Autolycum* has attracted criticism from scholars, with Marcovich, for instance, commenting that 'the work as a whole is ill-organised, highly repetitious and even redundant'.[17] It is, however, possible to isolate the main apologetic themes addressed in *Ad Autolycum*; these are the nature of God, the creation of the cosmos, the origin and nature of humankind, the salvation of humankind and the story of human history from earliest times down to the present day.[18] Presentation of the positive material promoting Christianity is, however, interspersed in each book with quite lengthy sections criticising various aspects of Greek culture and (especially) religion.[19]

Early in Book 1 the nature of God emerges as an important theme in response to a question from Autolycus asking Theophilus who his God is[20] and much of the first Book is devoted to answering this question. The avowedly monotheistic picture of God which is painted in the early chapters of this Book (Chapters 2-7) contrasts with the strongly worded attack on Graeco-Roman religion and its idolatry that follows later (particularly in Chapters 9 and 10).

Book 2 has two main sections. The first occupies Chapters 1-8 and consists of a series of attacks on Greek culture, notably (in Chapters 5 and 6), the ideas of Hesiod. This is followed, from Chapter 9 onwards, by a long section recounting the narrative of much of the Book of Genesis and including the text of Genesis 1-3 verbatim. This section is interspersed with comments on the scriptural text by Theophilus himself.

Book 3 consists of three main sections. The first (Chapters 1-8) is occupied (again) by a wide-ranging attack on Greek culture as it is found in the literature of poets, philosophers and historians. The second

---

    2.31.3'.

13. Rogers, *Theophilus*, pp. 15-16.
14. *AA* 2.1.1.
15. *AA* 2.1.2.
16. *AA* 3.1.1.
17. Marcovich, *AA*, p. 3. Grant has a similar view, although he expresses it more diplomatically: 'Theophilus' arrangement of his materials . . . leaves something to be desired' (Grant, *AA*, p. xi).
18. For a detailed list of the contents of *AA*: Marcovich, *AA*, pp. 4-14.
19. E.g. *AA* 1.9-1.10, 2.2-2.8 and 3.1-3.8.
20. *AA* 2.1.1.

(Chapters 9-15) describes some positive Christian virtues and includes (in Chapter 9) a version of the Decalogue. The third section (Chapters 16-30) comprises a chronology from the creation of the world to Theophilus' own time.

Such is the broad structure of *Ad Autolycum*. However, the key issue for this book is the use which Theophilus makes of the Jewish scriptures in the presentation of his arguments. In Book 1 his responses to Autolycus' question, Who is your God? make some, although limited, reference to the Jewish scriptures. Allusions can be identified, most notably, to Job and the Psalms[21] in Chapters 6 and 7, when Theophilus is discussing the nature of God. He does not, however, specify the sources of his allusions and his arguments do not depend on the texts to which he refers being identified as scriptural.

In Books 2 and 3 explicit and extensive references are made to the Jewish scriptures. The most obvious instance of this is the inclusion in Book 2 of lengthy extracts from Genesis; they are identified as such and Theophilus provides commentaries to demonstrate the unique value of these ancient texts. In Book 3 the chronology he presents is derived from the scriptures (ultimately, if not immediately) and it is those texts which are the key source of the factual material driving his argument.

In considering how *Ad Autolycum* should be read, some of the same issues are encountered as was the case with Justin's *First Apology* and Tatian's *Oratio*. *Ad Autolycum* presents itself as part of an ongoing debate, dealing with particular questions about, and objections to, Christianity, although none of the other components of the debate (real or implied) that may once have existed now survive. The author presents himself as a convert to Christianity[22] and his addressee, Autolycus, as a non-Christian with whom he has friendly relations.[23] It is clear from literary references in *Ad Autolycum* that Theophilus had a measure of Greek education, as did his (real or imaginary) addressee.[24] Nothing is known of

---

21. E.g. *AA* 1.6.4 (Job) and 1.7.1 (Psalms). Lists of Jewish scriptural quotations and allusions are at Grant, *AA*, pp. 148-49, and Marcovich, *AA*, pp. 141-44. For discussion of allusions to Job: S.E. Parsons, *Ancient Apologetic Exegesis: Introducing and Recovering Theophilus's World* (Cambridge: James Clarke & Co., 2015), pp. 58-64.

22. *AA* 1.14.1.

23. This is shown by the polite manner in which Autolycus is addressed by Theophilus at the beginning of each book, in spite of the disagreements between them on the issues discussed ('friend', *AA* 1.1.2, 'O excellent Autolycus', *AA* 2.1.1 and 'greetings' *AA* 3.1.1).

24. Lists of non-scriptural references: Grant, *AA*, pp. 151-53, and Marcovich, *AA*, pp. 146-47.

Autolycus from sources external to the work; whether he actually existed and, if so, whether he had the characteristics ascribed to him cannot be established.[25] Engberg suggests that *Ad Autolycum* does represent a real debate between two real historical figures but that Theophilus also had a wider audience in view, among both Christians and non-Christians.[26] This could well be the case, although, as with Justin and Tatian, it is not possible to be sure whether there was a genuine external audience; the form of the work could merely be a frame for material which was directed internally. *Ad Autolycum* was read and preserved by Christians but there is no surviving evidence to suggest that it was known to non-Christians.[27] Thus, the audience could have been external, or it could have been among Christians alone, or it could have straddled the borderlines between Christians and non-Christians. These are familiar issues from discussion of Justin and Tatian in previous chapters and with Theophilus they are no easier to resolve. Nonetheless, *Ad Autolycum* is concerned with matters of controversy between Christians and non-Christians and in all probability addresses topics of debate that were live issues in the context in which Theophilus was writing.

The Scholarly Context

Scholarship on Theophilus has tended to concern itself with theological issues that arise in *Ad Autolycum*. Cases in point are the work of Grant,[28] the one book-length work on Theophilus by Rogers[29] and articles, such as those by Curry (on the theogony of Theophilus)[30] and Bentivegna (on the apparent absence of Christ from Theophilus' theology).[31] Writers on Theophilus have also been interested in the external influences on

---

25. The author of the most extensive work to date on Theophilus considers that Autolycus probably was a real person, while still recognising the possibility that he could be fictional (Rogers, *Theophilus*, pp. 6-7).
26. Engberg, 'Conversion', pp. 86-87.
27. Caution should, however, be exercised in drawing conclusions from this, given the low rate of survival of texts.
28. Grant, *Greek Apologists*, pp. xx. Theophilus was the subject of Grant's Harvard doctoral dissertation in the 1940s and he retained a lifelong interest in *Ad Autolycum*, which spawned a series of articles over a number of years, e.g. R.M. Grant, 'The Problem of Theophilus', *HTR*, vol. 43 (1950), pp. 179-96.
29. Rogers, *Theophilus*.
30. C. Curry, 'The Theogony of Theophilus', *VC*, vol. 42 (1988), pp. 318-26.
31. J. Bentivegna, 'A Christianity without Christ by Theophilus of Antioch', in E.A. Livingstone, ed., *SP*, vol. 13, no. 2 (Berlin: Akademie-Verlag, 1975), pp. 107-130.

Theophilus' thought, with some scholars, such as Grant and Rogers, emphasising Jewish influences, while others, such as McVey[32] and Schoedel,[33] stress connections with Graeco-Roman ideas.

Some works dealing with theological issues touch on Theophilus' use of the scriptures but without making it a subject of major interest.[34] None of them considers how Theophilus regarded or used the scriptures, however. Rogers examines his subject on an issue by issue basis, but Theophilus' approach to scripture is not one of his themes or chapter topics.[35] A recent doctoral thesis by Boccabello on Theophilus' treatment of Greek myth bears to some extent on his treatment of scripture in *Ad Autolycum*, since the way Theophilus interprets myth is seen as a foil for his interpretation of ideas from scripture. Thus, there is some discussion of comparisons and contrasts to be drawn between scripture and Greek myth, although Boccabello's interest is very much in Theophilus' treatment of myth and not scripture.[36]

The one work in which the role of the Jewish scriptures in *Ad Autolycum* is central is Grant's article, 'The Bible of Theophilus',[37] the counterpart to his article on 'Tatian and the Bible' discussed in Chapter 3 above. Grant rightly recognises the importance of the Jewish scriptures for Theophilus; he identifies the scriptural texts drawn on and the nature of their Septuagintal sources[38] and for this the work is exceptionally useful. He does not, however, consider how Theophilus uses the scriptures in his arguments and thus does not address the issues which are of prime importance to this book. A more recent article by Simonetti highlights themes relating to Theophilus' use of the scriptures, such as

32. K.E. McVey, 'The Use of Stoic Cosmogony in Theophilus of Antioch's Hexamaeron', in M.S. Burrows and P. Rorem, eds, *Biblical Hermeneutics in Historical Perspective: Studies in Honor of Karlfried Froehlich on His Sixtieth Birthday* (Grand Rapids: Eerdmans, 1991), pp. 32-58.

33. W.R. Schoedel, 'Theophilus of Antioch: Jewish Christian?', *Illinois Classical Studies*, vol. 18 (1993), pp. 279-97.

34. E.g. Bentivegna, 'Christianity without Christ'; Curry, 'Theogony of Theophilus'; Schoedel, 'Theophilus of Antioch: Jewish Christian?'; McVey, 'The Use of Stoic Cosmogony in Theophilus of Antioch's Hexamaeron'.

35. Rogers, *Theophilus*.

36. J.S. Boccabello, 'Cosmological Allegoresis of Greek Myth in Theophilus of Antioch's Ad Autolycum' (DPhil, University of Oxford, 2011).

37. R.M. Grant, 'The Bible of Theophilus of Antioch', *JBL*, vol. 66 (1947), pp. 173-96.

38. Grant, 'Bible of Theophilus', pp. 174-77, argues that the texts which Theophilus quotes often agree with the 'Lucianic' version of the Septuagint but reaches the overall conclusion that 'the attempt to establish a single type of text for Theophilus' Septuagint is a failure' (p. 177).

the concept of inspiration, but is too brief to develop them extensively.[39] Other works, such as those by Bolgiani[40] and Zeegers-Vander Vorst,[41] address very specific issues concerning the interpretation of scriptural texts in *Ad Autolycum* but they do not engage with the broader themes discussed here.

The title of Parsons' recent work, *Ancient Apologetic Exegesis* (already cited), suggests a focus on Theophilus' use of scripture for apologetic purposes. Parsons certainly is interested in the relationship between Theophilus and scripture and also in his presentation of arguments, and his work is concerned with four specific issues. The first, which has worried a number of scholars,[42] is why Theophilus, writing as a Christian apologist, says so little about Christ, and particularly his role in salvation; Parson's answer is that *Ad Autolycum* should be viewed as a protreptic work designed 'to draw outsiders towards Christianity,'[43] so detailed treatment of soteriological issues would be out of place. His second issue concerns the prevalence of orality in the ancient world; he argues that, as a consequence of this, scholarly interest in a text like *Ad Autolycum* should extend beyond actual quotations to allusions and echoes of scripture. His third point is that the structure of *Ad Autolycum* should be seen as an example of 'judicial rhetoric' in which writers of scripture function as witnesses presenting evidence; while his fourth concerns the way that scriptural anthologies and *testimonia* are used in *Ad Autolycum*.

A complication arises from Parsons' use of the term 'scripture' to include New Testament texts, which are outside the remit of this book. His work provides new insights across a range of topics, however. It is welcome, for instance, following Skarsaune's trailblazing work on Justin, to find a scholar attempting to identify the use of *testimonia* by another second-century writer, although Parson's conclusion is that in *Ad Autolycum* such usage 'is relatively sparse compared with their rich use in early and mid-second-century writers such as Pseudo-Barnabas and

39. M. Simonetti, 'La Sacra Scrittura in Teofilo d'Antiochia', in J. Fontaine and C. Kannengiesser, eds, *Epektasis: Mélanges patristiques offerts au Cardinal Jean Daniélou* (Paris: Beauchesne, 1972), pp. 197-207.

40. F. Bolgiani, 'L'ascesi di Noé: A proposito di Theoph., ad Autol., III, 19', in F. Paulo and M. Barrera, eds, *Forma futuri: Studi in onore del Cardinale Michele Pellegrino* (Torino: Bottega d'Erasmo, 1975), pp. 295-333.

41. N. Zeegers-Vander Vorst, 'La création de l'homme (Gn 1,26) chez Théophile d'Antioche', *VC*, vol. 30 (1976), pp. 258-67, and 'Satan, Ève et le serpent chez Théophile d'Antioche', *VC*, vol. 35 (1981), pp. 152-69.

42. E.g. Bentivegna, 'Christianity without Christ'; Rogers, *Theophilus*, pp. 158-59.

43. Parsons, *Ancient Apologetic Exegesis*, p. 156; Rogers, *Theophilus*, pp. 153-72, also characterises Theophilus' theology as 'protreptic'.

Justin'.[44] Parsons' discussion of allusions and echoes is less relevant for this book than might be expected, however, since so many of the instances he identifies relate to New Testament texts.[45] His contention that allusions to Job play a part in Theophilus' account of the nature of God in Book 1 is, however, well made.[46] Overall, Parsons provides a useful addition to the literature on Theophilus. However, the issues he discusses only overlap to a small extent with the concerns of this book. Exploring the way Christian authors present the Jewish scriptures to a non-Christian world – central to this thesis – is not within Parsons' remit and he does not attempt to address two issues that are of particular importance here: the use of the Jewish scriptures as a source of accurate history and the inclusion in *Ad Autolycum* of a commentary on Genesis.[47]

The Approach Taken here

This review of previous scholarship has shown that a number of different approaches can be taken to this text. It can be analysed theologically, for instance, or examined within the intellectual context of its time, either Jewish or Graeco-Roman. In this book, in line with the way the text presents itself, it will be considered as apologetic and examined for the use the author makes of the Jewish scriptures in his arguments, a relatively neglected topic in studies of *Ad Autolycum* hitherto.

As with the *First Apology* and the *Oratio*, the issue of audience cannot be resolved definitively and a number of possibilities remain open. It is fruitful again to consider Theophilus' audience against the categories identified by Barclay. The declared audience is the single individual, Autolycus, named in the text. The intended audience is, as already noted, difficult to determine; it could be internal or external to the Christian community (or both) or it could located somewhere on the borderlands between the two. The implied audience, given the wide range and generalised nature of the arguments is to be found among educated Graeco-Romans more generally, and not limited to Autolycus, but external to Christianity and widely drawn. It is this implied audience which is relevant to the analysis of arguments undertaken here.

Thus, as with the texts examined in Chapters 2 and 3 above, *Ad Autolycum* will be treated here as a repository of arguments which may be studied for what they reveal about the use of the Jewish scriptures by

---

44. Parsons, *Ancient Apologetic Exegesis*, p. 155.
45. Ibid., pp. 38-44.
46. Ibid., pp. 58-64.
47. Ibid., pp. 40-41, has only a brief discussion.

a second-century Christian convert occupied in debates (real or implied) with non-Christians. In order to avoid the convoluted phraseology which would be necessary to recognise this, however, *Ad Autolycum*'s audience, like those of the *First Apology* and the *Oratio*, will be referred to throughout as if it is external to Christianity and in line with the way the text presents itself.

It will be shown in what follows that for Theophilus, as for Justin, the Jewish scriptures are prophetic texts and their authors are prophets. The scriptures are, however, also characterised by Theophilus in other ways, most notably, as a source of accurate chronological information for the history of the world and as a source of theological insights into truths about God, Creation and the nature of humankind, as revealed in the Book of Genesis. Before exploring these issues in detail, however, Theophilus' view of the nature of the scriptures and of their prophetic authorship will first be considered. What is important here emerges not just from the explicit comments he makes, but also from the way he treats the scriptures in what he says. In a number of respects, his approach is found to be similar to that of Justin (and to a lesser extent Tatian), although there are also clear points of difference.

The Nature of the 'Sacred Writings'

Theophilus very clearly asserts the importance of the Jewish scriptures for him:

> I too did not believe that it [resurrection] would take place, but, having now considered these matters, I believe. At that time I encountered [ἐπιτυχὼν] the Sacred Writings of the holy prophets, who through the Spirit of God foretold past events in the way that they happened, present events in the way that they are happening, and future events in the order in which they will be accomplished.[48]

It has already been noted that reference to an encounter with the Jewish scriptures as a trigger for conversion is a recurring theme in early Christian apologetic works,[49] including those of Justin and Tatian, but that it is difficult to judge how literally such comments should be taken. Whether or not Theophilus' comments are to any extent autobiographical, however, he is unquestionably claiming that the

---

48. *AA* 1.14.1.
49. Engberg, 'From among You Are We', pp. 49-77.

scriptures were critical for his conversion. He describes the scriptural texts as prophetic, dividing prophecies into those relating to past events, those relating to the present and those relating to the future in a way that echoes Justin. He also recommends the scriptures as a source of guidance for salvation: 'If you wish, you too should reverently read [ἔντυχε] the prophetic writings; they will guide you most clearly how to escape eternal punishments and obtain the eternal benefits of God.'[50] Such explanatory comments are introduced because the audience does not have prior familiarity with the Sacred Writings. By contrast, Theophilus does not at any stage describe or explain references to Graeco-Roman literature; this would be unnecessary since his Greek-educated audience would already be familiar with them.

In referring to the scriptures Theophilus does not use a standard term; he employs a number of different formulations, although for the most part he follows the reference in the conversion account quoted above in emphasising that the scriptures are both written and sacred. Thus, his terms tend to involve a combination of either ἱερός (holy), ἅγιος (sacred) or θεῖος (divine) with some form of γράφω (write) or βίβλος (book) and the following phrases are found: 'ἡ ἁγία γραφή',[51] 'ἡ θεία γραφή',[52] 'διὰ τῶν ἁγίων γραφῶν',[53] 'ἐν ταῖς ἁγίαις γραφαῖς',[54] 'τὰς ἱερὰς βίβλους'[55] and 'τα ἱερὰ γράμματα'.[56] In what follows the phrase 'Sacred Writings' will be used as the collective term for Theophilus' description of the texts.

Like the two authors already discussed, Theophilus presents the Jewish scriptures as sacred texts of very ancient origin, with the most recent prophetic author referred to dating from the reign of King Darius in the sixth century BCE.[57] He makes no reference to the Septuagint legend – which featured so strongly in Justin's account – to explain the historical origin of the Sacred Writings. As in Justin's *First Apology* and Tatian's *Oratio*, in *Ad Autolycum* scriptures are always quoted in Greek; there are three references suggesting that they were originally written in Hebrew – and showing that Theophilus knows this – but the point is not emphasised.[58]

---

50. *AA* 1.14.3.
51. *AA* 2.13.7.
52. *AA* 2.18.1.
53. *AA* 2.30.7.
54. *AA* 3.11.7.
55. *AA* 3.20.6.
56. *AA* 3.26.1.
57. *AA* 3.23.2: 'The last of the prophets, Zacharias by name, flourished in the reign of Darius.'
58. The three references are at *AA* 2.12.5, when Theophilus is discussing the

The Texts which Make up the Sacred Writings

Like Justin and Tatian, Theophilus never accompanies the phrase 'Sacred Writings' with a definition or list of contents, so what view he takes of their scope remains unclear. He may have regarded them as a settled collection of books but, as was suggested in the case of Tatian, he could have looked on them more in the nature of a tradition of writings, consisting of a number of texts, whose make-up was not necessarily fixed. It is, however, possible to build up a picture of what the Sacred Writings comprise from the references Theophilus makes and these suggest that he has a wider range of texts in view than either Justin or Tatian.

The texts which are unambiguously referred to in *Ad Autolycum* are: first, the early chapters of Genesis, quoted at length and described in the following terms: 'these things the Sacred Writings teach first',[59] a phraseology suggesting that reference is being made to a collection of which the early chapters of Genesis are the beginning; second, the later chapters of Genesis which feature in summary narrative (with some quotations);[60] third, texts containing the Jewish law (at least in extracts);[61] fourth, prophetic texts, again, at least in extracts;[62] and, fifth, the outline chronology of human history from the Garden of Eden to the return from the Babylonian Exile as recounted in the Jewish scriptures.[63]

The only complete texts to which Theophilus unequivocally has access are the early chapters of Genesis which he quotes in full.[64] His references to later chapters of Genesis, to the Jewish law and to prophetic texts could come directly from the Septuagint. However, they could also be from other texts, such as 'Rewritten Bible' works, or from collections of extracts; if the latter, then their ultimate source is, however, likely to be the full text of the Jewish scriptures. The chronological material referred to could, similarly, be derived from historical summaries of the contents of the scriptures or directly from the Sacred Writings.

Hexaemeron and says, 'what the Hebrews call Sabbath is rendered "hebdomad" [ἑβδομάς] in Greek', at 2.24.3, where he says, 'The Hebrew word Eden means delight', and at 3.19.2, where he refers to 'Noah, whose Hebrew name is translated in Greek as rest'.

59. *AA* 2.10.10.
60. E.g. *AA* 2.29, which summarises the story of Cain and Abel and contains three quotations from Genesis 4.
61. Theophilus' version of the Decalogue is at *AA* 3.9.1-5.
62. Quotations from prophetic books are found in *AA* 3.11-14.
63. *AA* 3.24-25.
64. *AA* 2.10-21.

Whether or not Theophilus is engaging with the texts themselves or with dependent summaries, his use of material from the Jewish scriptures to construct a continuous chronology shows an awareness of these texts as a series, providing a connected narrative of historical events from Creation to the Babylonian exile or, expressed textually, from Genesis to 2 Kings/2 Chronicles. At least some of the texts of the Jewish scriptures – at least by implication – appear therefore to form a collection with a coherent organising principle, that is a chronological one; they are not a grouping of otherwise unconnected writings. In this respect, Theophilius presents the Jewish scriptures in a very different light from Justin and Tatian.

On occasion, Theophilus refers to a written source using a different description, the 'Genesis of the World' (Γένεσις κόσμου), although what is meant by this phrase is problematic. Theophilus tells the story of Cain and Abel partly through quotations from Genesis 4 and partly in his own words. His account cannot be described as a paraphrase, since he introduces elements of his own not in the Genesis narrative – saying, for example, that it is Satan who incites Cain to kill Abel[65] – and he leaves out some elements – such as the sacrifices to God by the two brothers – that are in the Genesis narrative.[66] He says that further information is to be found in a book (βίβλος) called Γένεσις κόσμου.[67] There are three later references which may be to the same source, all of them relating to an (unspecified) earlier place in the text. The first occurs when Theophilus describes the descendants of Cain and Seth and refers to the existence of a 'partial account elsewhere' – additional to the Sacred Writings – with the parenthetic comment 'as we have said above'.[68] The other two occur when the story of Noah is being discussed; he describes how 'an account of the story of Noah . . . is available for us in the book [βίβλος, again] which we mentioned before'[69] and he later comments: 'As for the three sons of Noah and their relationships and their genealogies, we have a brief catalogue in the book [βίβλος, again] we mentioned previously.'[70]

If these three references are all to the same text – as seems most likely – then the book entitled Γένεσις κόσμου contains at a minimum the stories of Cain and Abel, of Noah and of the sons of Noah and

---

65. *AA* 2.29.3.
66. Genesis 4:3-5.
67. *AA* 2.29.2.
68. *AA* 2.30.7.
69. *AA* 2.30.10.
70. *AA* 2.31.3.

also genealogical material. Use of the term '*βίβλος*' implies a discrete text rather than a collection of quotations and to judge from the contents referred to this could well be Genesis or at least a portion of it. Commenting on *Γένεσις κόσμου*, Bardy says firmly that: 'This title obviously indicates *Genesis*.'[71] Grant, with less assurance, comments that it is 'possibly, but not certainly,' a reference to Genesis.[72] Theophilus could, however, be referring to some text other than Genesis and there are two reasons for thinking that this may be so: first, as already noted, the Cain and Abel narrative in *Ad Autolycum* is not the same as Genesis; and, second, there is an apparent distinction between two texts, one referred to as the 'Sacred Writings' and another simply as a '*βίβλος*'. If Theophilus is accessing some other source called *Γένεσις κόσμου*, separate from Genesis, it is unlikely to be wholly independent, however; it is most likely a text that is partly, and probably mainly, dependent on Genesis. The most likely candidates are either a source belonging to the Hellenistic-Jewish 'Rewritten Bible' tradition, referred to in Chapter 1 above, or, alternatively, another work by Theophilus himself; indeed, when discussing the story of the deluge, Theophilus says that he provides explanations in another work, and this could be the same *Γένεσις κόσμου*.[73]

The Prophets as Authors of the Sacred Writings

The authors of the Sacred Writings are described by Theophilus as prophets. He refers to them in the plural, showing that there were a number of them: 'There were not just one or two of them but more at various times and seasons.'[74] Like Justin, Theophilus says little about the prophets. However, he does say that they came from among the Hebrews, using the phrases '*παρὰ Ἑβραίοις*'[75] and '*ἐν Ἑβραίοις*',[76] and comments that the term '*Ἑβραίοις*' is synonymous with '*Ἰουδαίοις*', the Jews.[77]

---

71. Bardy, *AA*, p. 171, n. 5.
72. Grant, *AA*, p. 73, n.
73. *AA* 3.19.3: 'we have explained in another work [*ἐν ἑτέρῳ λόγῳ ἐδηλώσαμεν*]': this assumes that in using the first-person plural Theophilus refers to himself.
74. *AA* 2.9.2.
75. *AA* 2.9.2.
76. *AA* 2.35.15.
77. *AA* 3.9.6. Usage of 'Hebrew' and 'Jew' in ancient texts is often more complex than the simple identity of the two terms described here by Theophilus: Lieu, *Christian Identity*, pp. 240-49.

Prophets are sometimes named individually when they are quoted: Moses,[78] David,[79] Solomon,[80] Isaiah,[81] Jeremiah,[82] Hosea,[83] Habbakuk,[84] Ezekiel,[85] Joel,[86] Zechariah[87] and Malachi.[88] Snippets of information about individual prophets are provided only rarely and briefly; for instance, Theophilus says that 'Moses . . . lived many years before Solomon'[89] and that Solomon 'was a king and prophet'.[90] Essentially, however, the prophets are presented, as in Justin's *First Apology*, as little more than names.

Collectively the prophets are described as 'illiterate men [ἀγράμματοι] and shepherds and uneducated [ἰδιῶται]',[91] suggesting that their prophetic insights do not derive from learning and education. Theophilus does not mention the legend of the Septuagint which was so important to Justin; and whether, like Justin, Theophilus thought that the prophetic sayings were originally delivered orally and only later written down is unclear. The works of the prophets clearly exist as texts which can be read,[92] however, and they must, therefore, have been committed to writing at some stage. He refers to 'the antiquity of our writings'[93] and describes the Sacred Writings as 'older than all other writers',[94] suggesting that he thought the commitment of the prophecies to writing took place at a very early stage; he may have thought, like Justin, that the prophets did it themselves. Like Justin, he says that the preservation of the ancient texts is attributable to the Jews, since it is 'from them we possess the Sacred Writings [οἱ Ἑβραῖοι . . . ἀφ᾽ ὧν . . . τὰς ἱερὰς βίβλους ἔχομεν]'.[95] The Greek Library at Alexandria – important to Justin – is, however, never mentioned.

---

78. *AA* 3.18.5.
79. *AA* 2.35.12.
80. *AA* 3.13.5.
81. *AA* 2.35.5.
82. *AA* 2.35.8.
83. *AA* 2.35.4.
84. *AA* 2.35.13.
85. *AA* 3.11.4.
86. *AA* 3.12.6.
87. *AA* 3.12.7.
88. *AA* 2.38.1.
89. *AA* 2.10.7.
90. *AA* 3.13.2.
91. *AA* 2.35.15. An echo of the description of the Apostles Peter and John in Acts 4.13 as ἀγράμματοι and ἰδιῶται: Marcovich, *AA*, p. 88, n.
92. *AA* 1.14.1.
93. *AA* 3.1.1.
94. *AA* 3.20.6.
95. *AA* 3.20.6.

For Theophilus the prophets' status derives from the fact that they were inspired by God – a sentiment again familiar from Justin and Tatian – and this is how they acquired their knowledge and insights: hence, the use of the terms '*ἱερός*' (holy) and '*ἅγιος*' (sacred). Theophilus does not use Justin's phrase, 'Prophetic Spirit' but his terminology conveys a similar sense that it is a spirit, which ultimately comes from God, that inspires the prophets. Thus, he says that the prophets foretold 'through the spirit of God [*διὰ πνεύματος θεοῦ*]'[96] and that they 'were possessed by a holy spirit [*πνεύματος ἁγίου*] and became prophets and were inspired and instructed by God himself, were taught by God and became holy and righteous'.[97] Theophilus does, however, use other terms to denote the intermediary between God and the prophets, saying: 'It was the Spirit of God and Beginning and Sophia and Power of the Most High who came down into the prophets and spoke through them about the creation of the world and all the rest'.[98] He also uses logos with a similar sense: 'Moses . . . – or rather, the Logos of God speaking through him as an instrument – says: "In the Beginning God made heaven and earth."'[99] Why Theophilus uses a number of different terms in this way is unclear; perhaps he did not regard the particular words he uses – which in any case he does not define – as having precise meanings or indeed as being especially significant. The important point he wishes to convey is that the prophets' words were divinely inspired and he uses the term 'spirit' (*πνεῦμα*) most commonly to denote this.[100]

If the Sacred Writings are the product of divine inspiration, then it follows that they must be true. Theophilus says that: 'those who wish to can read what was said through them and acquire accurate knowledge of the truth and not be misled by speculation and pointless labour'.[101] (The factual accuracy of the Sacred Writings is an issue that will recur when their role as historical sources is discussed below.) One aspect of the truthfulness of the scriptures is that they are *σύμφωνος* (consistent).[102] This theme occurs in both Justin and Tatian but Theophilus gives it greater emphasis. The term 'consistent' sounds somewhat bland in English translation. However, to Theophilus it is a significant virtue and

---

96.   *AA* 1.14.1.
97.   *AA* 2.9.1.
98.   *AA* 2.10.5.
99.   *AA* 2.10.7.
100. Marcovich, *AA*, p. 183, lists the 25 occurrences of the word '*πνεῦμα*' in the text.
101. *AA* 2.35.14.
102. This is probably the least bad translation. Grant sometimes renders *σύμφωνος* as 'consistent' (e.g. *AA* 2.9.2) and sometimes as 'harmonious' (*AA* 2.35.9). Boccabello, 'Cosmological Allegoresis', pp. 232-36, uses 'harmony' throughout.

he refers to the prophets' consistency on a number of occasions.[103] Since there are a number of prophets, it is important, if the truthfulness of what they say is to be credible, that they are consistent with one another and that their messages do not conflict. He paints a positive picture of the concept of consistency by combining the term 'σύμφωνα' with φίλα (agreeably) several times[104] and contrasts σύμφωνος with ἀσύμφωνος (inconsistent),[105] the quality – or rather the defect – found in Greek poets and philosophers.[106]

Although prophets are central to Theophilus' understanding of the scriptures, since collectively they are its authors, he does not define what a prophet is. It is, however, possible to glean from *Ad Autolycum* what prophets do and the kind of texts they produce. There are similarities with Justin in this respect, in that Theophilus sees prophets as authors who produce texts with a wide range of types of content, including not just prophecy, in the sense of foretelling the future, but also ethical and legal material, accounts of the origin of the cosmos and of the very early history of humankind.

Foretelling the future is a critical part of the prophets' role, to which Theophilus refers more than once. As noted above, he says in his conversion account that they foretold past events as they happened, present events as they are happening and future events as they will happen.[107] Later, he repeats this sentiment when he says that prophets described 'events which had previously occurred, events in their own time and events which are now being fulfilled in our times'.[108] Since former events occurred as predicted by the prophets, so other events predicted, but not yet fulfilled, will occur in the future; this is an argument familiar from Justin. Theophilus limits himself to generalised statements about prophecy, however; he does not cite individual prophecies nor seek to match them with their fulfilments, as Justin does.

The prophets do more than foretell the future; they describe events in the distant past which they had not themselves experienced, a point, again, familiar from Justin. Thus, the prophet Moses[109] gives accounts of Creation and of events in the Garden of Eden which took place long

---

103. *AA* 2.9.2, 2.10.1, 2.35.9 and 3.17.4.
104. *AA* 2.9.2, 2.35.9 and 3.17.4.
105. Again, 'inconsistency' is probably the least bad translation: Boccabello, 'Cosmological Allegoresis', pp. 232-36, uses 'discordant'.
106. *AA* 2.5.1, 2.8.2, 2.8.5 and 3.3.1.
107. *AA* 1.14.1.
108. *AA* 2.9.2.
109. For Moses as a prophet, see *AA* 2.30.8 and 3.18.5.

before he was born. This is possible because prophets receive knowledge from God: 'they were judged worthy of receiving the reward of becoming instruments of God and of containing Wisdom from him. Through this Wisdom they spoke about the creation of the world.'[110]

The prophets also recount ethical precepts – again, as in Justin – and proclaim God's law, two categories which in practice overlap: 'God . . . gave a law and sent the holy prophets to proclaim and to teach the human race so that each one of us might become sober. . . . They also taught us to refrain from unlawful idolatry and adultery and murder, fornication, theft, covetousness, perjury, anger, and all licentiousness and uncleanness.'[111] Theophilus gives a version of the Decalogue, which he calls a 'holy law' (νόμον ἅγιον),[112] although it diverges from the Septuagint text of Exodus 20. It was not unusual in Jewish and early Christian texts for both the order and the contents of the Decalogue to vary.[113] In *Ad Autolycum* the commandments not to take the Lord's name in vain and to observe the Sabbath are omitted and three injunctions from Exodus 23 are added: not to pervert the judgement of the poor human being in judging him, not to kill the innocent and righteous human being and not to vindicate the ungodly human being.[114] Moses is described as the minister (διάκονος) 'of this divine law'[115] and several chapters follow which contain further ethical precepts enunciated by prophets, grouped around the themes of repentance,[116] justice[117] and chastity.[118]

Theophilus' use of the term prophet is not limited to figures from the Jewish tradition; he also applies it to the Sibyl, a well-known and long-established prophetic figure from the Graeco-Roman tradition. Modern scholars regard the texts known as the Sibylline Oracles as Hellenistic-Jewish texts of uncertain date, whose origins are obscure;[119] to Theophilus,

---

110. *AA* 2.9.1.

111. *AA* 2.34.4-5.

112. *AA* 3.9.1.

113. R.A. Freund, 'The Decalogue in Early Judaism and Christianity', in C.A. Evans and J.A. Sanders, eds, *The Function of Scripture in Early Jewish and Christian Tradition* (Sheffield: Sheffield Academic Press, 1998), pp. 124-41; J.C. de Vos, *Rezeption und Wirkung des Dekalogs in jüdischen und christlichen Schriften bis 200 n. Chr.* (Leiden: Brill, 2016), pp. 270-363, especially 290-96.

114. *AA* 3.9.2-5. See Grant, 'Bible of Theophilus', pp. 175-76, and R.M. Grant, 'The Decalogue in Early Christianity', *HTR*, vol. 40 (1947), pp. 1-17.

115. *AA* 3.9.6.

116. *AA* 3.11.

117. *AA* 3.12.

118. *AA* 3.13. This section also contains two citations from the Gospel of Matthew, described as being from 'the gospel voice' (ἡ εὐαγγέλιος φωνὴ) (3.13.3).

119. For Sibylline traditions, see the works cited in Chapter 2, fn. 183. In spite of

however, they have a Greek provenance and he describes their author as 'the Sibyl who was a prophetess among the Greeks and the other nations'.[120] Although a number of early Christian texts treated the Sybilline Oracles as non-Christian witnesses to the truth,[121] Theophilus is the first extant Christian writer to give them a high profile and to quote extensively from them.[122] The role these texts play in his argument is not wholly clear, although the strongly monotheistic sentiments expressed by the Sibyl in the passages Theophilus quotes are certainly consistent with his own thinking. The Sibylline Oracles are first introduced after Theophilus has been discussing the Hebrew prophets in positive terms, and reference to them demonstrates that prophecy is not a feature of the Hebrew tradition alone but is also found among the Greeks. The Sibyl is introduced with minimal explanation, so it can be assumed that she is already familiar to Theophilus' audience. He includes a lengthy extract of 84 lines from the Third Sibylline Oracle and afterwards comments approvingly, 'that these statements are true and useful and just and lovely is obvious to all people'.[123] In general, he draws a sharp distinction between the Hebrew prophets, whom he admires, on the one hand, and poets and philosophers from among the Greeks whom he heavily criticises, on the other;[124] the Sibyl does not fit neatly into this framework, however, for, while she is described as being from 'among the Greeks',[125] she is referred to approvingly; she appears to have much in common with the Hebrew prophets, since she herself is a prophetess. When Theophilus refers to the consistency to be found among the divinely-inspired prophets, he includes the Sibyl along with the Hebrew prophets[126] and, when he later distinguishes between prophets on the one hand and 'poets and philosophers' (who are Greek) on the other, he brackets the Sibyl with the prophets.[127]

its title, Lightfoot, *Sibylline Oracles*, pp. 3-253, contains useful material on the Third Oracle.

120. *AA* 2.36.1.

121. G.J.M. Bartelink, 'Die *Oracula Sibyllina* in den frühchristlichen griechischen Schriften von Justin bis Origenes (150-250 nach Chr.)', in J. den Boeft and A. Hilhorst, eds, *Early Christian Poetry: A Collection of Essays* (Leiden: Brill, 1993), pp. 23-33.

122. Lightfoot, *Sibylline Oracles*, p. 82.

123. *AA* 2.36.16.

124. In *AA* 2.37, after the main Sibylline extract in *AA* 2.36, Theophilus cites some Greek writers, who expressed sentiments of which he approves, but criticises them by invoking the theft theory which has been referred to in previous chapters, saying that 'they stole these things from the law and the prophets' (*AA* 2.37.16).

125. *AA* 2.9.2.

126. *AA* 2.9.2.

127. *AA* 2.38.3. Lightfoot, *Sibylline Oracles*, p. 82.

After including the lengthy extract from the Third Sibylline Oracle, Theophilus, curiously, makes very little further comment about it. Before the quotation begins he says, briefly, that the Sibyl 'at the beginning of her prophecy rebukes the human race'.[128] At the end of the quotation – in addition to the statement of general approval already noted – he comments merely that 'those who behave in an evil way must necessarily be punished according to the worth of their actions'.[129] There are two other, much briefer, references to Sibylline prophecies in *Ad Autolycum* and the prophetess is named in both instances: the first is a three-line extract quoted to support the argument that gods are not generated;[130] and the second is a nine-line extract cited in connection with the story of the Tower of Babel.[131] For Theophilus, the Sibylline Oracles are a much less important source of prophetic insight than the Hebrew prophets but their inclusion shows at least that, for him, divinely-inspired prophecy is not purely the preserve of the Jewish tradition.

The Use of the Sacred Writings in *Ad Autolycum*

Thus, the Sacred Writings are presented by Theophilus as divinely inspired texts composed by prophets and, like Tatian, he uses these texts to support his arguments for Christianity. His interest is in Creation, in the origin, nature and salvation of humankind and in human history from the earliest times to the present day. However, he uses the scriptures more directly than Tatian in that he quotes from them extensively. When wishing to highlight moral points, Theophilus follows Justin's technique of providing brief selective quotations; an example is Theophilus' account of repentance,[132] which is developed through a series of quotations from Deuteronomy, Baruch, Isaiah, Ezekiel and Jeremiah, in some cases accompanying them with explanatory comments in the manner of Justin. This is (methodologically) familiar territory. Theophilus charts a new direction, however, when he introduces two extensive passages from the Jewish scriptures and employs a commentary format as the mechanism for presenting his own teachings; how he does this will be considered further below.

Justin, Tatian and Theophilus share a wish that readers should become more familiar with the scriptures through direct exposure to the texts, although they adopt different strategies to achieve this. Justin quotes

---

128. *AA* 2.36.1.
129. *AA* 2.36.16.
130. *AA* 2.3.2.
131. *AA* 2.31.6.
132. *AA* 3.11.1-6.

relatively short extracts, Tatian barely quotes at all (leaving engagement with texts to a later occasion), while Theophilus adopts the novel approach of quoting at length, no doubt recognising that his readers are unfamiliar with them. He explicitly encourages them to tackle the texts for themselves, saying: 'For those who wish to can read what was said through them [the prophets] and acquire accurate knowledge of the truth.'[133] Perhaps more important than what he says, however, is what he does, in laying before them extensive extracts from Genesis quoted verbatim.

Thus, while Theophilus' approach to the scriptures overlaps to a considerable degree with those of Justin and Tatian, there are also novel features in *Ad Autolycum* in both content and form. In terms of *content*, Theophilus uses the Jewish scriptures as the source for an accurate history of the world from the beginning of time to the return of the Jews from the Babylonian Exile. In terms of *form*, Theophilus not only sets out two extended extracts from the Jewish scriptures that are complete and coherent narratives, but he accompanies each with a commentary, a technique which, as will be shown, parallels the treatment of highly regarded texts in Graeco-Roman culture.

The Sacred Writings as a Source for Accurate History

Theophilus asserts that the Sacred Writings are true and claims that they are an important source providing accurate information about past events in human history. The second half of Book 3 is devoted to a demonstration of this. Neither Justin nor Tatian treated the Jewish scriptures as history in this way, so *Ad Autolycum* contains something novel in extant Christian apologetic writing in this respect.[134]

Justin has been shown to use prophetic material to tell the story of the life of Jesus Christ and the mission of the Apostles and to explain their significance. He also referred to prophecies about public events, such as the defeat of the Jews by the Romans, although he was not seeking to construct a general history. Tatian is also interested in historical events but very specifically in demonstrating that Moses was more ancient than Homer and, indeed, more ancient than the whole of Greek culture. Moreover, to achieve his objective he cites evidence from Greek, Chaldean, Phoenician and Egyptian sources and makes barely any use of the Jewish scriptures for this purpose.

---

133. *AA* 2.35.14.
134. For the broader historical perspective: M. Wallraff, 'The Beginning of Christian Universal History from Tatian to Julius Africanus', *ZAC*, vol. 14 (2011), pp. 540-55.

Theophilus adopts a different strategy, preferring to use the Sacred Writings as evidence in support of historical arguments: 'Hence it is obvious how our Sacred Writings are proved to be more ancient and more true than the writings of the Greeks and the Egyptians or any other historiographers.'[135] For Theophilus, the value of the Sacred Writings as a source for history is due to two factors which have already been noted: 'the antiquity of the prophetic writings and the divine nature of our message.'[136]

By contrast with the Sacred Writings, Greek historians only go back in time a certain distance and cannot deal with more ancient history: 'For most writers, such as Herodotus and Thucydides and Xenophon and the other historiographers, begin their accounts at about the reign of Cyrus and Darius, since they are unable to make accurate statements about the ancient times prior to them.'[137] Moreover, the divine nature of the message of the Sacred Writings gives them a factual accuracy denied to other sources. Thus, Theophilus highlights inaccuracies in the work of the Egyptian historian Manetho who, he says, claimed – contrary to the testimony in the Sacred Writings – that the Hebrews were expelled from Egypt because of leprosy and who was unable to establish a correct chronology of the events surrounding the Exodus.[138] Consequently, his history does not have the factual reliability of the Sacred Writings.

Theophilus' chronology begins with Adam, follows the narrative of the Jewish scriptures through the period of the Flood and the Patriarchs, the migration to and return from Egypt, the period of the Judges and the Monarchy up to the Babylonian Exile and ends with the return from the Exile under Cyrus the Persian.[139] He does not say in so many words that this chronology derives from the Sacred Writings but various comments strongly imply this. Thus, he begins by 'going back to the first beginning of the creation of the world, which Moses the minister of God described',[140] a comment which reads very like a description of the early chapters of Genesis. He also says that he is only able to provide such information 'with God's help',[141] asserting that: 'I ask favour from the one God that I may speak the whole truth accurately according to his will.'[142] These remarks indicate that he considers his source to be divinely inspired and this is a

---

135. *AA* 3.26.1.
136. *AA* 3.29.1.
137. *AA* 3.26.1.
138. *AA* 3.21.1.
139. *AA* 3.24-3.25.
140. *AA* 3.23.5.
141. *AA* 3.23.5.
142. *AA* 3.23.7.

characteristic of the Sacred Writings. Moreover, at two points Theophilus refers to the accuracy of the Sacred Writings as a historical source, the first before he sets out his chronology and the second afterwards. On the first occasion he says: 'Hence it is obvious how our Sacred Writings are proved to be more ancient and more true than the writings of the Greeks and the Egyptians or any other historiographers'[143] and on the second:

> From the compilation of the periods of time and from all that has been said, the antiquity of the prophetic writings and the divine nature of our message are obvious. This message is not recent in origin, nor are our writings, as some suppose, mythical and false, but actually more ancient and more trustworthy.[144]

Theophilus' chronological narrative is bald, with little more than names and lengths of time, for instance:

> Isaac . . . lived 60 years until he had issue and begot Jacob: Jacob lived 130 years before the migration to Egypt. . . . The sojourning of the Hebrews in Egypt lasted 430 years, and after their exodus from the land of Egypt they lived in what is called the desert for 40 years. The total, then, is 3,938 years to the time when Moses died.[145]

The computation of lengths of time is clearly important and a number of sub-totals are included in the course of the narrative, so that from Adam to the Deluge is 2,242 years,[146] to Abraham is 3,278 years,[147] to the death of Moses is 3,938 years[148] and to 'the sojourning in the land of Babylon is 4,954 years, 6 months and 10 days'.[149]

Theophilus does not make any further use of the numbers emerging from his computations and no arguments are built upon them, so it must be asked why he accords them the importance he evidently does. Two points can be made. First, the large size of the numbers produced by computing totals shows the great length of time which has elapsed

143. *AA* 3.26.1.
144. *AA* 3.29.1.
145. *AA* 3.24.3.
146. *AA* 3.24.1.
147. *AA* 3.24.2.
148. *AA* 3.24.3.
149. *AA* 3.25.3.

from Adam to the present day and attests to the antiquity of the events being recounted. Second, the precision of the computations, to the year, and ultimately to the day, demonstrates the great accuracy of the Sacred Writings as a historical record.

There are only two brief references to Theophilus' historical account being anything more than a chronology of events. The first is his comment that the Babylonian captivity was a consequence of the sins of the Jewish people: 'since the people remained in their sins and did not repent, in accordance with the prophecy of Jeremiah, a king of Babylon named Nebuchadnezzar went up to Judaea. He transferred the people of the Jews to Babylon and destroyed the temple which Solomon had built.'[150] The second is his observation that the beginning and the end of the Babylonian captivity were prophesied by God speaking through Jeremiah: 'Just as God foretold through the prophet Jeremiah that the people would be led captive to Babylon, so he indicated in advance that they would come back again to their own land after 70 years.'[151] These comments are exceptional, however, since, for the most part, Theophilus' interest in the Sacred Writings as a historical record is purely in the chronology which they provide. The events referred to are not accorded any intrinsic interest beyond enabling numbers of years to be counted and, indeed, Theophilus says as much: 'Our concern is not with material for loquacity but with making clear the length of time from the beginning of the world.'[152]

The historical narrative is told entirely through the story of the Jewish people, at least up to the time of Cyrus, which is, of course, a consequence of using a Jewish source. The other peoples who inhabited the region at the same time and were the Jews' neighbours are only mentioned when they are part of the Jews' narrative history.[153] There is virtually no sense that the narrative is an account of the relationship of God with the Jewish people, however. Theophilus' does not treat his historical narrative as a source of theological or ethical insights, despite the strong interest in theological issues he displays elsewhere in *Ad Autolycum*.

From the end of the Babylonian Exile onwards, Theophilus utilises a historical source from outside the Sacred Writings. He does not refer to later texts from the Jewish scriptures which contain historical material, such as Ezra and Nehemiah or 1 and 2 Maccabees. He does not state why;

---

150. *AA* 3.25.3.
151. *AA* 3.25.4.
152. *AA* 3.26.3. B. Pouderon, *Les apologistes grecs du IIe siècle* (Paris: Éditions du Cerf, 2005), p. 249, comments on Theophilus' lack of interest in the significance of historical events.
153. E.g. the reference to the Midianites in *AA* 3.24.4.

perhaps he did not know these texts[154] or perhaps the task of establishing a chronology from them was too difficult (which in the case of Maccabees, for instance, would be readily understandable). It may, however, be that he regarded his Roman source as more reliable; or he may have considered that use of a Roman source was better suited to his purpose, since he was engaging with a Graeco-Roman audience who may well have been familiar with the source, or at least with the material contained in it. In any event, he switches at the death of Cyrus to the source described as 'Chryseros the Nomenclator, a freedman of M. Aurelius Verus'[155] – and thus a contemporary of Theophilus – and the chronology then becomes that of the history of Rome rather than the Jews. This enables Theophilus to bring his account right up to the death of Emperor Marcus Aurelius in 180 CE, an event computed to be 5,695 years (with additional months and days) from the creation of the world.[156]

One consequence of using Chryseros the Nomenclator as the authoritative source for his later chronology is that Theophilus makes no mention of Jesus Christ as a historical figure, a point noted by both Bardy and Pouderon.[157] Thus, the account of the chronology of the Jewish scriptures includes a series of names of significant historical figures ending with Cyrus, and the earlier history of the Jews is not presented as leading up to, or culminating in, the figure who might be expected to be of prime importance to a Christian apologist. Theophilus' interest is, however, historical and not soteriological. Bardy's suggestion that reference to Christ is omitted because the argument from antiquity would lose all its force if the beginnings of Christianity were dated to the time of Jesus is a compelling one;[158] moreover, since *Ad Autolycum* is an apologetic work, use of a Graeco-Roman source for chronological information is an appropriate strategy since the external audience would be more likely to accept its reliability.

Theophilus' chronology is the first extant example of a form that would become significant for Christian literature, as later authors from the third century onwards developed their chronologies.[159] Caution

---

154. At *AA* 1.4.5 Theophilus appears to be quoting from 2 Macc 7:28, although he may have taken this isolated reference from a summary or quotation source.

155. *AA* 3.27.3. Chryseros is not otherwise known: 'Our sole source on Chryseros is the Christian apologist Theophilus of Antioch', BNJ article on Chryseros by V. Costa. M. Aurelius Verus is normally styled Marcus Aurelius, Emperor from 161 to 180 CE.

156. *AA* 3.28.7.

157. Bardy, *AA*, p. 53; Pouderon, *Les apologistes grecs*, p. 248.

158. Bardy, *AA*, p. 53.

159. W. Adler, *Time Immemorial: Archaic History and Its Sources in Christian*

should be exercised in crediting Theophilus with too much originality, however, for his work has parallels, and, indeed, roots, in existing traditions of non-Christian historical literature.

From the third century BCE onwards, interest in writing works of general history with a wide chronological sweep developed in Hellenistic culture[160] and, although many of these have not survived, they are known to have been written; histories by Nicolaus of Damascus[161] and Timagenes of Alexandria[162] are cases in point. Some historians wrote accounts, like Theophilus, stretching back to the earliest times, indeed to Creation. Examples of this are the works of Diodorus Siculus[163] and Philo of Biblos,[164] each of whose histories commenced with an account of the creation of the world. The Jews had a long tradition of historical writing of their own but they came to be influenced by Hellenistic practice.[165] Theophilus' history is told largely through an account of the Jews and this has counterparts in the works of Berossus,[166] who in the third century BCE wrote a history of the Babylonians, and Manetho,[167] the third-century-BCE historian of the Egyptians; in both these cases, as with Theophilus, part of the purpose was to demonstrate, and, indeed, celebrate, the antiquity of the people whose history was being narrated.[168] Theophilus had some familiarity with the contents of the works of both Berossus and Manetho – whether or not he actually knew their texts directly – as will be discussed below.

Chronography from Julius Africanus to George Syncellus (Washington, DC: Dumbarton Oaks, 1989).

160. Mortley, *Idea of Universal History.*

161. BNP article on Nicolaus by K. Meister. He was active in the first century BCE.

162. BNP article on Timagenes by K Meister. He was also active in the first century BCE.

163. Diodorus Siculus, *Library of History*, 1.4.6, gives an outline of the chronological scope of the work from before the Trojan War to the campaigns of Julius Caesar. He wrote in the first century BCE.

164. Philo of Biblos, *The Phoenician History: Introduction, Critical Text, Translation and Notes*, ed. by H.W. Attridge and R.A. Oden Jr (Washington, DC: Catholic Biblical Association of America, 1981). He was active in the first to second century CE.

165. G.E. Sterling, 'The Jewish Appropriation of Hellenistic Historiography', in J. Marincola, ed., *A Companion to Greek and Roman Historiography*, 2 vols (Oxford: Blackwell Publishing, 2007), 1, pp. 231-43.

166. BNP article on Berossus by B. Pongratz-Leisten.

167. BNP article on Manetho by R. Krauss.

168. For the apologetic historiography of these authors: Sterling, *Historiography and Self-Definition*, pp. 103-36.

Thus, Theophilus' chronology fulfils a number of objectives. First, it demonstrates the antiquity of the Jewish people and their traditions from which Christianity was derived. Second, it shows the authority and status of the Sacred Writings that provided the source for his accurate historical account. Third, in drawing material from a Roman source as well as from the Jewish scriptures, Theophilus made his chronology universal so it became, not an account of the Jewish people only, but, in its later stages, a chronology of the whole world. Jewish chronology thus acquires a central historical position as the precursor to the chronology of the Roman Empire.

Grant[169] and Hardwick[170] have described how Theophilus drew a significant amount of his material from *Against Apion* by Josephus.[171] The Jewish apologist's aims were similar to those of Theophilus in that he sought to demonstrate to a non-Jewish audience the great antiquity of the Jewish people, particularly compared with the relatively recent origins of Greek culture. Like Tatian, however, he cites non-Jewish sources in support of his argument, rather than the Jewish texts Theophilus uses. Theophilus only names Josephus once and, then, not with reference to *Against Apion*, but as the author of a history of the Jewish war against the Romans.[172] *Against Apion* is an important source for *Ad Autolycum*. However, it is the material in the text of Josephus – references to the writings of Manetho[173] and the second-century-BCE writer Menander of Ephesus,[174] to evidence from Tyrian sources[175] and from Berossus[176] – rather than the views or arguments of Josephus himself, on which Theophilus draws. Thus, for Theophilus, Josephus' text is merely a conduit to reach the writings of Berossus, Manetho and Menander and, in building his own chronology, he adopts a different strategy from Josephus, relying principally on the Jewish sacred writings as the source of his evidence and not – as Josephus does – on non-Jewish historians.

---

169. Grant, 'Bible of Theophilus', pp. 191-96.
170. M.E. Hardwick, *Josephus as an Historical Source in Patristic Literature through Eusebius* (Atlanta: Scholars Press, 1989), pp. 11-14, and M. Hardwick, 'Contra Apionem and Christian Apologetics', in L.H. Feldman and J.R. Levison, eds, *Josephus'* Contra Apionem: *Studies in Its Character and Context with a Latin Concordance to the Portion Missing in Greek* (Leiden: Brill, 1996), pp. 369-402, 371-78.
171. The references are listed in Marcovich, *AA*, p. 147.
172. *AA* 3.23.1.
173. *AA* 3.20.1 and 3.21.1-6.
174. *AA* 3.22.3-7.
175. *AA* 3.22.1.
176. *AA* 3.29.7.

Ad Autolycum as a Commentary on the Sacred Writings

As well as presenting the Sacred Writings as a source for accurate history, Theophilus also provides his readers with textual commentary on them. A considerable portion of Book 2 is devoted to this. Having criticised Greek literature and the ideas they contain at length,[177] he then presents his own alternative literary tradition, the Sacred Writings. He quotes in full the Creation narrative from Genesis 1:1-2:3[178] and the narrative of the Garden of Eden from Genesis 2:8-3:19.[179] Unlike Justin or Tatian, he presents these extracts from the Sacred Writings as continuous narratives. He provides two complete and coherent sections of Genesis, giving each an overall description or title; the Creation narrative is labelled the 'Hexaemeros'[180] and the Garden of Eden narrative 'the history of man and paradise'.[181]

Theophilus supplies a commentary to explain the texts to his audience. The term commentary does not appear in *Ad Autolycum* but describes well the process in which Theophilus is engaged. In employing a form which would be familiar to his Graeco-Roman audience, Theophilus follows Tatian in drawing on the resources of literary criticism, although he does so very differently. Moreover, there is a similarity with Justin in formal terms for, just as the Proof from Prophecy is included within Justin's *First Apology* (a work with the overall form of a petition), so Theophilus' commentary is part of a larger text which is framed as a communication addressed to Autolycus.

The commentary accompanying each Genesis extract goes sequentially through the text, providing a succession of comments to aid readers' understanding and appreciation. Theophilus explains little of what he is doing. At the commencement of the Creation narrative he says that 'these things the Sacred Writings teach first'[182] and, when the text ends, he goes straight into his commentary. He begins the Garden of Eden narrative with: 'The writings thus contain the words of the sacred history [Τὰ δὲ ῥητὰ τῆς ἱστορίας τῆς ἱερᾶς]'[183] and, when the quoted extract finishes, he again moves into his commentary. Theophilus says nothing about the process he is following in commenting on texts but an understanding of his approach emerges from examining what he does.

---

177. *AA* 2.1-8.
178. *AA* 2.10-11.
179. *AA* 2.20-21.
180. *AA* 2.12.1.
181. *AA* 2.21.5.
182. *AA* 2.10.10.
183. *AA* 2.20.1.

A commentary on the Jewish scriptures is something new in surviving Christian texts of the time.[184] Scholars have been particularly interested in exploring the possible Jewish roots of Theophilus' work[185] but it will be examined here in the context of the Graeco-Roman commentary tradition. In Chapter 2 above it was noted that the practice of writing commentaries on highly regarded texts was well-established by the late Hellenistic period; reference was made there to the *Anonymous Commentary on Plato's* Theaetetus and this can act as a useful comparator for *Ad Autolycum*. There is no suggestion that Theophilus knew the *Anonymous Commentary*; commentaries of this kind would, however, have been familiar to those, like Theophilus and his audience, who had received a Graeco-Roman literary education. Chapter 2 included a summary (not repeated here) of the useful analysis in the Introduction to Bastianini and Sedley's edition of the *Commentary*[186] which describes the approach taken by its anonymous author.

The *Anonymous Commentary* is predicated on a number of implicit assumptions which are relevant to the comparison with *Ad Autolycum*. The Platonic text being commented on must be accepted as having a high status if it is to merit such close and extended attention; the issues which arise in commenting on it are both textual and interpretative; and the *Theaetetus* is a text which can, and by the time the *Commentary* was written had been, interpreted in a number of different ways. It is not always a straightforward text, so the reader needs guidance to understand it properly; indeed, the anonymous author of the *Commentary* observes that Plato never sets out his ideas plainly, leaving the reader (or perhaps he means the commentator) to expand on what he says and explain what he means.[187]

Rather than comparing point by point the two commentators' methods, the approach here will be to examine what Theophilus does and judge this, where relevant, against the background provided by the

---

184. Fragments survive of a commentary by Herakleon on a New Testament text, the Gospel of John, from earlier in the second century: *Fragments of Heracleon*, ed. by A.E. Brooke (Cambridge: Cambridge University Press, 1891); W. Löhr, 'Gnostic and Manichaean Interpretation', in NCHB1, pp. 584-604, 586-87.

185. E.g. R.M. Grant, 'Theophilus of Antioch to Autolycus', *HTR*, vol. 40 (1947), pp. 227-56, especially 237-41.

186. *Anonymous Commentary* (*AC*), pp. 257-59.

187. *AC*, p. 258: 'This way of proceeding is justified by A's [the anonymous author] (LIX 12-21) observation that Plato never makes his own theory clear, leaving to the reader the task of working it out'. In the Aristotelian tradition obscurity of expression was almost expected and, indeed, taken as a sign of authenticity; hence, the need for commentaries to explain texts: Tuominen, *Ancient commentators*, p. 3.

Anonymous Commentary. There are points of similarity but also points of divergence, with the latter often arising from the difference in the circumstances in which the commentaries were written. The author of the *Anonymous Commentary* was writing about a text that was familiar to his audience and accepted as being highly regarded; his task was to explain it and on occasions to argue for his own interpretation over those of other commentators. Theophilus in *Ad Autolycum* was writing a commentary on a text which was unfamiliar to his audience and his task was less to distinguish between rival interpretations of the Sacred Writings (although he occasionally does this) so much as to argue for the superiority of these texts over the rival non-Christian non-Jewish alternatives which might be familiar to his readers. Providing a commentary on the Sacred Writings was therefore part of Theophilus' apologetic strategy.

Clearly, by devoting so much space to the early chapters of Genesis, Theophilus presents his Sacred Writings as a text that is a source of ideas about Creation and the nature of humankind which should be regarded highly. Like the author of the *Anonymous Commentary*, Theophilus goes sequentially through the text. A clear example of this is 2.15-2.19, where he discusses each day of the week in the Creation narrative in turn from the fourth day to the seventh.[188] Theophilus differs from the Anonymous author in quoting the whole text of the section under consideration at the outset and then providing a commentary.[189] The Anonymous Commentator, by contrast, quotes extracts one at a time and comments immediately on each of them; furthermore, he only quotes selectively and, although his extracts collectively comprise more than half of Plato's text, this is still some way short of the complete text which Theophilus provides.[190] Theophilus is not explicit but this difference of approach most likely results from the fact that Theophilus' audience was unfamiliar with the text, so he wanted to bring their attention to the whole section of text to be discussed before commenting on it. The audience of the *Anonymous Commentary* would have known Plato's *Theaetetus* already – or at least have had ready access to it – so the whole text did not need to be quoted by the commentator at the outset, and he is able to move straight into citing and commenting on specific passages.

---

188. *AA* 2.15 discusses the fourth day, 2.16, the fifth day, 2.17-2.18, the sixth day and 2.19, the seventh day.

189. This comment is subject to the proviso that in *AA* 2.10 at the start of the Creation account, some comments are interspersed with the Genesis text, although this is not Theophilus' practice thereafter.

190. *AC*, pp. 256-57.

Like the *Anonymous Commentary* Theophilus' commentary at times discusses detailed points in the text. He picks on a number of individual words and phrases and either explains in simple terms what they mean – 'What he [the prophet Moses] calls earth is equivalent to a base and foundation. Abyss is the multitude of the waters'[191] – or explains their significance – '"Darkness" is mentioned because the heaven created by God was like a lid covering the waters with the earth.'[192] Later, he lights on use of the first-person plural in Genesis 1:26, describing the creation of humankind:

> When God said: 'Let us make man after our image and likeness' he first reveals the dignity of man. For after creating everything else through the Logos,[193] God considered all this as secondary; the creation of man he regarded as the only work worthy of his own hands. Furthermore, God is found saying 'Let us make man after the image and likeness' as if he needed assistance; but he said 'Let us make' to none other than his own Logos and his own Sophia.[194]

Genesis 1:26 is a text which attracted varying interpretations from ancient commentators.[195] Theophilus explains that it should be read not to mean that God needed help from others when he created man,[196] but that, while in the previous stages of Creation God had acted through the Logos, the creation of man was uniquely worthy of action on the part of God himself because of the special status humankind was to enjoy. The first-person plural is therefore used by God, when addressing the Logos and the Sophia,[197] in order to show that God is involving himself together with them in the act of creation.

---

191. *AA* 2.13.3.
192. *AA* 2.13.3.
193. Grant renders λόγῳ as 'by a word'. Marcovich gives it a capital lambda, indicating that the text is referring to the Logos, rather than simply 'a word', and it is this latter textual reading which underpins the translation here.
194. *AA* 2.18.1-2.
195. E.g. *Dialogue with Trypho* 62.1-5. For Philo of Alexandria: *On the Creation of the Cosmos According to Moses: Introduction, Translation and Commentary*, by D.T. Runia (Atlanta: SBL, 2001), pp. 65-66.
196. This could refer to an alternative reading of Genesis 1:26-27 that Theophilus was aware was then current.
197. Theophilus refers elsewhere to 'the triad of God and his Logos and his Sophia' (*AA* 2.15.4) and to the involvement of both the Logos and the Sophia in primal creation: 'God made everything through his Logos and the Sophia' (*AA* 1.7.3).

A final example of detailed textual comment is found when Theophilus picks apart the order in which words appear in the Sacred Writings to identify a point of particular significance. Discussing Genesis 1.1, 'ἐν ἀρχῇ ἐποίησεν ὁ θεὸς τὸν οὐρανὸν καὶ τὴν γῆν' (In the beginning God made heaven and earth), Theophilus draws attention to the fact that the terms 'ἀρχῇ' and 'ἐποίησεν' appear before 'θεὸς', commenting as follows: 'First he mentioned beginning and creation, and only then introduced God, for it is not fitting to refer to God idly and in vain.'[198] His point is presumably that the subject ὁ θεὸς might be expected to appear at or closer to the beginning of the sentence and before the verb ἐποίησεν. When Theophilus refers elsewhere to God's act of creation using his own words, he places θεὸς before ἐποίησεν, so this would appear to be what he regards as the normal word order.[199]

These references show Theophilus, as a commentator well might, and as the Anonymous Commentator does, explaining specific words in the text. The *Anonymous Commentary* also includes paraphrase and exegesis – with the proviso previously noted that the distinction between these two is not always clear-cut – and considers issues and problems raised by the text. Theophilus is similarly interested in going beyond detailed textual questions in order to explain what the text says and how it should be understood; indeed, he bears out the comment in the *Anonymous Commentary*, referred to earlier, to the effect that Plato never sets out his ideas plainly and leaves the reader to work out what he means. Differences do arise, however, between *Ad Autolycum* and the *Anonymous Commentary* and these can (broadly speaking) be attributed to the fact that *Ad Autolycum* is an apologetic text unlike the *Anonymous Commentary*; commentary on the Sacred Writings is an apologetic strategy and Theophilus uses approaches and techniques which serve this purpose.

An example of paraphrase and exegesis is Theophilus' commentary on the passage in Genesis 2 describing how God created paradise and placed Adam in it. Theophilus provides some paraphrasing of the Genesis text when he describes God's creation of the Garden, with its two trees of life and of knowledge, and later describes how God placed man in paradise 'to work it and to guard it'.[200] He also adds two interpretative points. First, he clarifies where the location of paradise is; not somewhere far distant but located under the same heaven as the earth: 'By the expressions "also from the earth" and "to the east" the Sacred Writings clearly teach us

---

198. *AA* 2.10.7.
199. *AA* 1.7.3. The same is true of *AA* 1.4.5, although in that case Theophilus appears to be quoting 2 Maccabees 7.28 (Marcovich, *AA*, p. 19, n.).
200. *AA* 2.24.5.

that paradise is under this very heaven under which are the east and the earth.'[201] Second, he explains that, at least in terms of its beauty, paradise is in an intermediate state between earth and heaven, just as humankind is in an intermediate state between the mortal and the immortal. This is a hook on which he hangs an account of the essential nature of humankind as having potential for mortality or immortality:

> God transferred humankind out of the earth from which it was made into paradise, providing the opportunity for progress, so that by growing and becoming perfect, and furthermore having been declared a god, it might also ascend into heaven and possess immortality. For humankind was created in an intermediate state, neither wholly mortal nor entirely immortal, but capable of either state; similarly the place paradise – as regards beauty – was created intermediate between the world and heaven.[202]

A slightly different example of paraphrase and exegesis is provided when Theophilus discusses the tree of knowledge and the fall of humankind described in Genesis 2-3. The balance here tilts away from paraphrase and more towards exegesis. There is still an element of paraphrase, for instance, in Theophilus' description of the tree of knowledge, although it is brief and most of his commentary is concerned with two exegetical points. Theophilus writes as the Anonymous Commentator does when he expounds the meaning of Plato's text. First, to explain the relationship between God and Adam, Theophilus compares the latter to a child who should obey his parent and then adds some more general comments about the nature of children: 'For it is a sacred matter, not only before God but in the face of humankind, to obey one's parents in simplicity and without malice; and if children must obey their parents, how much more must they obey the God and Father of the universe!'[203] Second, he emphasises that it was not the commandment not to eat the fruit which led to the Fall, but rather Adam's disobedience of the commandment and, again, he imports a general homiletic statement: 'when a law commands abstinence from something and someone does not obey, it is clearly not the law which results in punishment but the disobedience and the transgression.'[204] Theophilus' reading is that God

---

201. *AA* 2.24.3.
202. *AA* 2.24.6-7.
203. *AA* 2.25.4.
204. *AA* 2.25.6.

sought to test Adam but, by disobeying God's command, Adam failed the test. Thus, responsibility for the Fall lay with Adam: 'So also for the first-formed human being, disobedience resulted in his expulsion from paradise.'[205]

Exegesis can lead to issues being identified which call for more extended discussion, especially when the text is found to contain problems or difficulties which require explanation. One of the functions of the *Anonymous Commentary* was to consider difficult issues which arose in Plato's text and to propose solutions, and there are parallels to this in *Ad Autolycum* when Theophilus identifies an issue or a question and seeks to explain or answer it. One example is when Theophilus asks why God created Eve as he did out of the body of Adam rather than simply *de novo*. His rather surprising – and ingenious – explanation is that God had foreknowledge that human beings would erroneously identify a multitude of gods and he wanted to prevent it being thought that one of those gods had made man and another had made woman; hence, his statement that God 'did not make the two separately'.[206] He then gives an additional explanation of God's action by saying that he made the woman out of the man's side 'so that the man's love for her might be the greater'.[207] In a second example, Theophilus asks the question: how could God be described as walking in paradise when it is the nature of God not to be confined in one place? His response is that it is the Logos generated by God who is present in the garden and not God himself. The Logos has a divine nature but is nevertheless able to be in a particular place: 'Since the Logos is God and derived his nature from God, the Father of the universe, whenever he wishes, sends him into some place where he is present and is heard and seen. He is sent by God and is found in a place.'[208]

When tackling a problematic issue, the Anonymous Commentator sometimes considers more than one rival interpretation of Plato's text and discusses which should be preferred. There are instances of this in *Ad Autolycum*, although they are neither numerous nor prominent. When discussing the tree of knowledge and the fall of humankind,

---

205. *AA* 2.25.8.
206. *AA* 2.28.2: the translation here follows the substitution by Marcovich (*AA*, p. 78, n.) of οὐκ (not) for the manuscript οὖν (therefore) and of ἀμφίς (literally, apart) for the manuscript ἄμφω (both). It is possible that there was a theory extant at the time that one god created Adam and another Eve and that Theophilus is explicitly refuting it.
207. *AA* 2.28.3.
208. *AA* 2.22.6.

Theophilus refers twice to rival interpretations of Genesis, first saying, 'For the tree did not contain death, as some suppose'[209] and later, when discussing God's relationship with Adam, 'Therefore God was not jealous, as some suppose, in commanding him not to eat of the tree of knowledge.'[210] Recognition that other interpretations exist does not lead Theophilus to specify what these are or to discuss their relative merits and, from the brevity of his comments, it is clearly not his intention to dwell on these issues. His commentary essentially promotes a single reading of the Sacred Writings – his own – and gives little consideration to others that might exist. In this respect, his approach is consistent with the approaches taken by Justin and Tatian when they discussed texts or ideas from their authoritative writings.

This is not to say that Theophilus is not concerned with combatting competing ideas, rather that his interest is in promoting the claims of the Sacred Writings against rival claims which derive from the Greek literary tradition. After his extended quotation from the Genesis Creation narrative, and before his detailed comments on that text, he refers first in general terms to the quality of the Genesis text, contrasting it with the unsatisfactory accounts of Creation found in Greek literature.[211] Speaking of the Genesis account of Creation he writes: 'No one . . . even if he were to live ten thousand years . . . would be competent to say anything adequately in regard to these matters, because of the surpassing greatness and riches of the Wisdom of God to be found in this Hexaemeros quoted above.'[212] He notes that many have tried to provide Creation accounts but subjects them to a blanket condemnation; even though he recognises that they have 'imitated' Genesis or 'taken it as their starting point',[213] the claims made by philosophers, historians and poets are characterised by 'the abundance of their nonsense and the absence of even the slightest measure of truth in their writings'.[214]

This does not really explain why Theophilus considers the Greek accounts of Creation to be wrong. However, his criticisms become more specific as he singles out the poet Hesiod for attack and contrasts the latter's Creation account unfavourably with Genesis. First, he attacks

---

209. *AA* 2.25.1.
210. *AA* 2.25.3: the translation here follows Marcovich's addition of the words τοῦ ξύλου (of the tree) which are not in the manuscript.
211. The variety of approaches to Creation among the Greek philosophical schools was noted in Chapter 3 above: Sedley, *Creationism*.
212. *AA* 2.12.1.
213. *AA* 2.12.2: an echo of the theft theory referred to earlier.
214. *AA* 2.12.3.

Hesiod for claiming that Erebus, Earth and Eros were created out of Chaos to rule over gods and men and describes his account as 'foolish and false and entirely alien to the truth'.[215] Second, he argues that, whereas Genesis begins with the creation of the heavens, Hesiod begins erroneously with the creation of earthly things: 'Furthermore, as for his [Hesiod's] notion of describing creation by starting from beneath, with what is earthly, it is merely human and mean and, indeed, quite feeble in relation to God'.[216] Condemning alternative Greek accounts of Creation reflects a broader theme already found in Justin and Tatian: the contrast between the contents of the Sacred Writings on the one hand and the Greek literary tradition on the other, always presented to the detriment of the latter.

The parallels between *Ad Autolycum* and the *Anonymous Commentary* are therefore considerable. There are, however, also differences, notably in the way that Theophilus uses techniques that go beyond expounding and explaining what is in the text, in order to advance his apologetic purpose.[217] The first is the identification of types to which attention is drawn to uncover hidden significance in the text; the second is the addition of descriptive details not in the Genesis text which are used to draw out points Theophilus wishes to share with his readers; while the third is the use of a word or phrase as a trigger or starting point for a discussion of issues only distantly related to the surface content of the text.

The word 'type', τύπος, appears a number of times in *Ad Autolycum*,[218] when Theophilus identifies references in the Sacred Writings which he reads as types of entities external to the text and uses them to expose meanings not found on the surface of the words. Thus, Theophilus follows Justin in invoking symbols to explain the meaning of texts. An example is Theophilus' discussion of the fourth day of creation which includes the creation of the sun and the moon. He identifies these two

---

215. *AA* 2.12.6: the translation here follows the substitution by Marcovich (*AA*, p. 58, n.) of ψυδρὸν (false) for the manuscript ψυχρὸν (frigid).

216. *AA* 2.13.1.

217. Parsons, *Ancient Apologetic Exegesis*, p. 41, points the way by commenting that 'unlike many modern commentators, he [Theophilus] did not provide an intentionally impassive, verse-by-verse exposition. Rather he commented on the Genesis text specifically to support his own apologetic polemic.'

218. Marcovich, *AA*, p. 189, lists eight occurrences of τύπος or τύποι, all in Book 2. In one instance, at 2.13.4. Grant, *AA*, p. 48, n., follows the eighteenth-century editor Maran in substituting τόπον (place) for the manuscript reading τύπον (type) (even though he acknowledges that Maran 'did not make direct use of the manuscripts', p. xxii).

heavenly bodies as types, the sun as a type of God and the moon as a type of humankind and the contrast between the qualities of the two physical entities, sun and moon, is used to point up differences between human and divine natures:

> As the sun greatly surpasses the moon in power and brightness, so God greatly surpasses humankind; and just as the sun always remains full and does not wane, so God always remains perfect and is full of all power, intelligence, wisdom, immortality and all good things. But the moon wanes every month and virtually dies, for it exists as a type of humankind; then it is reborn and waxes as a pattern of future resurrection.[219]

In other cases, types have a prophetic edge when the text of Genesis is found to foreshadow later occurrences. God's blessing of sea creatures on the fifth day of creation is a type of the redemption of humankind in the future: 'those created from the waters were blessed by God so that this might serve as a pattern of humankind's future reception of repentance and remission of sins through water and a bath of regeneration'.[220] On the sixth day when land creatures are created, but are *not* blessed by God, they become a type of human beings in the future who 'are ignorant of God and sin against him and have regard to earthly things and do not repent'.[221]

Introducing types in this way enables Theophilus to make points not apparent from the surface of the text of Genesis but significant for his apologetic purpose. A somewhat complex example is found in Theophilus' discussion of the fourth day of creation, the day 'the luminaries came into existence'.[222] This prompts him to backtrack and identify the first three days prior to the fourth, retrospectively, as 'types of the triad of God and his Logos and his Sophia'.[223] The fourth entity is humankind which Theophilus adds to the triad and which needs the light supplied by the luminaries created on the fourth day.

A second technique used by Theophilus is to embellish the Genesis narrative with additional details which are not in the original text and to use these to identify issues of significance. Genesis describes the creation of the heavenly bodies on the fourth day but says nothing about there

---

219. *AA* 2.15.2-3.
220. *AA* 2.16.2.
221. *AA* 2.17.2.
222. *AA* 2.15.1.
223. *AA* 2.15.4.

being different types of star. Theophilus, however, describes three different ranks of star, the brightest, the less bright and the least bright, which are the planets. He then goes on to describe how these correspond to three sorts of human beings: the brightest stars correspond to those who 'exist in imitation of the prophets' and 'remain steadfast', the less bright stars are 'types of the people of the righteous', while those called planets are 'a type of the human beings who depart from God, abandoning his laws and ordinances'.[224] Theophilus is here filling out the Genesis narrative, which makes no reference to different sorts of star, and providing additional details which he uses to identify different types of human beings.

Something similar occurs with the creation of sea creatures and birds on the fifth day. The Genesis account simply describes the act of creation and concludes with the words: 'And God saw that they were good.'[225] Theophilus introduces the adjective '*σαρκοβόρα*' (carnivorous) to describe the birds created by God, a term not in Genesis. This enables him to identify two sorts of creature, which can crudely be described as the good and the bad; one sort 'remain in their natural state, not injuring those weaker than themselves but observing the law of God and eating from the seeds of the earth',[226] while the other sort 'transgress the law of God, eating flesh and injuring those weaker than themselves'.[227] The addition of the term 'carnivorous' is necessary to make this distinction, since the key difference between the two sorts of creature is that the good is herbivorous and the bad carnivorous. Theophilus then equates the two sorts of creature with two sorts of people: on the one hand, the righteous, 'who keep the law of God, do not bite or injure anyone but live in a holy and just manner',[228] while, on the other hand, the 'robbers and murderers and the godless are like great fish and wild animals and carnivorous birds; they virtually consume those weaker than themselves'.[229] Hence, a small addition to the Genesis text – introduction of the adjective 'carnivorous' – enables Theophilus to develop a distinction of his own between two sorts of creature and to use this to differentiate between righteous and unrighteous human beings.

The third technique employed by Theophilus is to use the text of Genesis as a springboard for a discussion, which wanders far from the content of the text that generates it, so that the ensuing debate can scarcely

---

224. *AA* 2.15.5-6.
225. Genesis 1:21 (*NETS*).
226. *AA* 2.16.3.
227. Ibid.
228. Ibid.
229. Ibid.

be described as illuminating the originating text. The most extended
example of this is the discussion of 'sea', which is triggered by Genesis
1:10, where God is described as gathering together the waters beneath
the firmament to form seas. Theophilus lights on the word 'sea', which
he interprets symbolically, equating it to the world and highlighting two
features of it not mentioned in Genesis. The first is that the sea does not
dry up because of the constant nourishment provided by the rivers and
springs which flow into it. Theophilus equates this with 'the law of God and
the prophets flowing and gushing forth with sweetness and compassion
and justice and the teaching of the holy commandments of God'.[230]
Theophilus' second observation is that the sea contains islands, some
of which are 'habitable and well-watered and fertile',[231] while others are
'rocky and waterless and barren, full of wild beasts and uninhabitable'.[232]
Islands are also interpreted symbolically, with the first group equating to
the 'holy churches' in which human beings can take refuge and find truth,
while the second equate to sources of heresy; if human beings approach
these for refuge, they are destroyed by erroneous heretical teachings.
Nothing of all this is found, or even hinted at, in the Genesis text and it is
only by seizing on the trigger provided by the term 'sea' that Theophilus
is enabled to develop his argument in two novel directions.

Use of such techniques enables Theophilus to consider a number of
issues and it will be noted that they all relate to a favourite theme of his,
the nature of humankind.[233] This is a particular concern for Theophilus,
as is evident when his commentary discusses verses in which the nature
of humankind is the subject being considered on the surface of the text.
Thus, when Theophilus discusses the creation of humankind in Genesis
1:26, he describes how this 'first reveals the dignity of mankind' and,
having explained the use of the first-person plural (as discussed above),
he then makes further comments on the divine creation of humankind:

> When he [God] had made human beings and blessed them
> so that they would increase and multiply and fill the earth,
> he subordinated to them all other beings as subjects and
> slaves. He also determined that human beings should from
> the beginning have a diet derived from the fruits of the earth
> and seeds and herbs and fruit trees.[234]

---

230. *AA* 2.14.2.
231. *AA* 2.14.3.
232. *AA* 2.14.4.
233. Discussed in Rogers, *Theophilus*, pp. 33-72.
234. *AA* 2.18.3: translation follows the addition to the text in Marcovich, *AA*, p. 65,

Later, when describing God's establishment of the Garden of Eden, he again considers aspects of the nature of humankind; he paraphrases Genesis briefly and says: 'God transferred humankind out of the earth from which it was made into paradise, providing the opportunity for progress, so that by growing and becoming perfect, and furthermore having been declared a god, it might also ascend into heaven'.[235]

Given Theophilus' interest in the nature of humankind when it is the overt subject of the Genesis text, it is not surprising that it is also the principal theme when he explores meanings below the surface of the words and a number of examples will illustrate this. One reference already noted is the distinction Theophilus draws between those who are saved and those who are not when discussing islands in the sea;[236] the salvation of humankind is also a theme when the waxing of the moon is equated to humankind's future resurrection[237] and when the blessing of newly-created sea creatures is equated with the future salvation of humankind.[238] A favourite theme of Theophilus is the division of human beings into the good and the bad and three examples of this appear in his commentary on the Creation narrative: first, there is a threefold division into 'those who remain steadfast', 'the people of the righteous', and 'the people who depart from God';[239] second, a distinction is drawn between those who keep and those who transgress the law of God;[240] and, third, humankind is divided into 'those who repent of their iniquities and live righteously' and 'those who are ignorant of God and sin against him'.[241]

Theophilus uses the identification of these issues below the surface of the text to advance his own teaching on the nature of humankind and he does this inside, and as part of, his commentary on the Sacred Writings. Thus, while he presents complete texts to his audience, the effect of using the methodology of the commentary is to break those texts up into small sections and, then, as he explains them, to create something new, which is his picture of the nature of humankind. There are affinities here with the way Justin combines his readings of individual prophetic texts into a narrative of the life of Jesus. The commentary technique which

---

n., of the word '$\pi\lambda\eta\theta\acute{v}\nu\varepsilon\sigma\theta\alpha\iota$' (multiply) not in the manuscript, by analogy with Genesis 1:28.

235. *AA* 2.24.6: Droge, *Homer or Moses?*, pp. 102-23, emphasises the importance of the 'Idea of Progress' in *AA*.

236. *AA* 2.14.3-5.

237. *AA* 2.15.3.

238. *AA* 2.16.2.

239. *AA* 2.15.5-6.

240. *AA* 2.16.3.

241. *AA* 2.17.3-4.

Theophilus uses also means that his doctrines on humankind appear to be in some way derived from the Sacred Writings, even though close scrutiny shows that Theophilus' comments relate scarcely at all to the surface meaning of the Genesis text he is purporting to discuss. Thus, by including these comments as part of his commentary, Theophilus is hoping that some of the gloss of the Sacred Writings will rub off onto the views he expresses on the nature of humankind and thus give his views enhanced status.

The early chapters of Genesis are clearly important to Theophilus and, in the previous chapter they were found to be important to Tatian as well. There is, however, a very clear contrast in the way the two writers present and make use of these texts. Tatian drew important ideas from Genesis but limited actual quotations to two key phrases, 'in the beginning' and 'the image and likeness of God'; his account betrayed no sense of Genesis 1-3 as a narrative text. Theophilus, by contrast, quotes the whole Creation narrative as a coherent entity and provides a point-by-point commentary, using it as a vehicle to expound his own ideas. This is a clear example of two writers using the same scriptural text in their apologetic arguments but doing so in completely different ways.

Ad Autolycum and Graeco-Roman Literary Culture

Examining the detail of Theophilus' text in a number of respects has pointed up various connections with texts from the Graeco-Roman tradition. Standing back from the detail now and seeking to locate *Ad Autolycum* within the context of Graeco-Roman literary culture more generally, there are similarities with Justin's *First Apology*. On the one hand, Theophilus uses an overarching form – that of a communication between two friends – as the frame for his work. This form was very familiar in Graeco-Roman culture, as is evidenced by the extensive use of letter-writing as a means of communication between individuals, with such texts often being collected together and circulated more widely.[242] There are parallels here with Justin's use of the public, and popular, petition form. On the other hand, Theophilus makes use within his overall framework of more specific forms of writing, the historical chronology and the commentary on a highly regarded text. Such forms would be familiar to Graeco-Roman audiences from their own traditions and they are used by Theophilus to serve his apologetic intentions. Justin's Proof from Prophecy exhibited parallels with a number of Graeco-Roman literary forms; with *Ad Autolycum*, however, the position is more

---

242. Stowers, *Letter Writing*.

straightforward, since, as has been shown, direct parallels can be drawn between the historical chronologies and commentaries in the Graeco-Roman literary tradition and the use of these forms by Theophilus.

Characters in the Text

In discussing Justin's *First Apology* and Tatian's *Oratio*, the place in the text occupied by both the Graeco-Romans and the Jews was considered and this is also relevant to *Ad Autolycum*. Here the attitude towards Graeco-Roman culture is essentially a hostile one. There are numerous references to Greek literature,[243] which is treated as an entity, with terms employed, such as 'the writings of the poets and philosophers'[244] or 'what has been said by philosophers, historians and poets'.[245] This Greek literary tradition is subjected to volleys of criticism at intervals in *Ad Autolycum*.[246] Theophilus draws strong contrasts between the shortcomings of Greek literature – including its mythological contents – and the merits of the Sacred Writings; thus, the qualities of antiquity, truthfulness and consistency possessed by the Sacred Writings are contrasted with the comparative novelty of the Greek literary tradition,[247] the falsity of its contents[248] and the inconsistency of its authors.[249] The consequence is that, like Justin and Tatian, Theophilus leaves no room for accommodation between the Sacred Writings and the Greek literary tradition and the battle of the literatures produces the same result: that acceptance of the one entails rejection of the other.

The Jews are given a more positive presentation in *Ad Autolycum* than in either Justin's *First Apology* or Tatian's *Oratio*. They are not criticised as they are by Justin and are not referred to as barbarian[250] as

---

243. Grant, *AA*, pp. 151-53, and Marcovich, *AA*, pp. 146-47.

244. *AA* 2.3.8.

245. *AA* 2.12.3. There are a number of other formulations, e.g. 'historians and poets and so-called philosophers' (2.8.1) and 'so-called wise men or poets or historiographers' (2.33.1).

246. Most notably, at *AA* 2.1-8 and 3.2-8.

247. E.g. 'For most writers, such as Herodotus and Thucydides and Xenophon and the other historiographers, begin their accounts at about the reigns of Cyrus and Darius, since they are unable to make accurate statements about the ancient times prior to them' (*AA* 3.26.1).

248. E.g. 'So unwillingly they admit that they do not know the truth. Inspired by demons and puffed up by them, they said what they said through them' (*AA* 2.8.7).

249. E.g. 'their statements are inconsistent and most of them demolished their own doctrines. They not only refuted one another but in some instances even nullified their own doctrines' (*AA* 3.3.1).

250. The word 'barbarian' appears only once in *AA*, at 3.26.2, where it refers to the

they are by Tatian. Indeed, Theophilus refers to the Jews in uncritical terms as the predecessors of present-day Christians, saying, 'These Hebrews were our forefathers, and from them we possess the sacred writings'[251] and, later, refers to '*our* sacred writings'[252] (italics added) as if Jews and Christians should not be differentiated from each other. These references are relatively low-key. However, a higher profile is given to the Jews in Theophilus' chronology of human history from the origins of the world. This is presented from the perspective of the Jews and their history is thus accorded a prominence which it did not have in either Justin's or Tatian's works; from the Garden of Eden to the return from the Babylonian exile, it is the Jews whose chronology is described.

Conclusion

The Jewish scriptures were instrumental in Theophilus' conversion to Christianity and he uses material from these ancient and inspired texts to support his apologetic arguments. In his handling of the Jewish scriptures, Theophilus betrays considerable similarities with the works of Justin and Tatian, not least in the importance he attaches to the prophetic and the philosophical. However, two novel features, not found in the work of the other two authors, are introduced: use of the scriptures as a source for the accurate history of the world; and employment of commentary techniques to explain how texts should be read.

These novelties lead Theophilus to extend the scope of the way the scriptures are handled in different argumentative contexts, thus demonstrating the extent of the flexibility available to Christian writers in the second century in their use of the Jewish scriptures. Employing the scriptures in Book 3 of *Ad Autolycum* to support a chronological case leads to a presentation of the Sacred Writings as a collection made up of a much broader spread of texts and one which has the coherence of an overall narrative sweep. Using the commentary format in Book 2 to apply to texts which are not previously known to his audience leads Theophilus to extract from the Sacred Writings complete, self-contained narratives of the Creation and the Garden of Eden; they are taken verbatim from the Sacred Writings and the length of the extracts contrasts markedly with the isolated and comparatively brief prophetic sayings quoted by Justin.

Persian kings, Darius and Cyrus: Marcovich, *AA*, p. 159.

251. *AA* 3.20.6.
252. *AA* 3.26.1.

The sharpness of this contrast must be tempered to some degree, however, since Theophilus comments only to a limited extent on the two Genesis extracts as complete narratives; for the most part, he breaks the texts up (as commentators tend to do) and comments separately on each short passage. Like Justin, he seeks to isolate hidden messages concealed in the texts. Theophilus does not re-assemble the hidden messages to construct a narrative of the life of Jesus as Justin does, however, but he does use what he finds to focus on the subject of most interest to him – the nature of humankind – and to this extent his approach might be regarded as reflecting (albeit somewhat dimly) that of Justin.

The form of Theophilus' chronological argument would have been familiar to his audience, because it draws on an existing literary tradition, although he Christianises it to support his apologetic argument. It could well have been effective in debate in the second-century context because the argument is presented coherently, the detailed evidence put forward is fully supported by the documentary sources cited and the accumulation of the evidence validates well the overall conclusion.

What impact the commentary on Genesis 1-3 might have had on an external audience is problematic. The commentary is presented in a form which would have been familiar to those who had experienced Graeco-Roman education in which highly regarded texts were similarly examined. Theophilus therefore shows in a very concrete way how the Sacred Writings could, and should, be regarded as analogous to the foundational texts of the Graeco-Roman literary tradition. The contents of his commentary are, however, fashioned to support apologetic objectives and, since Theophilus' promotion of Christianity entailed the rejection of the Graeco-Roman literary tradition and of the myths which were often its subject-matter, the arguments in his commentary might well not have appealed to an external audience which retained a high regard for that literary and cultural tradition.

While, like Justin and Tatian, Theophilus promotes Christianity and heaps criticism on the Graeco-Roman traditions of philosophy and mythological religion, he does not suggest an alternative focus for allegiance in barbarian culture, with the Barbarian Writings at their core, as Tatian does. Thus, some ambiguity lingers as to the precise location of his Christianity in relation to Greek culture, although there is no doubt that he places the Sacred Writings inherited from Judaism at the heart of it.

Chapter 5
Conclusion

This book began by highlighting the extensive references which some second-century Christian apologists make to the Jewish scriptures. To explore why this should be the case, three texts with implied Graeco-Roman audiences have now been considered in detail. Their literary strategies and the role the Jewish scriptures play in them have been examined. This final chapter highlights some of the more general themes which have emerged and suggests some avenues for further research.

It was not inevitable that these authors should have used scriptural texts to support their arguments; it was clearly a conscious choice on their part, since other apologetic works of the time do not do so. Justin does not draw on the scriptures to support the arguments in his *Second Apology* and the important concept of the *Logos Spermatikos* is introduced and developed without reference to the scriptures.[1] Athenagoras in his *Legatio*, dated to 176-180 CE,[2] hardly refers to the scriptures at all,[3] even though his arguments have been noted as being strikingly similar to Justin's.[4] Moreover, looking beyond Christianity to the mystery cults which were also attracting new adherents in this period, significant and successful movements – such as those of Isis and Mithras – were concerned with mythologies and rituals and not the promotion of ancient scriptures.[5]

In the three texts examined here, however, the Jewish scriptures *are* presented as a critically defining feature of Christianity. The authors all stress the significance of exposure to the Jewish scriptures for their

---

1.   Referred to in the *Second Apology* 7.1 and 13.3.
2.   Athenagoras, *Legatio*, p. xi.
3.   Athenagoras, *Legatio*, p. 154.
4.   S. Parvis, 'Justin Martyr and the Apologetic Tradition', pp. 123-25.
5.   H. Bowden, *Mystery Cults in the Ancient World* (London: Thames & Hudson, 2010).

own conversion narratives and the importance they attach to them is reflected in the way these texts are used in their apologetic arguments. The strategy of these apologists is to portray Christianity to Graeco-Roman audiences as grounded in ancient authoritative texts, which they promote as the route into Christianity both for themselves and for others. Thus, the scriptures are instrumental in shaping the way the new religion presents itself externally, as it strives to engage with, and challenge, the culture and traditions of the non-Jewish world.

All three authors encourage their audiences to read the scriptures for themselves. They do not rely on summaries of scriptural material, nor do they compose 'Rewritten Bible' works as the Jewish apologist Josephus did in his *Jewish Antiquities*. It is an important feature of the works of Justin and Theophilus that they quote verbatim from the texts of the Jewish scriptures, while Tatian's protreptic approach offers readers direct exposure to the texts on later occasions. The Jewish scriptures are not, however, handed over to the audiences for them to read as they wish; the apologists always accompany textual references with their own interpretations of them and thus seek to retain control of the meaning they will have for readers.

The appeal to the Jewish scriptures in these apologetic works represents a new and decisive step in the use of such texts by Christian writers. It was noted in Chapter 1 above that, when other second-century Christian works, such as the *Epistle of Barnabas* or, indeed, Justin's own *Dialogue with Trypho*, discussed the interpretation of these ancient scriptures, they did so in the context of dialogue with Jews and sought to differentiate their Christian readings of the scriptures from those of the Jews. What the apologists did was to take the scriptures out of the context of the Christian-Jewish dialogue, bring them into a non-Jewish Graeco-Roman debating arena and use them as a source of valuable material to support Christian apologetic arguments. This significant shift in the role of the scriptures was part of the broader process which turned Christianity from an offshoot of Second Temple Judaism in Palestine into a movement which sought to appeal much more widely to non-Jewish populations across the Roman Empire. The scriptures were clearly Jewish in origin but they were not one of the aspects of the Jewish heritage (like the dietary laws or circumcision) which Christianity abandoned. Instead, they became a central feature of the increasingly universalist Christian culture.

For the great value of the Jewish scriptures for the Christian apologists turns out to be that these ancient texts are a rich and flexible literary resource able to provide a variety of material to support a wide range of arguments: prophetic, philosophical, ethical and historical. Thus, the three authors utilise the scriptures extensively but, individually, they do so in very different ways, reflecting the different argumentative contexts in which each of their own works was written. Indeed, the extent to which they differ shows that these writers were not following a single model for the apologetic use of scripture; individual circumstance shaped the way the ancient texts were deployed in argument. It is no accident that each author uses a different descriptive term to denote the scriptures, one that reveals his own particular apologetic interest in the texts, so that with Justin the emphasis is on their prophetic nature, with Tatian on their barbarian origins and with Theophilus simply on their status as sacred texts.

The way that arguments were crafted in these apologetic works drew attention, in numerous respects, to affinities between the Jewish scriptures and various types of text which would have been familiar to their Graeco-Roman audiences. The references to Graeco-Roman literary culture, the techniques used to present arguments and the forms of writing in which the apologetic writings were themselves framed all served to underline such similarities. Moreover, in a number of respects, all three authors treat the scriptures in the same way as highly regarded texts from the Greek literary tradition would be treated, with the result that written works that originated in an alien culture have a guise of familiarity for a Graeco-Roman readership.

While introducing these texts into the world of Greek literary culture, however, the apologists make no attempt to claim that the Jewish scriptures belong to one of the established forms of Greek literature or to locate them within Greek literary culture more generally. They do not disguise the fact that, although the texts are written in Greek, they emanate from an alien culture. Indeed, this separate and distinctive Jewish scriptural tradition is presented as a rival to Greek culture; the apologists are antagonistic and confrontational towards Greek literary tradition and, as a consequence, the gulf between the two traditions is made to appear very wide and, indeed, unbridgeable. Acceptance of the claims the apologists make on the basis of the Jewish scriptures entails rejection of the Greek literary heritage and there is no suggestion that there should, or could, be an accommodation between the two.

Since the audience to which the apologists are introducing the Jewish scriptures had no (or very limited) prior familiarity with them, it is necessary for the origins and characteristics of these ancient texts to be explained and for the nature and extent of their authority to be justified. Moreover, to present the Jewish scriptures as a multi-authored collection of texts rather than a single work leads to comparisons and contrasts with the multi-author Greek literary tradition *as a whole*, rather than with particular works or writers within it. Homer and Moses are compared and contrasted only as the originators of their respective traditions – and then chiefly in terms of their relative antiquity. The apologists do not so much compare the Jewish scriptures with the works of Homer, but rather contrast them with the whole Greek literary tradition. Like the Greek tradition, the Jewish scriptures are not a clearly defined set of texts and it is not always obvious which writings are included under the umbrella headings used. Indeed, in the way the scriptures are portrayed, they have the character of a loosely characterised textual tradition on which the apologists draw for material.

The apologists are not merely promoting one particular set of highly regarded writings in place of another; they are arguing for the replacement of a *literary* tradition, in which different views are expressed in different texts, by a *scriptural* tradition containing a single coherent message. Moreover, the Jewish scriptures include prophetic material which highly regarded texts in the Greek tradition did not. To the extent that the Jewish scriptures were a set of sacred texts, inspired and, ultimately, authored, by God, they were radically different in nature from the texts in the Greek traditions of, for example, drama, philosophy and history. Thus, the apologists sought to introduce the very idea of scriptures to a Greek literary world which was not then acquainted with it.

The significance of the apologists' approach to the scriptures emerges more clearly when comparison is made with *Against Apion* by Josephus. The description of the scriptures given there is of a defined set of twenty-two books,[6] whose texts are fixed[7] and whose primary significance is as the source of Jewish law.[8] Josephus writes for an external Roman audience.[9] However, his stance is not that of a proselytiser, nor is he arguing that the scriptures should supplant the Graeco-Roman literary tradition. Rather, he is defending Judaism as a tradition and culture to be respected and admired in the face of a climate of hostility and criticism, writing in Barclay's words, 'to boost sympathy and support for the Judean people.'[10] The Christian apologists, whose aims include the encouragement of

---

6. The five of the Pentateuch by Moses, thirteen by other prophets and four containing 'hymns to God and instruction to people on life' (Barclay, *Against Apion* 1.38-1.40).
7. Ibid., 1.42.
8. Josephus' summary of the contents of the Jewish laws is given in ibid., 2.190-2.218.
9. Ibid., pp. xlv-li.
10. Ibid., p. liii.

outsiders to embrace the new religion, therefore go much further when they promote the scriptures as texts which their audience should read and whose message they should accept in place of texts from the literary culture in which they had been educated.

In the opening chapter reference was made to important works by Droge and Young. The fundamental theses of these two works have not been called into question, so Droge's account of the development of an early Christian history of culture and Young's argument for a battle of the literatures stand uncontested. Droge's work, however, paid insufficient attention to the central place of the Jewish scriptures in early Christian apologetic writings, while Young's did not consider fully enough the way early Christian authors employed the scriptures to support apologetic arguments. This book has therefore been able to build on the work of these two scholars, as well as to develop a fuller and richer understanding of the apologists, of their arguments and their use of scripture.

Bringing together investigation of apologetic literary strategies and scriptural interpretation has shown how the reading of the scriptures in the three works examined is driven by apologetic objectives. At one level, the selection of the texts these authors choose to cite is determined by the issues of debate with which they are engaged. A consequence of this is that large parts of the Jewish scriptures, notably the Jewish law emphasised by Josephus, do not feature strongly in these apologetic works, since they are not relevant to the arguments being made. Thus, a comparison of the apologists' presentations with the total scope of the Jewish scriptures as they came to be codified shows that only a small part of the whole is utilised.

The apologists' handling of particular texts from scripture reflect, at another level, the demands of their apologetic arguments. The technique they most commonly use is to break an extended text down into small sections, to interpret each of those sections and then to combine their readings of the individual portions of text to form something larger. Interpretation of a particular sentence or passage is therefore only the first step; readings of the individual passages are amalgamated to produce an overall meaning which then, most importantly, is used to support an apologetic argument. In this way, Justin's individual prophecies are added together to furnish an account of the life of Christ and the early growth of Christianity as foretold, Tatian's individual scriptural references are combined to build a Christian philosophy, while Theophilus' commentary on Genesis is used *inter alia* to present an account of the nature of humankind. Each writer seeks to persuade his audience of his case using evidence culled from the scriptures and each treats a sacred text as having a single interpretation rather than more than one possible reading. Since the scriptures are examined by these authors from a number of perspectives, however, and since they are deployed in various argumentative contexts, they may appear to be multi-layered texts which can be read from different standpoints.

In the opening chapter, reference was briefly made to the variety of approaches to scriptural interpretation found in second-century Christian texts. An additional ingredient has now been added to the mix by showing how the scriptures could also have an important role in supporting apologetic arguments directed at external audiences, in this case Graeco-Roman audiences, and how those arguments could shape the way the scriptures are interpreted. The question which arises from this is the extent to which the outcome is a distinctively apologetic mode of scriptural interpretation. This would be a fruitful issue for further research; and one way of investigating it would be to compare what has been found here with evidence from other texts whose audiences and argumentative contexts were markedly different. Thus, Justin's *Dialogue with Trypho*, whose implied audience at least was Jewish, forms an obvious source of possible comparison, particularly with the *First Apology*. Texts, which were directed towards an internal audience, that is, fellow Christians, and whose avowed purpose was to challenge alternative forms of Christianity, such as the work of the second-century Christian writer, Irenaeus,[11] could also be examined for purposes of comparison. In both these cases, scriptural interpretation forms an important feature of the argumentative battleground of the text and there is ample scope for comparison with the apologetic works studied here.

The meaning of scriptural texts is potentially problematic for Graeco-Roman audiences previously unfamiliar with them and the apologetic authors therefore routinely provide interpretations. Explaining texts is therefore an essential feature of their works; text and interpretation are coupled together and, indeed, appear inseparable. In the case of Justin, interpretation of scriptural texts through the lens of the Proof from Prophecy is especially prominent. A useful opportunity for further research would be to examine the Proof as a theme in early Christian writing more broadly. It has been unduly neglected hitherto;[12] yet the way prophetic texts should be interpreted features strongly in major Christian

---

11. For Irenaeus and the scriptures: Behr, *Irenaeus of Lyons*, pp. 124-40.

12. K. Fullerton, *Prophecy and Authority: A Study in the History of the Doctrine and Interpretation of Scripture* (New York: Macmillan, 1919), pp. 3-50, contains a relatively brief discussion, but since it dates from 1919 necessarily takes no account of several generations of modern scholarship.

works of the period following Justin, in Irenaeus' *Against the Heresies*,
Books 3 and 4,[13] in Tertullian's *Against Marcion*, Books 3 and 4 (both texts
refuting alternative forms of Christianity)[14] and in Origen's work on the
theory of scriptural interpretation, *On First Principles*, Book 4.[15]

The interpretation of passages from the Jewish scriptures is presented by Theophilus in the format of a commentary, the earliest extant
Christian example of the use of this form. A fruitful avenue for further
research would be to examine the development of Christian scriptural
commentaries as a form of writing, because, while the *contents* of the
extensive literature of patristic commentaries have been much studied,
the evolution of the commentary as a *form* would merit closer examination,[16] not least to establish whether later writers followed in
Theophilus' footsteps to any extent and the degree to which the emerging
Christian commentary tradition was influenced by Graeco-Roman pre-
cursors.

The need to highlight, for apologetic purposes, the antiquity of the
scriptures has the consequence that no appeal is made to Christian
writings, including those of the New Testament (which are inevitably
of recent date). Therefore, Christian texts play little part in these works,
even though the apologists betray some familiarity with earlier Christian
writings and indeed allude (although without acknowledgment) to texts
from the New Testament. As a result, the categories 'Old Testament'
and 'New Testament' are not used to refer to scriptural texts, since these
terms would have no meaning in a context in which there is no New
Testament. Further, the figure of Jesus Christ does not feature strongly
in these works, except insofar as he is the subject of ancient prophecies.

The low profile of Jesus also reflects the fact that Christianity is not
presented as the religion of a great man to be followed. This contrasts
with the approach used by Josephus in his *Jewish Antiquities* to retell
the narrative of the Jewish scriptures as a series of portraits of successive
leaders of the Jewish people.[17] The apologists do not present the ancient

---

13. Irénée de Lyon, *Contre les hérésies: Livre 3*, ed. by A. Rousseau and L. Doutreleau,
    2 vols (Paris: Éditions du Cerf, 1974); and Irénée de Lyon, *Contre les hérésies:
    Livre 4*, ed. by A. Rousseau, B. Hemmerdinger, L. Doutreleau and C. Mercier
    (Paris: Éditions du Cerf, 1965).
14. Tertullian, *Adversus Marcionem*, ed. by E. Evans, 2 vols (Oxford: Oxford
    University Press, 1972), 3 and 4.
15. Origen, *On First Principles: A Reader's Edition*, trans. by J. Behr (Oxford:
    Oxford University Press, 2019), 4.2.
16. For some interesting, though brief, comments on this, see Horbury, 'Old
    Testament interpretation', pp. 733-36.
17. Feldman, *Josephus's Interpretation*, pp. 74-131.

prophets who wrote the scriptural texts in this way even though they are important figures in their arguments. The prophets appear to be little more than names, and their qualities, other than their ability to utter prophecies, are barely described.

The strategy of presenting ancient scriptures to Graeco-Roman audiences as derived from Jewish roots is potentially problematic for the apologists' stance towards the Jews. While the scriptural texts inherited from Jewish tradition are valued not just for the material they contain but also for the antiquity to which they give concrete expression, the apologists do not disguise the fact that they are at odds with the Jews over how the scriptures should be interpreted. They seek to differentiate themselves from the Jews and to present the ancient texts as Christian in the battle of the literatures with Graeco-Roman culture. Given the somewhat paradoxical nature of this position, however, it is unsurprising that the strategies employed by the three authors display significant differences. Justin acknowledges, but plays down, the Jewish origin of the texts; Tatian makes no reference at all to Jews or Judaism and prefers to call the texts barbarian; while Theophilus treats the Jews in a low-key and uncritical way as the forerunners of present-day Christians.

At the outset, it was made clear that the texts would be discussed as if they are directed at external Graeco-Roman audiences, even though it remains uncertain whether this was actually the case. Following this approach through, it has proved possible to analyse the texts and reach coherent conclusions. This does not, of course, demonstrate that there *were* external audiences for these texts; indeed, the debate on this issue has not really been advanced in any direction. The most that can be said is that no difficulties have been encountered with treating the texts as externally directed. Such an approach has, however, placed limits on the reach of this book, which has not considered, and has not been able to consider, how interactions between Christians and Graeco-Roman audiences actually took place; rather it has been restricted to examining how Christian apologetic texts portray their side of the interactions.

The other side of such interactions is invisible to modern eyes, because any Graeco-Roman texts that may have existed have not survived. Even though direct evidence is lacking, however, it is worthwhile to reflect on what the responses from Graeco-Roman audiences might have been to the apologists' arguments and their use of the Jewish scriptures. Strategies which emphasise the ways in which the Jewish scriptures are made to appear familiar to those from a Greek cultural background and which treat them as highly regarded literature could have given persuasive power to the arguments which the apologists built upon the scriptures.

Moreover, positioning Christianity as rooted in very ancient traditions, for which clear evidence survives in the form of authoritative texts available for contemporaries to read, could have given it a high degree of credibility and attractiveness, although such an approach might have been more effective in removing the obstacles and difficulties which arose from Christianity's apparent novelty than in providing positive grounds for accepting the Christian case.

It would have been demanding a lot from the audiences not only to accept Christianity, but also to reject wholesale the Greek cultural tradition. Christianity could have appeared to be an attractive alternative to the Graeco-Roman mythological religion. However, the apologists never really make use of the scriptures to counter the rival claims of Greek philosophy. They limit themselves to presenting their own case, with support from the scriptures, and then criticising and disparaging the Greek alternative. This could well have been less than convincing for those who were educated in Greek philosophy.

If, however, members of their audiences were already dissatisfied with the traditions of Greek ideas and Greek culture – as the apologists claim that they themselves were when they first encountered the Jewish scriptures – and so were open to arguments in favour of something different, then an apologetic case supported by the scriptures could have been persuasive to them as a radical alternative. This was particularly so given the attraction at the time of doctrines based on Ancient Wisdom or derived from the founding texts of the philosophical schools.

Those who saw continuing value in the ideas of the Stoic or Platonic traditions or who simply retained a respect for the established authority of the Greek philosophical schools might have been more difficult to impress. An apologetic work which used ancient authoritative texts not only to advance its own case, but also to support arguments which were capable of dismantling the alternatives could have been attractive to them. In their own tradition, they could find this in authors like Galen, who used texts by Hippocrates to refute his opponents, or like Alexander of Aphrodisias, who drew on texts from Aristotle for a similar purpose; but this was not what the Christian apologists offered.

Bibliography

Texts

Aelii Aristidis Smyrnaei quae supersunt omnia, ed. by B. Keil, 2 vols (Berlin: Weidmann, 1893-98)

Aelius Aristides, *The Complete Works*, trans. by C.A. Behr, 2 vols (Leiden: Brill, 1981-86)

Alcinoos, *Enseignement des doctrines de Platon: Introduction, texte établi et commenté*, by J. Whittaker, trans. by P. Louis (Paris: Les Belles Lettres, 1990)

Alcinous, *The Handbook of Platonism*, trans. with an Introduction and Commentary by J. Dillon (Oxford: Clarendon Press, 1993)

Alexander of Aphrodisias, *On Fate: Text, Translation and Commentary*, ed. by R.W. Sharples (London: Duckworth, 1983)

Alkinoos, *Didaskalikos Lehrbuch der Grundsätze Platons: Einleitung, Text, Übersetzung und Anmerkungen*, ed. by O.F. Summerell and T. Zimmer (Berlin: de Gruyter, 2007)

Ancient Literary Criticism: The Principal Texts in New Translations, ed. by D.A. Russell and M. Winterbottom (Oxford: Clarendon Press, 1972)

The Apology of Aristides on Behalf of the Christians, ed. by J.R. Harris with an Appendix by J.A. Robinson (Cambridge: Cambridge University Press, 1891)

The Apostolic Fathers, ed. by B.D. Ehrman, LCL, 2 vols (Cambridge, MA: Harvard University Press, 2003)

Aristeas to Philocrates: *Letter of Aristeas*, ed. and trans. by M. Hadas (Eugene: Wipf & Stock, 1951)

Aristotle, *Posterior Analytics*, ed. by H. Tredennick, LCL 391 (Cambridge, MA: Harvard University Press, 1960)

———, *Posterior Analytics*, trans. by J. Barnes, 2nd edn (Oxford: Clarendon Press, 1993)

———, *Protrepticus: An Attempt at Reconstruction*, by I. Düring (Göteborg: Acta Universitatis Gothoburgensis, 1961)

Athenagoras, *Legatio and De Resurrectione*, ed. by W.R. Schoedel (Oxford: Clarendon Press, 1972)

Cassius Dio: *Roman History*, ed. by H. Cary and H.B. Foster, LCL, 9 vols (Cambridge, MA: Harvard University Press, 1914-27)

Commentarium in Platonis Theaetetum (the *Anonymous Commentary on Plato's*
    Theaetetus), ed. by G. Bastianini and D. Sedley, in F. Adorno et al., eds, *Corpus
    dei papiri filosofici greci e latini: Testi e lessico nei papiri di cultura greca e
    latina: Parte III: Commentari* (Florence: Olschki, 1995), pp. 227-562
Demetrius, *On Style*, trans. by D.C. Innes, in *Ancient Literary Criticism*, ed. by
    Russell and Winterbottom, pp. 171-215
Dio Chrysostom, *Discourses 37-60*, ed. by H.L. Crosby, LCL 376 (Cambridge, MA:
    Harvard University Press, 1946)
Diodorus Siculus, *Library of History*, ed. by C.H. Oldfather, LCL, 12 vols
    (Cambridge, MA: Harvard University Press, 1933-67)
Dionysius of Halicarnassus, *Critical Essays: Volume 1: Ancient Orators*, ed. by S.
    Usher, LCL 465 (Cambridge, MA: Harvard University Press, 1974)
———, *On Thucydides*, trans. by W.K. Pritchett (Berkeley: University of California
    Press, 1975)
———, *Roman Antiquities*, ed. by E. Cary LCL, 7 vols (Cambridge, MA: Harvard
    University Press, 1937-50)
1 Enoch 1: A Commentary on the Book of 1 Enoch, Chapters 1-36, 81-108, by G.W.
    Nickelsburg, ed. by K. Baltzer (Minneapolis: Fortress Press, 2001)
Eusebius, *The History of the Church from Christ to Constantine*, trans. by G.A.
    Williamson, rev. and ed. with a new introduction by A. Louth (London:
    Penguin, 1989)
The Exagoge *of Ezekiel*, ed. by H. Jacobson (Cambridge: Cambridge University
    Press, 1983)
Fourth Ezra: A Commentary on the Book of Fourth Ezra, by M.E. Stone
    (Minneapolis: Fortress Press, 1990)
Fragments from Hellenistic Jewish Authors, ed. by C.R. Holladay, 4 vols (Chico and
    Atlanta: Scholars Press, 1983-96), *Volume 1: Historians* (1983) and *Volume 2:
    Poets* (1989)
Galen, *Institutio Logica*, ed. by C. Kalbfleisch (Leipzig: Teubner, 1896)
———, *Institutio Logica: English Translation, Introduction and Commentary*, by J.S.
    Kieffer (Baltimore: John Hopkins University Press, 1964)
———, *On the Doctrines of Hippocrates and Plato*, ed. and trans. by P. de Lacy, 3
    vols (Berlin: Akademie-Verlag, 1978-84)
———, *On the Elements According to Hippocrates*, ed. and trans. by P. de Lacy
    (Berlin: Akademie-Verlag, 1996).
Gegen falsche Götter und falsche Bildung: Tatian, Rede an die Griechen, ed. by H.-G.
    Nesselrath (Tübingen: Mohr Siebeck, 2016)
Giannini, A., ed., *Paradoxographorum Graecorum Reliquiae* (Milan: Institutio
    Editorale Italiano, Milan 1966); trans. in W. Hansen, trans., *Phlegon of Tralles'
    Book of Marvels* (Exeter: University of Exeter Press, 1996)
'The Gospel of Truth', ed. by E. Thomassen and M. Meyer, in M. Meyer, ed., *The
    Nag Hammadi Scriptures* (New York: HarperOne, 2007), pp. 31-47
Greek and Latin Authors on Jews and Judaism, ed. by M. Stern, 3 vols (Jerusalem:
    Israel Academy of Sciences and Humanities, 1974-84)
*The Hellenistic Philosophers: Volume 1: Translations of the Principal Sources with
    Philosophical Commentary*, ed. by A.A. Long and D. Sedley (Cambridge:
    Cambridge University Press, 1987)

The Hellenistic Philosophers: Volume 2: Greek and Latin Texts with Notes and Bibliography, ed. by A.A. Long and D. Sedley (Cambridge: Cambridge University Press, 1989)

Heracleon, *Fragments of Heracleon*, ed. by A.E. Brooke (Cambridge: Cambridge University Press, 1891)

Héraclite, *Allégories d'Homère*, ed. and trans. by F. Buffière (Paris: Les Belles Lettres, 1962)

Heraclitus, *Homeric Problems*, ed. and trans. by D.A. Russell and D. Konstan (Atlanta: SBL, 2005)

Irénée de Lyon, *Contre les hérésies: Livre 1*, ed. by A. Rousseau and L. Doutreleau, 2 vols (Paris: Éditions du Cerf, 1979)

———, *Contre les hérésies: Livre 2*, ed. by A. Rousseau and L. Doutreleau, 2 vols (Paris: Éditions du Cerf, 1982)

———, *Contre les hérésies: Livre 3*, ed. by A. Rousseau and L. Doutreleau, 2 vols (Paris: Éditions du Cerf, 1974)

———, *Contre les hérésies: Livre 4*, ed. by A. Rousseau, B. Hemmerdinger, L. Doutreleau and C. Mercier (Paris: Éditions du Cerf, 1965)

Josephus, *Contra Apionem*, ed. by H. St J. Thackeray, LCL 186 (Cambridge, MA: Harvard University Press, 1926)

Josephus, *Jewish Antiquities*, ed. by H. St J. Thackeray, R. Marcus and L.H. Feldman, LCL, 9 vols (Cambridge, MA: Harvard University Press, 1930-65)

Josephus, Flavius, *Against Apion*, trans. by J.M.G. Barclay (Leiden: Brill, 2007)

———, *Judean Antiquities, Books 1-4*, trans. by L.H. Feldman (Leiden: Brill, 2004)

———, *Judean Antiquities, Books 5-7*, trans. by C. Begg and P. Spilsbury (Leiden: Brill, 2005)

———, *Judean Antiquities, Books 8-10*, trans. by C. Begg and P. Spilsbury (Leiden: Brill, 2005)

The Book of Jubilees, ed. by J.C. VanderKam, 2 vols (Leuven: Peeters, 1989)

Justin, *Apologie pour les Chrétiens*, ed. by C. Munier (Paris: Éditions du Cerf, 2006)

Justin Martyr, *Apologiae pro Christianis*, ed. by M. Marcovich (Berlin: de Gruyter, 1994)

———, *Dialogue with Trypho*, trans. by T.B. Falls, rev. by T.P. Halton and ed. by M. Slusser (Washington, DC: Catholic University of America Press, 2003)

———, *Dialogus cum Tryphone*, ed. by M. Marcovich (Berlin: de Gruyter, 1997)

———, *The First and Second Apologies*, trans. by L.W. Barnard (Mahwah: Paulist Press, 1997)

Justin, Philosopher and Martyr: *Apologies*, ed. by D. Minns and P. Parvis (Oxford: Oxford University Press, 2009)

Juvenal, *Satires*, ed. by S.M. Braund, LCL 91 (Cambridge, MA: Harvard University Press, 2004)

'Longinus', *On the Sublime*, ed. by D.A. Russell (Oxford: Clarendon Press, 1964)

Lucan, *Pharsalia*, ed. by J.D. Duff, LCL 220 (Cambridge, MA: Harvard University Press, 1928)

Lucian, *Selected Dialogues*, trans. by D. Costa (Oxford: Oxford University Press, 2005)

Maximus of Tyre, *Dissertationes*, ed. by M.B. Trapp (Stuttgart: Teubner, 1994)

———, *The Philosophical Orations*, trans. with an Introduction and Notes by M.B. Trapp (Oxford: Clarendon Press, 1997).

Origen, *Contra Celsum*, trans. by H. Chadwick (Cambridge: Cambridge University Press, 1953)

———, *On First Principles*, trans. by J. Behr (Oxford: Oxford University Press, 2019)

Pietersma, A., and B.G. Wright, *A New English Translation of the Septuagint and the Other Greek Translations Traditionally Included under that Title* (New York: Oxford University Press, 2007)

Philo, *De Legatione ad Gaium*, ed. by F.H. Colson, LCL 379 (Cambridge, MA: Harvard University Press, 1962)

———, *De Vita Mosis*, ed. by F.H. Colson, LCL, 2 vols (Cambridge, MA: Harvard University Press, 1935)

———, *On the Creation of the Cosmos According to Moses: Introduction, Translation and Commentary*, by D.T. Runia (Atlanta: SBL, 2001)

———, *Questions on Exodus*, trans. by R. Marcus, LCL 401 (Cambridge, MA: Harvard University Press, 1953)

———, *Questions on Genesis*, trans. by R. Marcus, LCL 380 (Cambridge, MA: Harvard University Press, 1953)

Philo of Biblos, *The Phoenician History: Introduction, Critical Text, Translation and Notes*, ed. by H.W. Attridge and R.A. Oden Jr (Washington, DC: Catholic Biblical Association of America, 1981)

Philostratus, *Lives of the Sophists*, ed. by W.C. Wright, LCL 134 (Cambridge, MA: Harvard University Press, 1921)

Phlegon of Tralles' Book of Marvels, trans. by W. Hansen (Exeter: University of Exeter Press, 1996)

Plato, *Ion*, ed. by H.N. Fowler and W.R.M. Lamb, LCL 164 (Cambridge, MA: Harvard University Press, 1925)

———, *Meno*, ed. by W.R.M. Lamb, LCL 165 (Cambridge, MA: Harvard University Press, 1924)

———, *Phaedrus*, ed. by H.N. Fowler, LCL 36 (Cambridge, MA: Harvard University Press, 1914)

———, *Republic*, ed. by C. Emlyn-Jones and W. Preddy, LCL, 2 vols (Cambridge, MA: Harvard University Press, 2013)

———, *Timaeus*, ed. by R.G. Bury, LCL 234 (Cambridge, MA: Harvard University Press, 1929)

Plutarch, *De E Apud Delphos, De Pythiae Oraculis* and *De Defectu Oraculorum*, ed. by F.C. Babbitt, LCL 306 (Cambridge, MA: Harvard University Press, 1936)

———, *De Iside et Osiride*, ed. by J.G. Griffiths (Cardiff: University of Wales Press, 1970)

———, *De Stoicorum Repugnantiis* and *De Communibus Notitiis adversus Stoicos*, in *Moralia: Volume 13, Part 2*, ed. by H. Cherniss, LCL 470 (Cambridge, MA: Harvard University Press, 1976)

———, *Lives: I: Life of Theseus and Romulus. Lycurgus and Numa. Solon and Publicola*, ed. by B. Perrin, LCL 46 (Cambridge, MA: Harvard University Press, 1914)

———, *Platonicae Quaestiones* and *De Animae Procratione in Timaeo*, in *Moralia: Volume 13, Part 1*, ed. by H. Cherniss, LCL 427 (Harvard University Press, Cambridge Mass 1976)

———, *Quomodo Adolescens Poetas Audire Debeat*, in *Moralia: Volume 1*, ed. by F.C. Babbitt, LCL 197 (Cambridge, MA: Harvard University Press, 1927)

Polybius, *The Histories*, ed. by W.R. Paton, rev. by F.W. Walbank and C. Habicht, LCL, 6 vols (Cambridge, MA: Harvard University Press, 2010-12)

Quintilian, *Institutio Oratoria*, ed. by D.A. Russell, LCL, 5 vols (Cambridge, MA: Harvard University Press, 2002)

Septuaginta, Vetus Testamentum Graecum: Vol. 1: Genesis, ed. by J.W. Wevers (Göttingen: Vandenhoeck & Ruprecht, 1974)

Sextus Empiricus, *Outlines of Pyrrhonism*, ed. by R.G. Bury, LCL 273 (Cambridge, MA: Harvard University Press, 1933)

———, *Outlines of Scepticism*, trans. by J. Annas and J. Barnes (Cambridge: Cambridge University Press, 1994)

The Sibylline Oracles: With Introduction, Translation, and Commentary on the First and Second Books, ed. by J.L. Lightfoot (Oxford: Oxford University Press, 2007)

Book III of the Sibylline Oracles and Its Social Setting: With an Introduction, Translation and Commentary, ed. by R. Buitenwerf (Leiden: Brill, 2003)

Suetonius, *Lives of the Caesars, Volume 1: Julius. Augustus. Tiberius. Gaius. Caligula*, ed. by J.C. Rolfe, LCL 31 (Cambridge, MA: Harvard University Press, 1914)

Tacitus, *Annals*, ed. by J. Jackson, LCL 312 (Cambridge, MA: Harvard University Press, 1937)

Tatian, *Oratio ad Graecos and Fragments*, ed. by M. Whittaker (Oxford: Clarendon Press, 1982)

Tatiani Oratio ad Graecos, ed. by M. Marcovich (Berlin: de Gruyter, 1995)

Tatianos, *Oratio ad Graecos: Rede an die Griechen*, ed. by J. Trelenberg (Tübingen: Mohr Siebeck, 2012)

Tertullian, *Adversus Marcionem*, ed. by E. Evans, 2 vols (Oxford: Oxford University Press, 1972)

Théophile d'Antioche: Trois livres à Autolycus, ed. by G. Bardy and trans. by J. Sender (Paris: Éditions du Cerf, 1948)

Theophili Antiocheni ad Autolycum, ed. by M. Marcovich (Berlin: de Gruyter, 1995)

Theophilus of Antioch, *Ad Autolycum*, ed. by R.M. Grant (Oxford: Clarendon Press, 1970)

Thesaurus Linguae Graecae, digital library ed. by M.C. Pantelia (Irvine: University of California, 2001-) (accessed online)

Virgil, *Eclogues, Georgics and Aeneid*, ed. by H.R. Fairclough and rev. by G.P. Goold, LCL, 2 vols (Cambridge, MA: Harvard University Press, 1999)

Secondary Works

Ackrill, J.L., *Aristotle the Philosopher* (Oxford: Clarendon Press, 1981)

Adler, W., *Time Immemorial: Archaic History and Its Sources in Christian Chronography from Julius Africanus to George Syncellus* (Washington, DC: Dumbarton Oaks, 1989)

Albl, M.C., *'And Scripture Cannot Be Broken': The Form and Function of the Early Christian* Testimonia *Collections* (Leiden: Brill, 1999)

Alexander, P.S., 'Retelling the Old Testament', in D.A. Carson and H.G.M. Williamson, eds, *It Is Written: Scripture Citing Scripture: Essays in Honour of Barnabas Lindars, SSF* (Cambridge: Cambridge University Press, 1988), pp. 99-121

Anderson, A.A., *The Book of Psalms: Volume 1: Introduction and Psalms 1-72* (London: Oliphants, 1972)

Anderson, G., *The Second Sophistic: A Cultural Phenomenon in the Roman Empire* (London: Routledge, 1993)

Andresen, C., 'Justin und der mittlere Platonismus', *ZNW*, vol. 44 (1952/53), pp. 157-95

———, *Logos und Nomos: Die Polemik des Kelsos wider das Christentum* (Berlin: de Gruyter, 1955)

Antonova, S.E., *Barbarian or Greek? The Charge of Barbarism and Early Christian Apologetics* (Leiden: Brill, 2019)

Arena, V., 'Roman Oratorical Invective', in W. Dominik and J. Hall, eds, *A Companion to Roman Rhetoric* (Oxford: Blackwell Publishing, 2007), pp. 149-60

Armstrong, A.H., 'Pagan and Christian Traditionalism in the First Three Centuries A.D.', in E.A. Livingstone, ed., *SP*, vol. 15, no. 1 (Berlin: Akademie-Verlag, 1984), pp. 414-31

Aune, D.E., 'Justin Martyr's Use of the Old Testament', *BETS*, vol. 9 (1966), pp. 179-97

———, *Prophecy in Early Christianity and the Ancient Mediterranean World* (Grand Rapids: Eerdmans, 1983)

Barclay, J.M.G., *Jews in the Mediterranean Diaspora from Alexander to Trajan (323 BCE-117 CE)* (Edinburgh: T. & T. Clark, 1996)

Barnard, L.W., 'The Heresy of Tatian – Once Again', *JEH*, vol. 19 (1968), pp. 1-10

———, *Justin Martyr: His Life and Thought* (Cambridge: Cambridge University Press, 1967)

Barnes, J., *Aristotle* (Oxford: Oxford University Press, 1982)

———, 'Galen, Christians, Logic', in J. Barnes, *Logical Matters: Essays in Ancient Philosophy II*, ed. by M. Bonelli (Oxford: Clarendon Press, 2012), pp. 1-21

———, 'Peripatetic Logic: 100 BC-AD 200', in R.W. Sharples and R. Sorabji, eds, *Greek and Roman Philosophy 100 BC-200 AD*, 2 vols (London: Institute of Classical Studies, University of London, 2007), 2, pp. 531-46

———, 'Proof Destroyed', in M. Schofield, M. Burnyeat and J. Barnes, eds, *Doubt and Dogmatism: Studies in Hellenistic Epistemology* (Oxford: Clarendon Press, 1980), pp. 161-81

Bartelink, G.J.M., 'Die *Oracula Sibyllina* in den frühchristlichen griechischen Schriften von Justin bis Origenes (150-250 nach Chr.)', in J. den Boeft and A. Hilhorst, eds, *Early Christian Poetry: A Collection of Essays* (Leiden: Brill, 1993), pp. 23-33

Barton, J., 'The Old Testament Canons', in NCHB1, pp. 145-64

———, *Oracles of God: Perceptions of Ancient Prophecy in Israel after the Exile* (London: Darton, Longman & Todd, 1986)

Bauckham, R., *Jesus and the Eyewitnesses: The Gospels as Eyewitness Testimony* (Grand Rapids: Eerdmans, 2006)

Behr, C.A., *Aelius Aristides and the* Sacred Tales (Amsterdam: Adolf M. Hakkert, 1968)

Behr, J., *The Formation of Christian Theology: Volume 1: The Way to Nicaea* (New York: St Vladimir's Seminary Press, 2001)

———, *Irenaeus of Lyons: Identifying Christianity* (Oxford: Oxford University Press, 2013)

Bellinzoni, A.J., *The Sayings of Jesus in the Writings of Justin Martyr* (Leiden: Brill, 1967)

Bentivegna, J., 'A Christianity without Christ by Theophilus of Antioch', in E.A. Livingstone, ed., *SP*, vol. 13, no. 2 (Berlin: Akademie-Verlag, 1975), pp. 107-30

Betegh, G., 'The Transmission of Ancient Wisdom: Texts, Doxographies, Libraries', in L.P. Gerson, ed., *The Cambridge History of Philosophy in Late Antiquity* (Cambridge: Cambridge University Press, 2010), Volume I, pp. 25-38

Betz, H.D., *Plutarch's Theological Writings and Early Christian Literature* (Leiden: Brill, 1975)

Bird, M.L., *Crossing Land and Sea: Jewish Missionary Activity in the Second Temple Period* (Peabody: Hendrickson, 2010)

Birnbaum, E., *The Place of Judaism in Philo's Thought: Israel, Jews and Proselytes* (Atlanta: Scholars Press, 1996)

Bobzien, S., 'Logic', in B. Inwood, ed., *The Cambridge Companion to the Stoics* (Cambridge: Cambridge University Press, 2003), pp. 85-123

Boccabello, J.S., 'Cosmological Allegoresis of Greek Myth in Theophilus of Antioch's Ad Autolycum' (DPhil, University of Oxford, 2011)

———, 'Why Would a Pagan Read Zechariah? Apologetics and Exegesis in the Second-Century Greek Apologists', in C. Tuckett, ed., *The Book of Zechariah and Its Influence* (Aldershot: Ashgate, 2003), pp. 135-44

Boer, W. den, *Private Morality in Greece and Rome: Some Historical Aspects* (Leiden: Brill, 1979)

Bolgiani, F., 'L'ascesi di Noé: A proposito di Theoph., ad Autol., III, 19', in F. Paulo and M. Barrera, eds, *Forma Futuri: Studi in onore del Cardinale Michele Pellegrino* (Torino: Bottega d'Erasmo, 1975), pp. 295-333

Bompaire, J., *Lucien écrivain: Imitation et création* (Paris: de Bocard, 1958)

Bonazzi, M., and C. Helmig, eds, *Platonic Stoicism-Stoic Platonism: The Dialogue between Platonism and Stoicism in Antiquity* (Leuven: Leuven University Press, 2007)

Bond, H.K., *Pontius Pilate in History and Interpretation* (Cambridge: Cambridge University Press, 1998)

Borgen, P., *Philo of Alexandria: An Exegete for His Time* (Leiden: Brill, 1997)

Boslooper, T., *The Virgin Birth* (London: SCM Press, 1962)

Bouquiaux-Simon, O., *Les lectures homériques de Lucien* (Bruxelles: Palais des Académies, 1968)

Bowden, H., *Mystery Cults in the Ancient World* (London: Thames & Hudson, 2010)

Bowman, A.K., P. Garnsey and D. Rathbone, eds, *The Cambridge Ancient History: Volume 11: The High Empire, A.D. 70-192*, 2nd edn (Cambridge: Cambridge University Press, 2000)

Bowman, A.K., P. Garnsey and A. Cameron, eds, *The Cambridge Ancient History: Volume 12: The Crisis of Empire, A.D. 193-337*, 2nd edn (Cambridge: Cambridge University Press, 2005)

Boys-Stones, G.R., *Post-Hellenistic Philosophy: A Study of Its Development from the Stoics to Origen* (Oxford: Oxford University Press, 2001)

Braun, M., *History and Romance in Graeco-Oriental Literature* (Oxford: Blackwell, 1938)

Brenk, F.E., *In Mist Appareled: Religious Themes in Plutarch's Moralia and Lives* (Leiden: Brill, 1980)

Brooke, G.J., 'Thematic Commentaries on Prophetic Scriptures', in M. Henze, ed., *Biblical Interpretation at Qumran* (Grand Rapids: Eerdmans, 2005), pp. 134-57

Brunschwig, J., 'Proof Defined', in M. Schofield, M. Burnyeat and J. Barnes, eds., *Doubt and Dogmatism: Studies in Hellenistic Epistemology* (Oxford: Clarendon Press, 1980), pp. 125-60

Buck, P.L., 'Justin Martyr's *Apologies*: Their Number, Destination, and Form', *JTS*, n.s. vol. 54 (2003), pp. 45-59

Buffière, F., *Les mythes d'Homère et la pensée grecque* (Paris: University of Paris, 1956)

Burke, G.T., 'Celsus and Justin: Carl Andresen Revisited', *ZNW*, vol. 76 (1985), pp. 107-16

Byrskog, S., *Story as History-History as Story: The Gospel Tradition in the Context of Ancient Oral History* (Tübingen: Mohr Siebeck, 2000)

Cancik, H., and H. Schneider, eds, *Brill's New Pauly: Encyclopaedia of the Ancient World*, English edition, ed. by C.F. Salazar (Leiden: Brill, 2002-) (ccessed via online edn [2006-])

Carleton Paget, J., *The Epistle of Barnabas: Outlook and Background* (Tübingen: J.C.B. Mohr [Paul Siebeck], 1994)

———, 'The Interpretation of the Bible in the Second Century', in NCHB1, pp. 549-83

———, *Jews, Christians and Jewish Christians in Antiquity* (Tübingen: Mohr Siebeck, 2010)

Carleton Paget, J., and J. Schaper, *The New Cambridge History of the Bible: Volume 1: From the Beginnings to 600* (Cambridge: Cambridge University Press, 2013)

Chadwick, H., 'Justin Martyr's Defence of Christianity', *BJRL*, vol. 47 (1965), pp. 275-97

Chadwick, H., *Early Christian Thought and the Classical Tradition: Studies in Justin, Clement and Origen* (Oxford: Clarendon Press, 1966)

Chadwick, H., 'Florilegium', in RAC, 7, pp. 1131-43

Clarke, G.W., 'The Date of the Oration of Tatian', *HTR*, vol. 60 (1967), pp. 123-26

Clarke M.L., *Higher Education in the Ancient World* (London: Routledge & Kegan Paul, 1971)

Collins II, J.H., *Exhortations to Philosophy: The Protreptics of Plato, Isocrates and Aristotle* (New York: Oxford University Press, 2015)

Collins, J.J., 'The "Apocryphal" Old Testament', in NCHB1, pp. 165-89

———, *Between Athens and Jerusalem: Jewish Identity in the Hellenistic Diaspora*, 2nd edn (Grand Rapids: Eerdmans, 2000)

Cook, J.G., *The Interpretation of the Old Testament in Greco-Roman Paganism* (Tübingen: Mohr Siebeck, 2004)

Craigie, P.C., *Psalms 1-50*, with 2004 supplement by M.E. Tate, 2nd edn (Nashville: Thomas Nelson, 2004)

Crivelli, P., 'Aristotle's Logic', in C. Shields, ed., *The Oxford Handbook of Aristotle* (Oxford: Oxford University Press, 2012), pp. 113-49

Curry, C., 'The Theogony of Theophilus', *VC*, vol. 42 (1988), pp. 318-26

Daniélou, J., *Gospel Message and Hellenistic Culture*, trans. by J.A. Baker (London: Darton, Longman & Todd, 1973)

Dauge, Y.A., *Le Barbare: Recherche sur la conception romaine de la barbarie et de la civilisation* (Brussels: Latomus, 1981)

Dawson, D., *Allegorical Readers and Cultural Revision in Ancient Alexandria* (Berkeley: University of California Press, 1992)

Diels, H., *Sibyllinische Blätter* (Berlin: Georg Reimer, 1890)

Dillon, J., *The Middle Platonists: A Study of Platonism 80 BC to AD 220* (London: Duckworth, 1977)

Dines, J.M., *The Septuagint* (Edinburgh: T. & T. Clark, 2004)

Dodd, C.H., *According to the Scriptures: The Sub-Structure of New Testament Theology* (London: Nisbet & Co., 1952)

Dodds, E.R., *The Greeks and the Irrational* (Berkeley: University of California Press, 1951)

Donaldson, T.L., *Judaism and the Gentiles: Jewish Patterns of Universalism (to 135 CE)* (Waco: Baylor University Press, 2007)

Dorival, G., 'L'apologétique chrétienne et la culture greque', in B. Pouderon and J. Doré, eds, *Les apologistes chrétiens et la culture grecque* (Paris: Beauchesne, 1998), pp. 423-65

Dorival, G., M. Harl and O. Munnich, *La Bible grecque des Septante: Du Judaïsme hellénistique au Christianisme ancien* (Paris: Éditions du Cerf, 1988)

Droge, A.J., *Homer or Moses? Early Christian Interpretation of the History of Culture* (Tübingen: J.C.B. Mohr [Paul Siebeck], 1989)

Eck, W., 'Provincial Administration and Finance', in CAH11, pp. 266-92

Edwards, M.J., 'Apologetics', in S.A. Harvey and D.G. Hunter, eds, *The Oxford Handbook of Early Christian Studies* (Oxford: Oxford University Press, 2008), pp. 549-64

———, 'Christianity A.D. 70-192', in CAH12, pp. 573-88

———, 'On the Platonic Schooling of Justin Martyr', *JTS*, n.s. vol. 42 (1991), pp. 17-34

Edwards, M.J., M.R. Goodman, S.R.F. Price and C. Rowland, 'Introduction: Apologetics in the Roman World', in M.J. Edwards, M.R. Goodman, S.R.F. Price and C. Rowland, eds, *Apologetics in the Roman Empire: Pagans, Jews and Christians* (Oxford: Oxford University Press, 1999), pp. 1-13

Elze, M., *Tatian und seine Theologie* (Göttingen: Vandenhoeck & Ruprecht, 1960)

Engberg, J., 'Conversion, Apologetic Argumentation and Polemic (Amongst Friends) in Second-Century Syria: Theophilus' *Ad Autolycum*', in M. Blömer, A. Lichtenberger and R. Raja, eds, *Religious Identities in the Levant from Alexander to Muhammed: Continuity and Change* (Turnhout: Brepols, 2015), pp. 83-94

———, '"From among You Are We. Made, not Born Are Christians": Apologists' Accounts of Conversion before 310 AD', in J. Ulrich, A.-C. Jacobsen and M. Kahlos, eds, *Continuity and Discontinuity in Early Christian Apologetics* (Frankfurt am Main: Peter Lang, 2009), pp. 49-77

Farrell, J., 'Roman Homer', in R. Fowler, ed., *The Cambridge Companion to Homer* (Cambridge: Cambridge University Press, 2004), pp. 263-69

Fascher, E., *ΠΡΟΦΗΤΗΣ: Eine sprach- und religionsgeschichtliche Untersuchung* (Giessen: Alfred Töpelmann, 1927)

Feeney, D.C., *The Gods in Epic: Poets and Critics of the Classical Tradition* (Oxford: Clarendon Press, 1991)

Feldman, L.H., *Jew and Gentile in the Ancient World: Attitudes and Interactions from Alexander to Justinian* (Princeton: Princeton University Press, 1993)

———, *Josephus's Interpretation of the Bible* (Berkeley: University of California Press, 1998)

———, *Studies in Josephus' Rewritten Bible* (Leiden: Brill, 1998)

Fernández Marcos, N., *The Septuagint in Context: Introduction to the Greek Version of the Bible*, trans. by W.G.E. Watson (Leiden: Brill, 2000)

Fiedrowicz, M., *Apologie im frühen Christentum: Die Kontroverse um den christlichen Wahrheitsanspruch in den ersten Jahrhunderten* (Paderborn: Ferdinand Schöningh, 2000)

Finkelberg, M., 'Canonising and Decanonising Homer: Reception of the Homeric Poems in Antiquity and Modernity', in M.R. Niehoff, ed., *Homer and the Bible in the Eyes of Ancient Interpreters* (Leiden: Brill, 2012), pp. 15-28

Finkelberg, M., and G.G. Stroumsa, 'Introduction: Before the Western Canon', in M. Finkelberg and G.G. Stroumsa, eds, *Homer, the Bible and Beyond: Literary and Religious Canons in the Ancient World* (Leiden: Brill, 2003), pp. 1-8

Fojtik, J.E., 'Tatian the Barbarian: Language, Education and Identity in the *Oratio ad Graecos*', in J. Ulrich, A.-C. Jacobsen and M. Kahlos, eds, *Continuity and Discontinuity in Early Christian Apologetics* (Frankfurt am Main: Peter Lang, 2009), pp. 23-34

Fraser, P.M., *Ptolemaic Alexandria*, 3 vols (Oxford: Clarendon Press, 1972)

Frede, M.A., 'Epilogue', in K. Algra, J. Barnes, J. Mansfeld and M. Schofield, eds, *The Cambridge History of Hellenistic Philosophy* (Cambridge: Cambridge University Press, 1999), pp. 771-97

———, *A Free Will: Origins of the Notion in Ancient Thought*, ed. by A.A. Long (Berkeley: University of California Press, 2011)

Freund, R.A., 'The Decalogue in Early Judaism and Christianity', in C.A. Evans and J.A. Sanders, eds, *The Function of Scripture in Early Jewish and Christian Tradition* (Sheffield: Sheffield Academic Press, 1998), pp. 124-41

Freund, S. '"Und wunderbar sind auch eure Dichter, die da lügen…" (Tat., orat. 22,7). Beobachtungen zu Gestalt, Auswahl und Funktion von Dichterzitaten in der griechischen Apologetik am Beispiel Tatians', in C. Schubert and A. von Stockhausen, eds, *Ad veram religionem reformare: frühchristliche Apologetik zwischen Anspruch und Wirklichkeit* (Erlangen: Erlangen Forschungen, 2006), pp. 97-121

Fullerton, K., *Prophecy and Authority: A Study in the History of the Doctrine and Interpretation of Scripture* (New York: Macmillan, 1919)

Gager, J.G., *Moses in Greco-Roman Paganism* (Nashville: Abingdon Press, 1972)

Gaines, R.N., 'Roman Rhetorical Handbooks', in W. Dominik and J. Hall, eds, *A Companion to Roman Rhetoric* (Oxford: Blackwell Publishing, 2007), pp. 163-80

Gamble, H.Y., *Books and Readers in the Early Church: A History of Early Christian Texts* (New Haven: Yale University Press, 1995)

Geffcken, J., *Zwei griechische Apologeten* (Leipzig: Teubner, 1907)

Gibbon, E., *The Decline and Fall of the Roman Empire*, 6 vols (London: Dent, 1910)

Gill, C., 'Psychology', in J. Warren, ed., *The Cambridge Companion to Epicureanism* (Cambridge: Cambridge University Press, 2009), pp. 125-41

Gillingham, S., *A Journey of Two Psalms: The Reception of Psalms 1 and 2 in Jewish and Christian Tradition* (Oxford: Oxford University Press, 2013)

Goldhill, S., ed., *Being Greek under Rome: Cultural Identity, the Second Sophistic and the Development of Empire* (Cambridge: Cambridge University Press, 2001)

Goodenough, E.R., 'Philo's Exposition of the Law and his *De Vita Mosis*', *HTR*, vol. 26 (1933), pp. 109-25

Goodenough, E.R., *The Theology of Justin Martyr* (Jena: Frommann, 1923)

Goodman, M., *Mission and Conversion: Proselytising in the Religious History of the Roman Empire* (Oxford: Clarendon Press, 1994)

Gradel, I., *Emperor Worship and Roman Religion* (Oxford: Clarendon Press, 2002)

Grant, R.M., 'The Bible of Theophilus of Antioch', *JBL*, vol. 66 (1947), pp. 173-96

———, 'The Date of Tatian's Oration', *HTR*, vol. 46 (1953), pp. 99-101

———, 'The Decalogue in Early Christianity', *HTR*, vol. 40 (1947), pp. 1-17

———, 'Forms and Occasions of the Greek Apologists', *SMSR*, vol. 52 (1986), pp. 213-26

———, *Greek Apologists of the Second Century* (London: SCM Press, 1988)

———, 'The Heresy of Tatian', *JTS*, vol. 5 (1954), pp. 62-68

———, 'The Problem of Theophilus', *HTR*, vol. 43 (1950), pp. 179-96

———, 'Studies in the Apologists', *HTR*, vol. 51 (1958), pp. 123-34

———, 'Tatian and the Bible', in K. Aland and F.L. Cross, eds, *SP* 1/1 (Berlin: Akademie-Verlag, 1957), pp. 297-306

———, 'Theophilus of Antioch to Autolycus', *HTR*, vol. 40 (1947), pp. 227-56

Grant, R.M., and D. Tracy, *A Short History of the Interpretation of the Bible*, 2nd edn, rev. and enlarged (London: SCM Press, 1984)

Grube, G.M.A., *The Greek and Roman Critics* (London: Methuen, 1965)

Gruen, E.S., *Heritage and Hellenism: The Reinvention of Jewish Tradition* (Berkeley: University of California Press, 1998)

———, *Rethinking the Other in Antiquity* (Princeton: Princeton University Press, 2010)

Guthrie, W.K.C., *A History of Greek Philosophy: Volume 6, Aristotle: An Encounter* (Cambridge: Cambridge University Press, 1981)

Haddad, R.M., *The Case for Christianity: St Justin Martyr's Arguments for Religious Liberty and Judicial Justice* (Lanham: Taylor Trade, 2010)

Hankinson, R.J., 'The Man and His Work', in R.J. Hankinson, ed., *The Cambridge Companion to Galen* (Cambridge: Cambridge University Press, 2008), pp. 1-33

———, *The Sceptics* (London: Routledge, 1995)

Hardwick, M.E., '*Contra Apionem* and Christian Apologetics', in L.H. Feldman and J.R. Levison, eds, *Josephus'* Contra Apionem: *Studies in its Character and Context with a Latin Concordance to the Portion Missing in Greek* (Leiden: Brill, 1996), pp. 369-402

———, *Josephus as an Historical Source in Patristic Literature through Eusebius* (Atlanta: Scholars Press, 1989)

Harnack, A., *The Expansion of Christianity in the First Three Centuries*, trans. by J. Moffat, 2 vols (London: Williams & Norgate, 1904-05)

———, *Die Überlieferung der griechischen Apologeten des zweiten Jahrhunderts in der alten Kirche und im Mittelalter*, 2 vols (Leipzig: Hinrichs, 1882)

Hatch, E., *The Influence of Greek Ideas on Christianity* (New York: Harper & Row, 1957)

Hatzimichali, M., 'The Texts of Plato and Aristotle in the First Century BC', in M. Schofield, ed., *Aristotle, Plato and Pythagoreanism in the First Century BC: New Directions for Philosophy* (Cambridge: Cambridge University Press, 2013), pp. 1-27

Hauken, T., *Petition and Response: An Epigraphic Study of Petitions to Roman Emperors, 181-249* (Bergen: The Norwegian Institute at Athens, 1998)

Hawthorne, G.F., 'Tatian and His Discourse to the Greeks', *HTR*, vol. 57 (1964), pp. 161-88

Hay, D.M., ed., *Both Literal and Allegorical: Studies in Philo of Alexandria's* Questions and Answers on Genesis and Exodus (Atlanta: Scholars Press, 1991)

Hays, R.B., *Echoes of Scripture in the Gospels* (Waco: Baylor University Press, 2016)

Hengel, M., *The Septuagint as Christian Scripture: Its Prehistory and the Problem of Its Canon*, trans. by M.E. Biddle (Edinburgh: T. & T. Clark, 2002)

Holfeder, H.H., 'Εὐσέβεια καὶ φιλοσοφία: Literarische Einheit und politischer Kontext von Justins Apologie (Teil I)', *ZNW*, vol. 68 (1977), pp. 48-66

Holmes, M.W., 'The Biblical Canon', in S.A. Harvey and D.G. Hunter, eds, *The Oxford Handbook of Early Christian Studies* (Oxford: Oxford University Press, 2008), pp. 406-26

Holte, R., 'Logos Spermatikos: Christianity and Ancient Philosophy according to St. Justin's Apologies', in *ST*, vol. 12 (1958), pp. 109-68

Honigman, S., *The Septuagint and Homeric Scholarship in Alexandria: A Study in the Narrative of the* Letter of Aristeas (London: Routledge, 2003)

Horbury, W., *Jewish War under Trajan and Hadrian* (Cambridge: Cambridge University Press, 2014)

———, 'Old Testament Interpretation in the Writings of the Church Fathers', in M.J. Mulder, ed., *Mikra: Text, Translation, Reading and Interpretation of the Hebrew Bible in Ancient Judaism and Early Christianity* (Assen: Van Gorcum, 1988), pp. 727-87

Householder, F.W., *Literary Quotation and Allusion in Lucian* (New York: Columbia University Press, 1941)

Hunt, E.J., *Christianity in the Second Century: The Case of Tatian* (London: Routledge, 2003)

Hyldahl, N., *Philosophie und Christentum: Eine Interpretation der Einleitung zum Dialog Justins* (Kopenhagen: Prostant apud Munksgaard, 1966)

Jacobsen, A.-C., *Christ, the Teacher of Salvation: A Study on Origen's Soteriology and Christology* (Münster: Aschendorff & Verlag, 2015)

Jaeger, W., *Aristotle: Fundamentals of the History of His Development*, trans. by R. Robinson, 2nd edn (Oxford: Oxford University Press, 1948)

Jobes, K.H., and M. Silva, *Invitation to the Septuagint* (Grand Rapids: Baker Academic, 2000)

Johnson, A.P., 'Early Christianity and the Classical Tradition', in D.S. Richter and W.A. Johnson, eds, *The Oxford Handbook of the Second Sophistic* (Oxford: Oxford University Press, 2017), pp. 625-38

Joly, R., *Christianisme et philosophie: Études sur Justin et les apologistes grecs du deuxième siècle* (Brussels: University of Brussels, 1973)

Jones, C.P., *Culture and Society in Lucian* (Cambridge, MA: Harvard University Press, 1986)

Karadimas, D., *Tatian's* Oratio ad Graecos: *Rhetoric and Philosophy/Theology* (Stockholm: Almqvist & Wiksell International, 2003)

Kelly, J.N.D., *Early Christian Doctrines*, 4th edn (London: Adam & Charles Black, London)

Kennedy, G.A., *The Art of Rhetoric in the Roman World 300 BC-AD 300* (Princeton: Princeton University Press, 1972)

Kennedy, G.A., *Classical Rhetoric and Its Christian and Secular Tradition from Ancient to Modern Times*, 2nd edn, rev. and enlarged (Chapel Hill: University of North Carolina Press, 1999)

Keresztes, P., 'The Literary Genre of Justin's First Apology', *VC*, vol. 19 (1965), pp. 99-110

Kittel, G., and G. Friedrich, eds, *Theological Dictionary of the New Testament*, ed. and trans. by G.W. Bromiley, 10 vols (Grand Rapids: Eerdmans, 1964-76)

Klauck, H.-J., *The Religious Context of Early Christianity: A Guide to Graeco-Roman Religions*, trans. by B. McNeil (London: T. & T. Clark, 2000)

Klauser, T., F.J. Dölger, G. Schöllgen, E. Dassmann and H. Leitzmann, *Reallexikon für Antike und Christentum: Sachwörterbuch zur Auseinandersetzung des Christentums mit der antiken Welt*, 27 vols (Stuttgart: Hiersemann, 1950-)

Koltun-Fromm, N., 'Re-imagining Tatian: The Damaging Effects of Polemical Rhetoric', *JECS*, vol. 16 (2008), pp. 1-30

Kukula, R.C., *Tatians sogenannte Apologie: Exegetisch-Chronologische Studie* (Leipzig: Teubner, 1900)

Lamberton, R., *Plutarch* (New Haven: Yale University Press, 2001)

Lampe, P., *From Paul to Valentinus: Christians at Rome in the First Two Centuries*, trans. by M. Steinhauser (London: Continuum, 2003)

Lawlor, H.J., 'Early Citations from the Book of Enoch', *Journal of Philology*, vol. 25 (1897), pp. 164-225

Lazzati, G., *L'Aristotele perduto e gli scrittori cristiani* (Milano: Società Editrice, 1938)

Liddell, H.G., R. Scott and H.S. Jones, *A Greek-English Lexicon*, 9th edn, rev. and augmented (Oxford: Clarendon Press, 1996)

Lieu, J.M., *Christian Identity in the Jewish and Graeco-Roman World* (Oxford: Oxford University Press, 2004)

———, *Image and Reality: The Jews in the World of the Christians in the Second Century* (London: T. & T. Clark, 1996)

———, *Marcion and the Making of a Heretic* (Cambridge: Cambridge University Press, 2015)

Lloyd, G.E.R., 'Galen and His Contemporaries', in R.J. Hankinson, ed., *The Cambridge Companion to Galen* (Cambridge: Cambridge University Press, 2008), pp. 34-48

———, 'Scholarship, Authority and Argument in Galen's *Quod Animi Mores*', in P. Manuli and M. Vegetti, eds, *Le opere psicologiche di Galeno* (Naples: Bibliopolis, 1988), pp. 11-42

Löhr, W.A., 'Das antike Christentum in zweiten Jahrhundert – neue Perspektiven seiner Erforshung', *TLZ*, vol. 127 (2002), pp. 247-62

———, 'Gnostic and Manichaean Interpretation', in NCHB1, pp. 584-604

———, 'The Theft of the Greeks: Christian Self-Definition in the Age of the Schools', *RHE*, vol. 95 (2000), pp. 403-26

Lössl, J., 'Date and Location of Tatian's *Ad Graecos*: Some Old and New Thoughts', in M. Vinzent and A. Brent, eds, *SP*, vol. 74 (Leuven: Peeters, 2016), pp. 43-55

———, 'Hermeneutics and the Doctrine of God in Tatian's *Ad Graecos*', in J. Baun, A. Cameron, M. Edwards and M. Vinzent, eds, *SP*, vol. 45 (Leuven: Peeters, 2010), pp. 409-12

———, 'Zwischen Christologie und Rhetorik: Zum Ausdruck "Kraft des Wortes" (λόγου δύναμις) in Tatians "Rede an die Griechen"', in F.R. Prostmeier and H.E. Lona, eds, *Logos der Vernunft – Logos des Glaubens* (Berlin: de Gruyter, 2010), pp. 129-47

MacBain, B., *Prodigy and Expiation: A Study in Religion and Politics in Republican Rome* (Brussels: Latomus, 1982)

Machiela, D.A., 'Once More, with Feeling: Rewritten Scripture in Ancient Judaism –A Review of Recent Developments', *JJS*, vol. 61 (2010), pp. 308-20

MacMullen, R., *Christianizing the Roman Empire (A.D. 100-400)* (New Haven: Yale University Press, 1984)

Malingrey, A.-M., *'Philosophia' Études d'un groupe de mots dans la littérature grecque, des présocratiques au IVe siècle après J.-C.* (Paris: C. Klincksieck, 1961)

Markschies, C., *Christian Theology and Its Institutions in the Early Roman Empire: Prolegomena to a History of Early Christian Theology*, trans. by W. Coppins (Waco: Baylor University Press, 2015)

Marrou, H.I., *A History of Education in Antiquity*, trans. by G. Lamb (London: Sheed & Ward, 1956)

May, G., *Creatio ex Nihilo: The Doctrine of 'Creation out of Nothing' in Early Christian Thought*, trans. by A.S. Worrall (Edinburgh: T. & T. Clark, 1994)

McDonald, L.M., 'Canon', in J.W. Rogerson and J.M. Lieu, eds, *The Oxford Handbook of Biblical Studies* (Oxford: Oxford University Press, 2006), pp. 777-809

McGehee, M., 'Why Tatian Never 'Apologized' to the Greeks', *JECS*, vol. 1 (1993), pp. 143-58

McKnight, S., *A Light among the Gentiles: Jewish Missionary Activity in the Second Temple Period* (Minneapolis: Fortress Press, 1991)

McVey, K.E., 'The Use of Stoic Cosmogony in Theophilus of Antioch's *Hexamaeron*', in M.S. Burrows and P. Rorem, eds, *Biblical Hermeneutics in Historical Perspective: Studies in Honor of Karlfried Froehlich on His Sixtieth Birthday* (Grand Rapids: Eerdmans, 1991), pp. 32-58

Metzger, B.M., and M.D. Coogan, eds, *The Oxford Guide to Ideas and Issues of the Bible* (Oxford: Oxford University Press, 2001)

Millar, F., *The Emperor in the Roman World (31 BC-AD 337)* (London: Duckworth, 1977)

———, *The Roman Near East 31 BC-AD 337* (Cambridge, MA: Harvard University Press, 1993)

Mitchell, M.M., 'The Emergence of the Written Record', in CHC1, pp. 177-94

Mitchell, M.M., et al., 'Part IV: Regional Varieties of Christianity in the First Three Centuries', in CHC1, pp. 295-412

Mitchell, M.M., and F.M. Young, eds, *The Cambridge History of Christianity: Volume 1: Origins to Constantine* (Cambridge: Cambridge University Press, 2006)

Moll, S., 'Justin and the Pontic Wolf', in S. Parvis and P. Foster, eds, *Justin Martyr and His Worlds* (Minneapolis: Fortress Press, 2007), pp. 145-51

Moo, J.A., *Creation, Nature and Hope in 4 Ezra* (Göttingen: Vandenhoeck & Ruprecht, 2011)

Morgan, T.J., *Literate Education in the Hellenistic and Roman Worlds* (Cambridge: Cambridge University Press, 1998)

Morison, B., 'Logic', in R.J. Hankinson, ed., *The Cambridge Companion to Galen* (Cambridge: Cambridge University Press, 2008), pp. 66-115

Mortley, R., *The Idea of Universal History from Hellenistic Philosophy to Early Christian Historiography* (Lampeter: Edwin Mellen Press, 1996)

Most, G.W., 'Hellenistic Allegory and Early Imperial Rhetoric', in R. Copeland and P.T. Struck, eds, *The Cambridge Companion to Allegory* (Cambridge: Cambridge University Press, 2010), pp. 26-38

Moyise, S., *Evoking Scripture: Seeing the Old Testament in the New* (London: T. & T. Clark, 2008).

Mueller, I., 'An Introduction to Stoic Logic', in J.M. Rist, ed., *The Stoics* (Berkeley: University of California Press, 1978), pp. 1-26

Nahm, C., 'The Debate on the "Platonism" of Justin Martyr', *SecCent*, vol. 9 (1992), pp. 129-51

Nasrallah, L., 'Mapping the World: Justin, Tatian, Lucian and the Second Sophistic', *HTR*, vol. 98 (2005), pp. 283-314

Nesselrath, H.-G., 'Two Syrians and Greek Paideia: Lucian and Tatian', in G.A. Xenis, ed., *Literature, Scholarship, Philosophy and History: Classical Studies in Memory of Ioannis Taifacos* (Stuttgart: Franz Steiner Verlag, 2015), pp. 129-42

Niehoff, M., *Jewish Exegesis and Homeric Scholarship in Alexandria* (Cambridge: Cambridge University Press, 2011)

———, *Philo of Alexandria: An Intellectual Biography* (New Haven: Yale University Press, 2018)

———, *Philo on Jewish Identity and Culture* (Tübingen: Mohr Siebeck, 2001)

Norelli, E., 'La critique du pluralisme grec dans le *Discours aux Grecs* de Tatien', in B. Pouderon and J. Doré, eds, *Les apologistes chrétiens et la culture grecque* (Paris: Beauchesne, 1998), pp. 81-120

Norris Jr, R.A., 'The Apologists', in F.M. Young, L. Ayres and A. Louth, eds, *The Cambridge History of Early Christian Literature* (Cambridge: Cambridge University Press, 2004), pp. 36-44

North, J.A., 'The Books of the *Pontifices*', in C. Moatti, ed., *La mémoire perdue: À la recherche des archives oubliées de l'administration romaine* (Rome: École Française de Rome, 1998), pp. 45-63

———, 'Diviners and Divination at Rome', in M. Beard and J.A. North, eds, *Pagan Priests: Religion and Power in the Ancient World* (London: Duckworth, 1990), pp. 51-71

Nuffelen, P. van, *Rethinking the Gods: Philosophical Readings of Religion in the Post-Hellenistic Period* (Cambridge: Cambridge University Press, 2011)

Nyström, D.E., *The Apology of Justin Martyr: Literary Strategies and the Defence of Christianity* (Tübingen: Mohr Siebeck, 2018)

Oakesmith, J., *The Religion of Plutarch: A Pagan Creed of Apostolic Times* (London: Longmans, Green & Co., 1902)

O'Hara, J.J., *Death and the Optimistic Prophecy in Virgil's* Aeneid (Princeton: Princeton University Press, 1990)

Osborn, E.F., *The Emergence of Christian Theology* (Cambridge: Cambridge University Press, 1993)

———, *Justin Martyr* (Tübingen: J.C.B. Mohr [Paul Siebeck], 1973)

Osborne, A.E., 'Tatian's Discourse to the Greeks: A Literary Analysis and Essay in Interpretation' (PhD, University of Cincinnati, 1969)

Parke, H.W., *Sibyls and Sibylline Prophecy in Classical Antiquity*, ed. by B.C. McGing (London: Routledge, 1988)

Parsons, S.E., *Ancient Apologetic Exegesis: Introducing and Recovering Theophilus's World* (Cambridge: James Clarke & Co., 2015)

Parvis, P., 'Justin Martyr', in P. Foster, ed., *Early Christian Thinkers: The Lives and Legacies of Twelve Key Figures* (London: SPCK, 2010), pp. 1-14

Parvis, S., 'Justin Martyr and the Apologetic Tradition', in S. Parvis and P. Foster, eds, *Justin Martyr and His Worlds* (Minneapolis: Fortress Press, 2007), pp. 115-27

Pellegrino, M., *Studi su l'antica apologetica* (Rome: Edizioni di Storia e Letteratura, 1947)

Pépin, J., *Mythe et allégorie: Les origines grecques et les contestations judéo-chrétiennes* (Paris: Aubier-Montaigne, 1958)

Petersen, W.L., *Tatian's Diatessaron: Its Creation, Dissemination, Significance and History in Scholarship* (Leiden: Brill, 1994)

———, 'Tatian the Assyrian', in A. Marjanen and P. Luomanen, eds, *A Companion to Second-Century 'Heretics'* (Leiden: Brill, 2005), pp. 125-58

Potter, D., *Prophets and Emperors: Human and Divine Authority from Augustus to Theodosius* (Cambridge, MA: Harvard University Press, 1994)

Pouderon, B., *Les apologistes grecs du IIe siècle* (Paris: Éditions du Cerf, 2005)

Pouderon, B., and J. Doré, eds, *Les apologistes chrétiens et la culture grecque* (Paris: Beauchesne, 1998)

Pretila, N.W., *Re-appropriating 'Marvellous Fables': Justin Martyr's Strategic Retrieval of Myth in* 1 Apology (Eugene: Pickwick Publications, 2014)

Prigent, P., *Justin et l'Ancient Testament: L'argumentation scriptuaire du Traité de Justin contre toutes les hérésies comme source principale du Dialogue avec Tryphon et de la Première Apologie* (Paris: Librairie Lecoffre, 1964)

Puech, A., *Les apologistes grecs du IIe siècle de notre ère* (Paris: Libraire Hachette, 1912)
———, *Recherches sur le Discours aux Grecs de Tatien* (Paris: F. Alcan, 1903)
Rajak, T., *Josephus: The Historian and His Society* (London: Duckworth, 1983)
———, *Translation and Survival: The Greek Bible of the Ancient Jewish Diaspora* (Oxford: Oxford University Press, 2009)
Reed, A.Y., *Fallen Angels and the History of Judaism and Christianity: The Reception of Enochic Literature* (Cambridge: Cambridge University Press, 2005)
Riesner, R., 'A Pre-Christian Jewish Mission?', in J. Ådna and H. Kvalbein, *The Mission of the Early Church to Jews and Gentiles* (Tübingen: Mohr Siebeck, 2000), pp. 211-50
Rigoglioso, M., *The Cult of Divine Birth in Ancient Greece* (New York: Palgrave Macmillan, 2009)
Robinson, C., *Lucian and His Influence in Europe* (London: Duckworth, 1979)
Rogers, R., *Theophilus of Antioch: The Life and Thought of a Second-Century Bishop* (Lanham: Lexington Books, 2000)
Rokéah, D., *Justin Martyr and the Jews* (Leiden: Brill, 2002)
Rosenmeyer, P.A., *Ancient Epistolary Fictions: The Letter in Greek Literature* (Cambridge: Cambridge University Press, 2001)
Rowland, C., *The Open Heaven: A Study of Apocalyptic in Judaism and Early Christianity* (London: SPCK, 1982)
Royse, J.R., 'The Works of Philo', in A. Kamesar, ed., *The Cambridge Companion to Philo* (Cambridge: Cambridge University Press, 2009), pp. 32-64
Runia, D.T., *Exegesis and Philosophy: Studies on Philo of Alexandria* (Aldershot: Variorum, 1990)
Russell, D.A., *Criticism in Antiquity*, 2nd edn (London: Duckworth, 1995)
Sandbach, F.H., *The Stoics* (London: Chatto & Windus, 1975)
Santangelo, F., *Divination, Prediction and the End of the Roman Republic* (Cambridge: Cambridge University Press, 2013)
Schaper, J., 'The Literary History of the Hebrew Bible', in NCHB1, pp. 105-44
Scheid, J., 'Les Livres Sibyllins at les archives des quindécemvirs', in C. Moatti, ed., *La mémoire perdue: À la recherche des archives oubliées de l'administration romaine* (Rome: École Française de Rome, 1998), pp. 11-26
Schmid, W., 'Ein rätselhafter Anachronismus bei Justinus Martyr', in W. Schmid, *Ausgewählte philologishe Schriften: Herausgegeben von Hartmut Erbse und Jochem Küppers* (Berlin: de Gruyter, 1984), pp. 333-37
Schoedel, W.R., 'Theophilus of Antioch: Jewish Christian?', *Illinois Classical Studies*, vol. 18 (1993), pp. 279-97
Schürer, E., *The History of the Jewish People in the Age of Jesus Christ (175 BC-AD 135)*, Vol. 3.i, ed. by G. Vermes, F. Millar and M. Goodman, new English rev. version (Edinburgh: T. & T. Clark, 1986)
Schwartz, D.R., 'Philo, His Family, and His Times', in A. Kamesar, ed., *The Cambridge Companion to Philo* (Cambridge: Cambridge University Press, 2009), pp. 9-31
Sedley, D., *Creationism and Its Critics in Antiquity* (Berkeley: University of California Press, 2007)

———, 'Philosophical Allegiance in the Greco-Roman world', in J. Barnes and M. Griffin, eds, *Philosophia Togata: Essays on Philosophy and Roman Society* (Oxford: Clarendon Press, 1989), pp. 97-119

———, 'Plato's *Auctoritas* and the Rebirth of the Commentary Tradition', in J. Barnes and M. Griffin, eds, *Philosophia Togata II: Plato and Aristotle at Rome* (Oxford: Clarendon Press, 1997), pp. 110-29

Sellars, J., *Stoicism* (Chesham: Acumen, 2006)

Shields, C., *Aristotle* (Abingdon: Routledge, 2007)

Shotwell, W.A., *The Biblical Exegesis of Justin Martyr* (London: SPCK, 1965)

Simon, M., *Verus Israel: A Study of the Relations between Christians and Jews in the Roman Empire AD 135-425*, trans. by H. McKeating (Oxford: Oxford University Press, 1986)

Simonetti, M., *Biblical Interpretation in the Early Church: An Historical Introduction to Patristic Exegesis*, trans. by J.A. Hughes (Edinburgh: T. & T. Clark, 1994)

———, 'La Sacra Scrittura in Teofilo d'Antiochia', in J. Fontaine and C. Kannengiesser, eds, *Epektasis: Mélanges patristiques offerts au Cardinal Jean Daniélou* (Paris: Beauchesne, 1972), pp. 197-207

Skarsaune, O., 'Ethnic Discourse in Early Christianity', in J. Carleton Paget and J. Lieu, eds, *Christianity in the Second Century* (Cambridge: Cambridge University Press, 2017), pp. 250-64

———, 'Justin and His Bible', in S. Parvis and P. Foster, eds, *Justin Martyr and His Worlds* (Minneapolis: Fortress Press, 2007), pp. 53-76

———, 'Justin and the Apologists', in D.J. Bingham, ed., *The Routledge Companion to Early Christian Thought* (London: Routledge, 2010), pp. 121-36

———, *The Proof from Prophecy: A Study in Justin Martyr's Proof-Text Tradition: Text-Type, Provenance, Theological Profile* (Leiden: Brill, 1987)

Skinner, Q., *Visions of Politics: Volume 1: Regarding Method* (Cambridge: Cambridge University Press, 2002)

Slusser, M., 'Justin Scholarship: Trends and Trajectories', in S. Parvis and P. Foster, eds, *Justin Martyr and His Worlds* (Minneapolis: Fortress Press, 2007), pp. 13-21

Smith, R., 'Aristotle's Theory of Demonstration', in G. Anagnostopoulos, ed., *A Companion to Aristotle* (Chichester: Wiley-Blackwell, 2009), pp. 51-65

———, 'Logic', in J. Barnes, ed., *The Cambridge Companion to Aristotle* (Cambridge: Cambridge University Press, 1995), pp. 27-65

Smit Sibinga, J., *The Old Testament Text of Justin Martyr: I: The Pentateuch* (Leiden: Brill, 1963)

Snyder, H.G., 'The Classroom in the Text: Exegetical Practices in Justin and Galen', in S.E. Porter and A.W. Pitts, eds, *Christian Origins and Greco-Roman Culture: Social and Literary Contexts for the New Testament* (Leiden: Brill, 2013), pp. 663-85

———, *Teachers and Texts in the Ancient World: Philosophers, Jews and Christians* (London: Routledge, 2000)

Stanton, G.N., 'The Spirit in the Writings of Justin Martyr', in G.N. Stanton, B.W. Longnecker and S.C. Barton, eds, *The Holy Spirit and Christian Origins: Essays in Honor of James D.G. Dunn* (Grand Rapids: Eerdmans, 2004), pp. 321-34

Stark, R., *The Rise of Christianity: A Sociologist Reconsiders History* (Princeton: Princeton University Press, 1996)

Sterling, G.E., *Historiography and Self-Definition: Josephos, Luke-Acts and Apologetic Historiography* (Leiden: Brill, 1992)

———, 'The Jewish Appropriation of Hellenistic Historiography', in J. Marincola, ed., *A Companion to Greek and Roman Historiography*, 2 vols (Oxford: Blackwell Publishing, 2007), 1, pp. 231-43

Stowers, S.K., *Letter Writing in Greco-Roman Antiquity* (Philadelphia: Westminster Press, 1986)

Stylianopoulos, T., *Justin Martyr and the Mosaic Law* (Missoula: Scholars Press, 1975)

Tarrant, R.J., 'Aspects of Virgil's Reception in Antiquity', in C. Martindale, ed., *The Cambridge Companion to Virgil* (Cambridge: Cambridge University Press, 1997), pp. 56-72

Tcherikover, V., 'Jewish Apologetic Literature Reconsidered', *Eos*, vol. 48 (1956), pp. 169-93

Temkin, O., *Hippocrates in a World of Pagans and Christians* (Baltimore: Johns Hopkins University Press, 1991)

Tieleman, T., 'Methodology', in R.J. Hankinson, ed., *The Cambridge Companion to Galen* (Cambridge: Cambridge University Press, 2008), pp. 49-65

Trakatellis, D.C., *The Pre-existence of Christ in Justin Martyr* (Missoula: Scholars Press, 1976)

Trapp, M., *Philosophy in the Roman Empire: Ethics, Politics and Society* (Aldershot: Ashgate, 2007)

Trombley, F., 'Overview: The Geographical Spread of Christianity', in CHC1, pp. 302-13

Tuominen, M., *The Ancient Commentators on Plato and Aristotle* (Stocksfield: Acumen, 2009)

Ulrich, E., 'The Notion and Definition of Canon', in L.M. McDonald and J.A. Sanders, eds, *The Canon Debate* (Peabody: Hendrickson, 2002), pp. 21-35

———, 'The Old Testament Text and Its Transmission', in NCHB1, pp. 83-104

VanderKam, J.C., *Enoch: A Man for All Generations* (Columbia: University of South Carolina Press, 1995)

———, '1 Enoch, Enochic Motifs, and Enoch in Early Christian Literature', in J.C. VanderKam and W. Adler, eds, *The Jewish Apocalyptic Heritage in Early Christianity* (Assen: Van Gorcum, 1996), pp. 33-101

VanderKam, J.C., and W. Adler, eds, *The Jewish Apocalyptic Heritage in Early Christianity* (Assen: Van Gorcum, 1996)

Vermes, G., *Scripture and Tradition in Judaism: Haggadic Studies*, 2nd rev. edn (Leiden: Brill, 1973)

Vos, J.C. de, *Rezeption und Wirkung des Dekalogs in jüdischen und christlichen Schriften bis 200 n. Chr.* (Leiden: Brill, 2016)

Wacholder, B.Z., 'Biblical Chronology in the Hellenistic World Chronicles', *HTR*, vol. 61 (1968), pp. 451-81

Wallraff, M., 'The Beginning of Christian Universal History from Tatian to Julius Africanus', *ZAC*, vol. 14 (2011), pp. 540-55

Walzer, R., *Galen on Jews and Christians* (London: Oxford University Press, 1949)

Wasserstein, A., and D.J. Wasserstein, *The Legend of the Septuagint from Classical Antiquity to Today* (Cambridge: Cambridge University Press, 2006)

Waszink, J.H., 'Some Observations on the Appreciation of "The Philosophy of the Barbarians" in Early Christian Literature', in L.J. Engels et al., eds, *Mélanges offerts à Mademoiselle Christine Mohrmann* (Utrecht: Spectrum, 1963), pp. 41-56

Whitmarsh, T., '"Greece is the World": Exile and Identity in the Second Sophistic', in S. Goldhill, ed., *Being Greek under Rome: Cultural Identity, the Second Sophistic and the Development of Empire* (Cambridge: Cambridge University Press, 2001), pp. 269-305

———, *The Second Sophistic* (Oxford: Oxford University Press, 2005)

Whittaker, M., 'Tatian's Educational Background', in E.A. Livingstone, ed., *SP*, vol. 13, no. 2 (Berlin: Akademie-Verlag, 1975), pp. 57-59

Williams, G., *Technique and Ideas in the* Aeneid (New Haven and London: Yale University Press, 1983)

Wilson, S.G., *Related Strangers: Jews and Christians 70-170 C.E.* (Minneapolis: Fortress Press, 1995)

Wootton, D., *Divine Right and Democracy: An Anthology of Political Writing in Stuart England* (Harmondsworth: Penguin, 1986)

Worthington, I., ed., *Brill's New Jacoby* (Leiden: Brill, 2007-) (accessed via online edn [2007-])

Young, F.M., *Biblical Exegesis and the Formation of Christian Culture* (Cambridge: Cambridge University Press, 1997)

———, 'Greek Apologists of the Second Century', in M.J. Edwards, M.R. Goodman, S.R.F. Price and C. Rowland, eds, *Apologetics in the Roman Empire: Pagans, Jews and Christians* (Oxford: Oxford University Press, 1999), pp. 81-104

Zeegers-Vander Vorst, N., *Les citations des poètes grecs chez les apologistes chrétiens du IIe siècle* (Louvain: Université de Louvain, 1972)

———, 'La création de l'homme (Gn 1,26) chez Théophile d'Antioche', *VC*, vol. 30 (1976), pp. 258-67

———, 'Satan, Ève et le serpent chez Théophile d'Antioche', *VC*, vol. 35 (1981), pp. 152-69

Index

You may also be interested in:

From Jewish Prophet to Gentile God:
The Origins and Development
of New Testament Christology
Maurice Casey

An important contribution to the debate on the development
of Christology in the apostolic era, tracing the evolution
of the historical figure of Jesus.

Based on the 1985 Cardbury Lectures delivered at the University of
Birmingham, England, this book describes and explains the origins and
development of New Testament Christology. Using both original sources
and established and recent scholarship, Casey presents a convincing
argument to support his Christological framework. He traces the
evolution through the Pauline Epistles and the Gospels of the historical
figure of Jesus, the Aramaic-speaking Jew, to his identification as Jesus
Christ, the Messiah and Son of God. The declaration of his deity in
John's Gospel is related to the Gentile self-identification of the Johannine
community.

This is the first book in the field of Christian origins to make serious
analytical use of the concept of identity. It includes new discussion and
explanation of early Christian belief in the Resurrection, the Virgin birth
and other elements of Christian dogma.

Lucid and cogently organised, *From Jewish Prophet to Gentile God*'s
conclusions are both logical and startling. Casey's work represents a
major advance in the study of Christology.

MAURICE CASEY is a lecturer in Theology at the University of Nottingham,
where he teaches ancient Judaism and Christian origins. He is a member
of the Studiorum Novi Testament Societas, and the author of *Son of
Man, The Interpretation and Influence of Daniel* (London, 1980) as well
as numerous seminar papers and articles.

Hardback ISBN: 9780227679203
Dimensions 234 × 156 mm / Pages 204pp
Published: 1 June 1991

BV - #0020 - 010921 - C0 - 234/156/13 - PB - 9780227177358 - Gloss Lamination